Also by Tony Massarotti

Big Papi: My Story of Big Dreams and Big Hits

A Tale of Two Cities:
The 2004 Yankees–Red Sox
Rivalry and the War for the Pennant

DYN

TONY MASSAROTTI

THE INSIDE STORY OF HOW THE **RED SOX**
BECAME A BASEBALL POWERHOUSE

ST. MARTIN'S PRESS ⧓ NEW YORK

www.stmartins.com

Book design by Jonathan Bennett

ISBN-13: 978-0-312-38567-5
ISBN-10: 0-312-38567-6

First Edition: April 2008

10   9   8   7   6   5   4   3   2   1

For Alexander and Xavier,
each of whom brought with him
what his father could not:
a World Series championship

Contents

Acknowledgments

BACK IN 2006, WHEN ST. MARTIN'S PRESS AGREED TO PUBLISH *Big Papi*, the memoirs of inimitable Boston Red Sox slugger David Ortiz, no one imagined that the work would end up on the prestigious *New York Times* bestseller list. At the time, too, no one knew that another partnership between the publisher and writer could be so close behind.

But then, nobody knew that the Boston Red Sox would soon be winning their second World Series in four seasons, either.

Yet here we are now, in early 2008, and the Red Sox are the most successful franchise in baseball, a seeming dynasty in the making. Under the stewardship of principal owner John Henry, chairman Tom Werner, president Larry Lucchino, and, of course, general manager Theo Epstein, the Red Sox have done more than build a wildly successful baseball and business operation. They have also changed how the world perceives them, an achievement previously unimaginable.

Along the way, through the inevitable ups and downs in the relationship between a writer and his subjects, the Red Sox have remained remarkably understanding and cooperative with those who have both praised and criticized them.

For that, they forever have my utmost respect.

As one would expect, the remainder of the Red Sox organization has followed the example set by ownership and management, beginning with Terry Francona, who has turned the role of Red Sox manager into one of the most distinguished jobs in professional sports. Under Francona's watch, the Red Sox clubhouse has remained a most professional place to work, even for those who, simply by the nature of their job, can be both intrusive and unwelcome.

As for the Red Sox players, for so long burdened with the weight of their ancestors, their play in recent years has led them to unprecedented heights in the long history of the franchise. As a result of their work, the Boston uniform is now equated with success. A special thanks goes to catcher and captain Jason Varitek, (and liaison Justin Taglianet of the Scott Boras Corporation); who has been with the Red Sox throughout this extraordinary time in their history and who graciously agreed to assist with this project. To him, no measure of thanks could ever be enough.

A special thanks, too, to baseball commissioner Bud Selig (and Major League Baseball senior vice president of public relations director Rich Levin), who was gracious enough to offer an invaluable endorsement to this project. The same is true of former Red Sox general manager Dan Duquette, whose sizable contributions to the success of the Red Sox should never go overlooked. And a heartfelt thank you to both *Sports Illustrated* senior baseball writer Tom Verducci and ESPN writer and analyst Buster Olney, two of the most respected baseball voices in the country and a pair of first-ballot Hall of Famers. For all of the sports media, people like Verducci and Olney continue to set a very high standard.

Beyond Red Sox upper management and the Boston clubhouse, eternal gratitude is due current Sox media relations director John Blake and his assistants, Pam Ganley and Drew Merle, as well as the entire Red Sox media-relations staff. Over the years, the Red Sox have dutifully tried to respond to all requests and questions, many of them downright unreasonable or silly. Given that reality, it sometimes seemed miraculous that Red Sox employees would even take calls anymore, especially when they knew who was calling.

And, for that matter, why.

Of course, given the time required to complete projects like this one, cooperation is required from many others. *Boston Herald* sports editor

Hank Hryniewicz, deputy sports editor Mark Murphy, and assistant editor Joe Thomas have remained receptive and understanding when they did not have to be. So, too, have Sunday sports editor Nate Dow, night editors Ed Brennen and Bill McIlwrath, and an entire cast of unrecognized copy editors who frequently make *Herald* writers look far more intelligent and knowledgeable than they really are.

Thanks, too, to *Herald* publisher Pat Purcell, photo editor Jim Mahoney, and vice president of promotions Gwen Gage for their willingness to support the independent interests of *Herald* writers.

And, as always, thanks to all the members of the *Herald* sportswriting staff, each of whom knowingly or unknowingly fosters thought and discussion while providing readers with the absolute best daily sports coverage in the city of Boston.

For that matter, thanks to all of our competitors at the *Boston Globe*, too, for reminding us that there is nothing wrong with healthy, spirited competition.

Naturally, no matter the quality or incentive behind any work, others must be willing to invest in it to make any endeavor worthwhile. Negotiations with St. Martin's Press were astonishingly easy in this case, thanks primarily to the efforts of literary agent Scott Waxman and his team, including Farley Chase, who helped market this book internationally. St. Martin's editor Marc Resnick embraced this idea from the start and remained incredibly patient throughout an extremely tight work schedule, and his assistant, Sarah Lumnah, was an invaluable liaison and aide. Joe Rinaldi, the publicity director at St. Martin's, continued to take every phone call with boundless energy and vigor.

Finally, a most special thanks to Alexander, Xavier, and Natalie, the last of whom continues to demonstrate unmatched patience and remains the best friend, partner, and mother that any reasonable person could hope for.

Or, for that matter, an unreasonable one, too.

Foreword

Most nights, it never fails. I'll come back to my locker after a game, after stopping in the trainer's room to get ice strapped to my shoulder or to my knees, and the reporters will be waiting for me. Tony Massarotti is usually one of the guys standing in back, listening, and a lot of the time he hangs around until everyone else clears out.

And then I'll wonder: What the heck does he want now?

I've been playing for the Boston Red Sox for over ten seasons now and sometimes I feel like I've never played anywhere else. Some guys like playing in a place like Boston and some guys don't, and I think the Red Sox have done a good job over the years of finding the ones that do. When you play for the Red Sox, you have to answer to the fans and to the media for just about everything, and a lot of guys can have problems with that. I've heard people say that New York is the same way, that it can be a tough place to play, especially when things might not be going so well.

Personally, none of that stuff ever bothered me too much. I've always felt like I hold myself to a higher standard to begin with, and I feel like I expect more from myself than anyone else does. That's just the way my parents taught me. If I'm not playing well or the team is losing, I always felt like I had to take responsibility for it and move on, then go out and try to fix whatever the problem was.

When I joined the Red Sox in 1997, I really didn't know much about

Boston. I played most of my minor-league career with the Seattle Mariners and I was with the Triple-A Tacoma Rainiers when Seattle traded me and Derek Lowe to the Red Sox for Heathcliff Slocumb. Even then, I thought the trade was probably a good thing for me. At the time, Seattle had a catcher named Dan Wilson, and Dan was a good player. He wasn't going anywhere. The only way I was going to get a chance to play in the major leagues was if something happened to Wilson or if the Mariners traded me, and I knew a trade was probably my best chance. The Red Sox needed a catcher, and I started getting real playing time there in 1998, when Scott Hatteberg and I split time behind the plate.

A year later, when Hatty got hurt, I caught 144 games and batted .276 with 20 home runs and 76 RBIs, and our pitching staff had a good year. That was the year Pedro Martinez joined the team. From that point on, I've caught most of the games the Red Sox have played and we've been in the playoff race just about every year, which is one of the things I love most about playing in Boston: you know that you're always going to have a chance because our fans and owners demand it.

Since I joined the Red Sox, a lot has happened and a lot has changed. Tony is one of the reporters who has been there to see all of it. I don't know if I would call anyone in the Boston media a real friend, but Tony is always someone whom I respected and trusted. I don't let many reporters get to know me very well, but he probably knows me as well as any of them. He knows our team, too. In a place like Boston, where there are so many members of the media, they all want the story and they all want the scoop. I understand that they're competitive, too. But when you're a player and all anyone wants to ask you about is controversy, it gets old fast. In baseball, there's a game to play just about everyday. There really isn't a lot of time to get distracted by the unimportant stuff, especially if you're someone like me, especially if you're a catcher. I take a lot of pride in preparing for games, and I try to be thorough. Before every game, I try to go over scouting reports and our game plan because I always looked at that as the most important part of my job. I don't have a lot of time to answer questions about who was on the team bus or who wasn't.

Besides, when you're on a team, you have to take care of that stuff internally. It's important. During the season, we see our teammates sometimes more than we see our families, and we have to do our best to take care of any problems, to be on the same page. If I have something to say to someone, I'll say it to him. I don't need to share it with the press.

Most of the time, when Tony's hanging around my locker, it's usually because he wants to talk baseball. It's actually one of the things I like about him. There have been times over the last ten or eleven years where he'll come in and ask me questions about pitches we throw to certain batters in certain situations, about our strategies, about our approach. Sometimes I'm surprised that he notices the things he does. Sometimes there's not a lot I can say. But I've always respected the fact that he's trying to learn something and that he's trying to get it right, even I can't necessarily tell him out of obligation to our team. After all, we're there to win. It's not like I can give away company secrets.

One time, when we were getting close to the end of the season, I remember Tony asking me to evaluate my performance, which is a hard thing to do. You don't always see it the way everyone else does. But one of Tony's assignments every year is to give us all grades on a report card that they print in the paper he works for, the *Boston Herald*, and I remember thinking that he might give me a bad grade. I didn't feel like I was having a great season that year—I don't even remember the specifics—but I also knew my year wasn't as bad as a lot of people thought. I was standing near the bat rack in our dugout at Fenway Park when Tony asked me the question, and I remember exactly what I said to him: "If you give me an F, we're going to have a fight." He laughed. I think I got a C.

In the last four or five years, especially, the Red Sox have had a lot of success. We've won two World Series—in 2004 and 2007—and each one was special. Until we won the championship in 2004, the Red Sox hadn't won a World Series since 1918, which was something people reminded us of all the time. It's the primary reason why that World Series meant so much to people, so much to us. It's also one of the biggest reasons winning it was so hard. Winning the World Series was hard in

2007, too, but it was hard in a different way. I think a lot of people expected us to win that year. I'm pretty sure now that no one will ask us about 1918 anymore because we've completely changed the way people look at the Red Sox, look at us, and that was a difficult thing to do. I know it's something we're all proud of.

Like just about every other player during my career, I've had a lot of people help me and teach me things, make me better. My first manager in Boston, Jimy Williams, really took time with young players like me and Trot Nixon and gave us a chance. Every teammate I've ever played with gave me support. I learned things from my first pitching coach, Joe Kerrigan, and I learned a lot of from Pedro, Martinez, too. I've had a chance to work with some of the best pitchers in baseball—Pedro, Curt Schilling, Josh Beckett, lots of others—and I've caught two no-hitters, one by D-Lowe, one by Hideo Nomo. I've played with lots of terrific teammates and I've played in the best baseball city in the big leagues, and I can't ever say enough about our fans. People ask me all the time about why we've been such a good team at home during my time in Boston and I always say the same thing. It's our fans. They really do make us a better team.

At the start of the 2007 season, I turned thirty-five-years old, and a lot of people were wondering if I was starting to slip. A lot of reporters asked me about my age during spring training, including Tony, and I'll tell you what I told them: I still feel like I have a lot left. Baseball has always been a big part of my life and I can't ever imagine being without it, and I know I can keep playing this game at a high level for a long time. I'll continue to work at it, continue to prepare, continue to learn. Those are things we all strive for, no matter what we do.

Hopefully, you'll learn something from this book. Maybe I will, too. But if Tony says anything bad about me, let me know. I can always challenge him to another fight.

—Jason Varitek
January 2008

1

HOW DID WE GET HERE?

GIVEN THE HISTORY OF HEARTACHE, MAYBE IT WAS ONLY FITTING that champagne settled on the brim of Theo Epstein's cap in the form of a single, solitary teardrop.

But in the immediate aftermath of Game 4 of the 2007 World Series, there was little regret in the visiting clubhouse at Coors Field, home of the National League champion—and terribly overmatched—Colorado Rockies. For the second time in four baseball seasons, the Boston Red Sox were champions. Epstein stood near the center of a room filled with Red Sox players old and young, as sure a sign as any that the Red Sox had undergone a transformation, that they had truly evolved, that these Red Sox, above all others, were *different*. For nearly a century, after all, the Red Sox had been a team weighed down by its past, haunted by ghosts, interminably arrested in its development. The Red Sox had not been regarded as losers as much as they had been looked upon as tragic failures, a team that unfailingly stumbled after coming *thisclose*.

But now, in the wake of a second World Series championship in less time than was typically required to earn a college degree, the Red Sox had graduated, matured, and blossomed into everything they had always thought they could be.

Better late than never.

"There's always luck involved, but this shows we've started to build a great organization," said a beaming Epstein, still two months shy of his 34th birthday. "It's nice that we have two [championships] now and that no one can say it was an accident."

Echoed Red Sox principal owner John Henry during the clubhouse celebration: "This means the first one wasn't a fluke. It means this is an organization capable of more things over time with great credentials. We're not just stat geeks. We're a well-rounded organization and we do everything we can all year to win."

Indeed, for all of the torture that the Red Sox and their fans had endured during the extensive history of the franchise, a funny thing happened during the final days of the 2007 baseball season: the Red Sox suddenly became the standard against which all other major-league teams were measured. From 2000 through 2006, years that marked the turn of the millennium and baseball's entrance into an entirely new age, not a single team in baseball won as many as two world championships. After the New York Yankees dynasty of 1996–2000 ended with the Yankees' victory over the New York Mets, the six subsequent seasons in major-league baseball produced champions in Phoenix, Anaheim, Miami, Boston, Chicago, and St. Louis. Baseball officials, beginning with commissioner Bud Selig, took this as a delightful sign that the game had reached an age of parity, that the gap between the richest teams and the poorest ones had so considerably dwindled that most every team entered every season with at least some measure of hope. Given the economic gap that had existed in baseball in the years immediately prior to all of that—the period of the latest Yankees dynasty—this was no small statement.

But in 2007, while becoming baseball's first repeat champions of a truly new age, the Red Sox took over first place in the American League East during the early stages of the season and never relinquished it. Subsequently, the Red Sox never really teetered so much as they paced themselves. The team's greatest challenge came during the best-of-seven American League Championship Series with the Cleveland Indians, against whom the Red Sox faced a series deficit of three games to one before steamrolling their opponents in the final three games, a comeback that was decisive and, at times, seemed inevitable.

Entering the World Series, the upstart Rockies had won an incredible 21 of 22 games, including all seven of their postseason contests against the Philadelphia Phillies and Arizona Diamondbacks, respectively, in the National League Division Series and National League Championship Series. The Rockies were so damned near perfect that they had more than a week off before their first game against the Red Sox, who had to play the maximum seven games against the Indians. And while much was made of Colorado's unusually long layoff—excluding the midseason respite known as the All-Star break, baseball teams rarely go more than one day without playing during the season—the reality was that Colorado simply was no match for a Red Sox club that had effectively led from wire to wire in the far more competitive American League.

As it turned out, the Rockies were a fitting opponent for a Red Sox organization whose identity seemed to change instantaneously, for all the world to see, in the shadow of the Rocky Mountains for which the Colorado team was named. How many times had the Red Sox been the team on a hot streak entering the big games, only to see their momentum dissolve? How many times, at the most inopportune moments, had the Red Sox reverted to their old selves and proved incapable of overcoming their demons? How many times had the Red Sox been in complete control—or so it seemed—only to come apart at the seams, prompting even the cruelest Red Sox adversaries to feel, of all things, pity?

How many times?

And always, without exception, the story seemed to end with the same refrain: *Same old Red Sox.*

But now, after so many years, the old rules no longer seemed to apply. As the Red Sox systematically took apart the Rockies in the World Series, the entire baseball world had time to think. For all of the nonsense penned (and recited) about baseball being a microcosm of life, for all of the poetry and romanticism and nostalgia, the Boston Red Sox dragged the 2007 World Series to new depths and completely sucked the life from what should have been the most climactic games of the baseball season. The long-standing theory is that the beauty of baseball comes in its pace, in its deliberate nature, in the fact that players have time to reassess before each and every pitch; the game never was intended to be played solely out of reaction or athleticism. The stops in play were part of the attraction, particularly to those who watched baseball and wrote about it, because the details changed constantly. Ball one. *The batter has the advantage.* Strike one. *The scale is balanced.* The subtleties triggered emotions, which played on the mind, which invariably got in the way.

Among all of those who played and watched baseball, the Red Sox and their fans knew that better than anyone.

Yet, in 2007, Boston's deconstruction of Colorado was so thorough, so swift, that there was never really any doubt. The Red Sox completely dominated the series, just as they had in 2004 against the St. Louis Cardinals, another team that proved terribly overmatched. During the 2007 World Series, for as much time as there was to think, to evaluate, and to reassess, the Red Sox had seemingly done the impossible: they had given onlookers virtually nothing to dwell on, because they were so vastly superior to the Colorado Rockies team opposite them.

So, in the absence of any drama on the field during the four games of the 2007 World Series, most of those watching from Colorado to Cape Cod (and beyond) turned their sights to the horizon, to what the future held in store. Wasn't that the logical thing to do? Some people spend their time dealing with the past; most are caught up in the present. Few enjoy the freedom to prepare for the future, to survey the landscape, to truly know that nothing is behind them and nothing is gaining, that the world before them is truly an endless vista of possibilities.

In the final days of the World Series, that was where the Red Sox found themselves. And that was where most everyone saw them. "It allows this organization to move forward," Red Sox catcher and captain Jason Varitek succinctly stated in the celebratory champagne drizzle of the visitors' clubhouse at Coors Field. "Instead of the piano on our backs or the weight of the entire Red Sox nation . . . once that was lifted, it built confidence. And that confidence pushes its way through a clubhouse over time."

He was right, of course.

The Red Sox were done doubting themselves.

Finally, in Boston, there was no looking back.

WITH THE Red Sox, always, some reconstruction of their history is required. To understand where the Red Sox are—or, more specifically, how far they have traveled—one must understand from where they came. For the first 20 years of the twentieth century, the Red Sox were the model franchise in major-league baseball. Boston won five of the first 15 World Series ever played, ending with a victory over the Chicago Cubs in six games in 1918.

Back then, no one could have imagined the decades of trauma that would ensue.

Over the next 85 baseball seasons, from 1919 through 2003, the Red Sox won more games than all but five franchises in baseball; they had a higher winning percentage than all but seven. All of that only made it more maddening—and downright inexplicable—that the Red Sox went that same, entire period without winning even a single World Series, prompting Red Sox followers to adopt the notion that there were greater forces at work, that perhaps they had sold their souls in a previous existence, that they were paying for sins of the past.

That they were, as many would come to believe, *cursed*.

In its essence, of course, the curse was nothing more than a clever gimmick concocted by author Dan Shaughnessy, a longtime reporter and columnist at the *Boston Globe* who created the concept as a lure for his landmark book, *The Curse of the Bambino*; figuratively, it came to represent so much more. While effectively mocking the Red Sox for selling the greatest player in baseball history (Babe Ruth, nicknamed "the Bambino") to their most hated rivals (the New York Yankees), Shaughnessy put forth the notion that the Red Sox were being eternally punished for committing an inexcusable blunder of monumental proportions.

Under normal circumstances, such a theory might have been mocked and ridiculed in a region so staid and conservative as the six-state region of New England, but the Red Sox did more than their part to support believers over a near century of masochism.

It wasn't just that the Red Sox lost, after all. It was how.

And more important, for how long.

For the Red Sox and their followers, as with most everyone else, the deepest wounds left scars. Where most teams hung championship banners to identify their most significant years, the Red Sox might as well have placed headstones in the outfield at Fenway Park. *Here lie the Red Sox of 1946, 1948, 1967, 1975, 1978, and 1986.* In four of those seasons, the Red Sox qualified for the World Series; in the two others, they probably should have. Had the Red Sox followed the laws of logic and won the World Series in three of those years—maybe even two or just one—there is no telling how the history of the organization might have changed, how differently the Sox might have fared. At the very least, there would have been no grounds for a curse, if only because one of the greatest and most curious droughts in the history of professional sports would have been cut in half. Relatively speaking, then, the psychological and emotional damage done to the Red Sox and their legions would have been relatively minimal.

Instead, the Sox became a historic case study on the cruel effects of deprivation.

The specifics of Boston's frustrating pursuit of a world title were not nearly as important individually as they were collectively, which is undoubtedly true of any spectacular failure. Like Jean Van de Velde at the 1999 British Open golf championship or Phil Mickelson at the 2006 U.S. Open, the Red Sox had countless opportunities to escape the trouble they had wrought for themselves, only to make matters worse. An errant tee shot might have been the start of it all, but there was considerable opportunity to minimize the damage. Ultimately, the mistakes piled up on one another like a series of lifetime indiscretions, resulting in a rap sheet that could be uncoiled like a roll of paper towels. By the end of it, the Red Sox had a well-earned reputation of being not losers, but something worse—chokers—a team with the talent to win and that frequently put itself in position to do so, only to crumble under the considerable weight of the Boston uniform at the most pivotal of times.

And so, 1946 became connected to 1948 and to 1967, 1975, 1978, and 1986 when, in reality, the years had absolutely nothing to do with one another.

Nonetheless, like victims of a serial killer, each team had its own story. In 1946, despite winning more regular-season games than any team in baseball, the Red Sox lost to the St. Louis Cardinals in seven games, the last of which was decided, according to lore, when Red Sox shortstop Johnny Pesky *held the ball* as Enos "Country" Slaughter scored the decisive run, from first base, on a single by Harry "the Hat" Walker; in 1967, a year that generally remains pure in the heart of every Red Sox follower, the "Impossible Dream" Red Sox came out of nowhere to win the American League pennant before succumbing to the Cardinals, and the godlike Bob Gibson; the '75 Sox lost to one of the greatest teams in history, the Big Red Machine known as the Cincinnati Reds, after a pair of unforgettable bloopers—the first a lollipop curveball from eccentric left-hander Bill "Spaceman" Lee that slugger Tony Perez hit into orbit for a home run, the second an RBI single from Joe Morgan (against rookie left-hander Jim Burton) that delivered the final and decisive run of the Series; in '78, the Red Sox blew a 14½-game lead to the hated Yankees and ended up paired against New York in a historic one-game playoff, a game Boston appeared to have in hand until lightweight Bucky "Fucking" Dent homered into the left-field screen; the '86 Sox had the World Series won—a 5–3 lead, two outs, bases empty in the bottom of the 10th inning of Game 6 at Shea Stadium, home of the New York Mets—before a succession of events that felt more like a mudslide, culminating in the unforgettable Mookie Wilson grounder that went through the legs of Sox first baseman Bill Buckner.

Naturally, the Red Sox' losses on all of those occasions were far more complicated than any one splinter of misfortune, but to acknowledge this would have destroyed the idea that the Red Sox were the unluckiest of sorry souls.

In '78 and '86, in particular, the breakdowns seemed especially cruel abuse, in part because the Red Sox collapsed against teams from New York, in part because they came nearer the end. By then, the weight of frustration and failure had piled up so high on the Red Sox and their fans that the slightest bump in the road created a crisis in confidence, awakened self-doubt. And so anytime the Red Sox subsequently found themselves in a position to succeed, those even remotely affiliated with the team could not help but handle defeat—and victory—in a most predictable manner.

When the Red Sox ultimately lost, they and their followers expected to.

And if the Sox were about to win, the Sox and their legion of doom all too often made the mistake of looking over their shoulders.

Among those who were unfamiliar to Boston, it was this latter phenomenon that took getting used to, though most never did. The Red Sox' fear of failure became so great during the 85-year period from 1919 to 2003 that it was inescapable. Most every good Red Sox team during that period made the mistake of trying to outrun the past instead of facing up to it, which helped create an antagonistic and tension-filled environment that only perpetuated the problem. Snarled inimitable and annoyed Red Sox ace Pedro Martinez when asked about the alleged curse during the 2001 Red Sox season: "Wake up the damn Bambino and have me face him. Maybe I'll drill him in the ass."

In reality, of course, there was no curse on the Red Sox, only the belief in one; at times, because their psyches and souls had been damaged, the curse seemed to be a self-fulfilling prophecy. The much greater problem that the Red Sox faced throughout their history was the fact that Boston played in the same league and, later, division as the mighty Yankees, their unrelenting rivals just 200 miles to the south. Prior to 1969, the only way to get to the World Series was to win the American League pennant during the regular season, which meant that the Red Sox had to finish ahead of New York (and everyone else in the American League) over the course of a full season. Baseball split to two divisions beginning in 1969, which added another tier of playoffs to the equation, but the Red Sox still had the same problem: Boston and New York were both in the AL East. It wasn't until 1995 that baseball introduced a football variable into the mix—the now-familiar wild card—which meant that a second-place finisher could finally be rewarded for its efforts and qualify for the postseason despite the absence of a division title.

Looking back, given the way the Yankees had hovered over the Red Sox for the large majority of the 20th century, one cannot help but think that the wild card was tailored almost exclusively for Boston, a city that simply could not grow beyond the shadow of its bigger, more accomplished sibling, no matter how hard it tried.

In Boston, as it would turn out, the wild card was not a curse, but a blessing.

FOR THE Red Sox, more than any other team in baseball, the irony was obvious. As much as the Red Sox learned to hate the Yankees, the ultimate goal in Boston was to become more like New York.

During the years of the last baseball dynasty—New York's reign from 1996 to 2000—the Yankees were perceived as an army of mercenaries, a team of high-priced players brought in exclusively for the purpose of winning championships. One of the most popular and obvious theories was that the Yankees bought their greatness, plain and simple, because New York had the most money. Unlike the National Football League, for example, Major League Baseball had an unbalanced economic structure that allowed large-market teams like the Yankees to generate far greater revenue than any other team—and to keep it—which allowed the Yankees to spend far more on their players. New York did not have to share its wares with Kansas City, for example, so most people believed that the financial gap between the Yankees and everyone else was nearly impossible to overcome. Thus, the Yankees seemed to be storing championship trophies in the attic as if they were jamming birthday cards into a shoe box.

In reality, the money was only part of the story. Relatively speaking, the Yankees spent as freely in the 1980s as they did at later points during their existence, yet New York went the entire decade without winning a world title. In fact, after winning the World Series in 1978—the team's 22nd championship during a span of 56 years—the Yankees did not win again until 1996. That title began a stretch during which New York won the World Series title four times in five years while *averaging* more than 97 wins per regular season, highlighted by a 1998 campaign during which New York went a historic 114-48, a record so eye-popping that those Yankees were regarded as one of the greatest teams of all time. That '98 Yankees team, too, went a sterling 11-1 in the postseason, including a four-game sweep of the outclassed San Diego Padres in the World Series; overall, from Game 3 of the 1996 World Series through Game 2 of the 2000 World Series, the Yankees won an incredible 14 straight World Series games, a record that still stands and that defined their greatness more than any other measure.

In theory, anyway, the World Series was intended to pit the two best teams in baseball against each other. Sweeps were supposed to be the exception rather than the rule. Yet as surely as the leaves changed color in October, the Yankees were humiliating opponents that were alleged to be their peers.

From 1996 to 2000, if the Yankees were the number one team in base-ball, it really didn't matter who was number two.

Still, those critics of baseball's economic system who credited New York's wealth alone for the Yankees' success missed the point. In 1996, the Yankee shortstop and the American League Rookie of the Year was none other than Derek Jeter, who was drafted and developed by the Yankees. For that matter, center fielder Bernie Williams was also drafted by the organization. Left-handed pitcher Andy Pettitte, left fielder Gerald Williams, backup catcher (and postseason hero) Jim Leyritz, and setup man extraordinaire Mariano Rivera were all products of the Yankee farm system, as was a catcher then relatively unknown, Jorge Posada. Of course, the key players of that group were Jeter, Bernie Williams, Pettitte, Rivera, and Posada, each of whom became a central figure in New York's run of success that extended well into the next decade.

For all that the Yankees spent on pitchers like David Cone, for instance, it was impossible to overstate the impact of the Yankees' scouting and player-development departments on the long-term success of the franchise. Always, the Yankees had been regarded as peerless when it came to evaluating young talent; in this case, it was especially true. According to baseball philosophy, the best players always play in the middle of the field, from the catcher out to center field. It is as if an axis were drawn directly down the middle of the diamond. That line pierces the pitcher's mound and second base, the center of the infield, which is shared by two players: the shortstop and the second baseman. The latter of those two players is generally considered less important, which leaves the shortstop as the most important infield position outside of the catcher and, of course, the pitcher.

In the case of the Yankees, here is what their farm system had produced as the team entered the final half of the 1990s: an All-Star catcher in Posada; a Hall of Fame shortstop in Jeter; an All-Star center fielder in Bernie Williams. As for Pettitte and Rivera, the former was an All-Star starter and the latter a Hall of Fame closer, providing the Yankees with fundamental building blocks in their starting rotation and bullpen for years to come.

For all of the talk about the Yankees' spending, then, the truth is that the Yankees built their foundation from the ground up, then spent lavishly on the furnishings that turned Yankee Stadium into a king's palace. During those years, the Yankees had the best of everything: youth, promise, and money.

As a result, as baseball continued to struggle through labor wars and economic crises, the Yankees had what every team wanted, a team that could win now *and* win later. Jeter was the centerpiece of a youthful group that would allow the Yankees an extended run at multiple championships; meanwhile, owner George Steinbrenner had the means (and the madness) to spend whatever was necessary to ensure that the Yankees fully exploited their empire at a time when the game's economic realities favored a larger-market team like the Yankees. All along, the goal was to balance youth and experience, hunger and wealth, all with the hope of giving each team, each year, the necessary ingredients to win a championship.

For much of the 1990s and beyond, that was what the Red Sox were up against.

And that, too, was their model.

IN BASEBALL, as the saying goes, any player can have one good year. The trick is to have several, over and over again, because consistency is the true challenge of the game. During a 162-game season over the span of six months, the best players produce every day, from April through September. And then they do it again the next year. And the next. And the next.

In the case of baseball *teams*, for obvious reasons, the challenge is even greater. A *team* frequently relies on the performance of all players. A *team* has far more variables. Injuries alone can undermine a club. Inevitably, there are contract disputes. And none of those things even begins to measure the day-to-day distractions that can affect any individual on a team, from marital difficulties to a child's illness to a death in the family.

In their history, like many teams, the Red Sox had their opportunities to make extended runs at multiple championships only to be thwarted. In 1967, for instance, the Red Sox lost slugger Tony Conigliaro for the season when he was struck in the eye by a pitch; his career—and life— were never really the same again. Following that season, 1967 American League Cy Young Award winner Jim Lonborg broke his leg skiing and never regained the greatness of his '67 campaign. Until the present day, the Sox of the mid- and late 1970s were, to many, the golden years of the franchise, largely because the Sox had a collection of good young players that included, among others, Jim Rice, Fred Lynn, and Carlton Fisk. In the case of the last, the Red Sox made the colossal administrative blunder of failing to mail Fisk's contract in time, allowing him to become a free agent following the 1980 season. Fisk subsequently agreed to a new deal with the Chicago White Sox, with whom he finished his career before being inducted into the Hall of Fame in 2000.

Regardless of the specifics in a season that featured a near miss, the Red Sox consistently succumbed to the pitfalls that prevented them from finishing the job.

At least until 2004.

And, to some extent, until 2007.

But by the time the Red Sox completed their sweep of the Colorado Rockies in the World Series, all of the pieces finally were in place. In Game 4, for instance, the Red Sox' winning pitcher was 23-year-old left-hander Jon Lester, a Washington State native who had been diagnosed with large-cell lymphoma slightly more than a year earlier. Boston's second baseman and leadoff man was the feisty 5-foot-9 (on stilts) Dustin Pedroia, who batted .317 during his first season (and .319 in his last 11 postseason games) en route to the 2007 American League Rookie of the Year Award. The team's center fielder was a 23-year-old budding phenom named Jacoby Ellsbury, who joined the club for good only in the final month of the season before displacing starter Coco Crisp in the World Series, during which Ellsbury went 7-for-16 (a .438 average) with four runs scored, four doubles, three RBIs, two walks, and a stolen base.

Indeed, unlike the 2004 Red Sox, who ended 86 years of futility by winning the World Series with a largely veteran team that underwent immediate renovations, the 2007 Red Sox were, finally, built for the long haul. Along with Lester, starters Josh Beckett and Daisuke Matsuzaka were both under team control through at least 2010; neither had yet to celebrate his 28th birthday. Closer Jonathan Papelbon turned 27 a few weeks after the World Series and was similarly under team control through 2011. Surrounding these young centerpieces of the Red Sox' future were accomplished veterans like Varitek and designated hitter David Ortiz, left fielder Manny Ramirez, and pitcher Curt Schilling. Among that group, only Schilling was eligible for free agency after the 2007 campaign, though the Red Sox subsequently signed him to a one-year contract that ensured Schilling would remain in Boston for at least 2008.

Even in the case of third baseman Mike Lowell, the free-agent-to-be who was named Most Valuable Player of the World Series, the Red Sox avoided a potential land mine. Other Sox players left the team following comparable seasons, but Lowell was retained by virtue of a three-year, $37.5 million contract ensuring that he, too, would be under the team's control through 2010.

So, as the Boston Red Sox completed the 2007 season with the World Series championship, they had done a great deal more than win a second world title in four years. Along the way, the Red Sox had extinguished decades of futility. They had erased the past. They had positioned themselves for the future and wiped away all self-doubt, as was evident in the actions and faces of their new generation, the 20-somethings like Lester and Pedroia and even Clay Buchholz, a minor-league pitcher who appeared briefly in Boston during the season and threw a no-hitter in his second major-league start. Couldn't people see now? The Red Sox had completely changed the direction and identity of the franchise defined by its monumental gaffes, replacing it with a team on which the older players cultivated the young as if they were their children; where players were no longer asked about past failures as much as they were about recent successes; where the name on the front of the team uniform—Red Sox—came to symbolize achievement, perseverance, commitment, dedication, relentlessness, and, yes, consistency.

"I noticed it when we played the [Los Angeles] Angels [in the American League Division Series]," Red Sox owner John Henry told *Sports*

Illustrated after the club defeated the Rockies in the World Series. "Red Sox fans were extremely confident. The expectation now is that the Red Sox are going to win."

Indeed it is.

But in between there and here, it was quite a journey.

STARTING FROM SCRATCH

ON ONE OF THE MOST SIGNIFICANT AND SYMBOLIC DAYS IN THE history of the storied Boston Red Sox, Fenway Park had the chaotic feel of a train station during that busiest time of the year.

But while the rest of New England prepared for Christmas on the afternoon of December 21, 2001, Red Sox general manager Dan Duquette quietly left the clamor of the Diamond Club, a nighttime members-only area that doubled as a daytime conference room for press briefings beneath the left-field grandstands at historic Fenway Park. Effectively nestled into the tight corner of Brookline Avenue and Lansdowne Street, the Diamond Club was a part of Fenway Park that most fans rarely saw. And at a time when the Red Sox were undergoing a massive makeover that began with changes in ownership and philosophy, Duquette stopped suddenly as he approached a doorway in a quiet corner of the room.

In more ways than one, Dan Duquette was on his way out.

And his blood was boiling.

"Tell your paper to let it go," Duquette sternly and uncharacteristically told a reporter who had trailed him following a press conference to announce the signing of the team's latest player acquisition. Duquette's voice rose. *"Let it go,"* he repeated more loudly. "We've done four or five things to help this team and that's all you guys keep writing about."

Finally, he erupted. *"Let it fucking go!"*

With that, the general manager of the Red Sox stormed off, head down, into the concourse that tunneled its way from one foul pole to another, behind and around home plate in one of America's most fabled ballparks. Duquette went past a concession stand and up a hidden, dusty, and dimly lit ramp, a passageway that climbed behind the left-field grandstand at Fenway like an old dirt road. (Only the locals knew it was there.) For someone like Duquette, who preferred solitude and frequently felt smothered in gatherings larger than a few, the ramp was a way to get around the old ballpark without interruption, distraction, attention. He could leave a jammed Diamond Club through that same door and quickly get to that ramp, which delivered him to the narrow aisle behind the last row of seats along the left-field foul line. Duquette could then slip through an oddly placed door cut into the brick that served as Fenway's skeleton—a storage room, perhaps?—and slink through a short tunnel of a hallway that delivered him into the corporate offices of one of the more chronicled teams in the history of professional sports.

At Fenway Park, as peculiar as it seemed, the back way into master control was essentially a walk-in closet, complete with mops, pails, and brooms that might as well have disguised the location of a safe house.

But then, after a day like this, who could blame Duquette for wanting to hide? Who could blame him for being angry, for feeling unappreciated and downright irrelevant?

Things at Fenway Park had begun moving quickly; it was entirely understandable for Duquette to feel as if he were losing control. In fewer than three months since the ugly collapse that marked the end of the 2001 Boston baseball season, Duquette had been trying to rebuild the Red Sox roster and restore the trust of the Boston fans. He had made a succession of maneuvers that had considerably altered the makeup of the team. But today, on an afternoon when Duquette had finalized his most significant move in a series of off-season transactions, the focus was on the much bigger picture: the transfer of Red Sox ownership, which would lead to even more dramatic change within a franchise that was forever fighting itself and its history, that needed a transfusion; and that change threatened the jobs and futures of virtually everyone associated with the franchise, beginning with a general manager who had been born, bred, and schooled in New England.

If Dan Duquette was frustrated, it was no wonder.

While many were speculating that the general manager of the Red Sox was about to be fired, Duquette was hoping to celebrate the signing of a dynamic new center fielder and leadoff man who could do great things for his baseball team.

Didn't anyone else recognize what Johnny Damon meant for Boston?

IN SOME respects, from the very beginning Dan Duquette was simply a man before his time.

Yet, by the end of Duquette's eight-year career as general manager of the Red Sox, many had forgotten that he arrived in Boston under comparable circumstances and with similar beliefs to those of his eventual successor, Theo Epstein, the boy who would be king. Duquette, like Epstein, was a local product who grew up in Massachusetts and had built a reputation working for a small-market team in the National League. He was regarded as one of the brighter young minds in the game, an innovative thinker who was open to some of baseball's newer and more radical theories. And just as Epstein would be seen several years later, Duquette was regarded as something of a Red Sox savior, the man who would bring the entire organization into a modern new age of baseball with an approach both aggressive and progressive.

Years later, couldn't people see? Duquette was from Dalton, Epstein from Brookline; Duquette had worked for the Montreal Expos, Epstein for the San Diego Padres; Duquette believed that baseball was moving into an entirely new era that included the use of statistics and quantitative analysis, just as Epstein did when the latter claimed the general manager's office at Fenway Park as an aspiring executive who had just landed his dream job in November 2002.

But in between, there was so much else that changed the picture, that prevented so many from seeing that Dan Duquette and Theo Epstein shared as many similarities as they did differences.

When Dan Duquette took over the Red Sox in January 1994, his initial objectives were the same as those of most every team in baseball, particularly the large-market clubs that had resources like the Red Sox. His goal was to make the Red Sox a perennial playoff contender, to make Boston a force in scouting and player development so that the club could be self-sufficient. (The subsequent administration voiced an almost identical plan; Epstein, in particular, would speak of the Red Sox becoming a scouting and player-development "machine" on the day he was formally hired as GM.) Indeed, if the best farms grew their own produce and livestock, the same was true of the best baseball teams; they drafted and nurtured their own players. Duquette's goal was to make the Red Sox a facsimile of the Atlanta Braves, an organization that had recently begun an unprecedented string of 14 consecutive National League East Division championships that would eventually extend through the 2005 season. (At that time, every baseball franchise wanted to be like the Braves.) And though Atlanta won just one World Series (1995) during that span of 14 seasons—the Braves also lost World Series in 1991, 1992, 1996, and 1999—Duquette was among the many who believed that Atlanta's philosophy was the best way to claim not merely one world championship, but several.

Keep knocking on the door, he reasoned, and you'll win your share.

In the end, for all of the criticism that Duquette took during his time in Boston, here is what people carelessly forgot: the Red Sox were a complete and utter mess when he got there. After posting just one losing season from 1967 to 1991, the Red Sox finished with more losses than wins in the three consecutive seasons from 1992 to 1994, the last of which was cut short by a historic work stoppage that resulted in a previously unthinkable cancellation of the World Series. (Regardless, the Red Sox were among the many teams who were not going to be playing in October.) And though Duquette had become general manager by then, though the 1994 Sox would become part of his official résumé,

Duquette argued later during his Red Sox career that he regarded the '94 club as more of a stepson, for the simplest reason: in baseball, teams generally were built from November through the middle of January. But Duquette officially took over the Boston baseball operation shortly before the start of spring training in February, so he had no influence over or connection to the players who would take the field on Opening Day 1994.

The bottom line? Just because Dan Duquette had chosen to live with these Red Sox, that didn't mean he had built the house.

Nonetheless, to his credit, Duquette acted aggressively from the start. At a time when baseball players and owners were in the midst of the labor war that ultimately wiped out the 1994 World Series, Duquette began tearing down walls and rebuilding the skeleton of the Boston baseball operation. When baseball's labor dispute extended into the off-season, teams and owners took a series of dramatic and political steps, first attempting to impose unilaterally a new set of business rules on the game, later going through the charade of reporting to spring training with minor leaguers whom the clubs had strong-armed into accepting the unwanted title of "replacement players." All of it was done with the intention of breaking the powerful players union (officially known as the Major League Baseball Players Association, or MLBPA) and changing a game that was undergoing an economic crisis.

In Boston and beyond, then, Duquette found himself in the midst of a major reconstruction.

Nonetheless, using the uncertainty in baseball to his advantage, Duquette acted more decisively than any other executive in the game. During the brief period that baseball attempted to impose new guidelines for, among other things, free agency, Duquette reached contractual agreements with three of the game's better players: starting pitcher Kevin Appier, then of the Kansas City Royals; closer John Wetteland, then of the Expos; and outfielder Sammy Sosa, then of the Chicago Cubs. And though the deals never came to fruition, though baseball owners and players ultimately settled their disputes and agreed on a new system that would negate the transactions that were made during the time of great uncertainty, Duquette gained. From the outset, his resourcefulness and aggressiveness were apparent to a rabid Red Sox fan base that had seen its team grow stale during the final years under affable general manager Lou Gorman. And when baseball owners and players finally settled on a new collective bargaining agreement that would serve as baseball's version of the Marshall Plan, Duquette was among the few prepared for the subsequent and resulting chaos.

Between the 1994 and 1995 seasons, when all of baseball was in flux, Duquette did more than merely rebuild the Red Sox; he made them better, faster, stronger. Shortly after the conclusion of the 1994 season, Duquette fired the manager he had inherited, overmatched incumbent Butch Hobson, and replaced him with Kevin Kennedy, who had served as a coach during Duquette's time in Montreal and more recently had been the manager of the Texas Rangers. Not much later, in a trade that gave the Red Sox instant relevance and marketability, Duquette dealt veteran outfielder Otis Nixon and third-base prospect Luis Ortiz to the Texas Rangers for glamorous slugger Jose Canseco, swapping the proverbial two ponies for a horse. Just like that, Canseco was reunited with Kennedy, with whom the player shared a strong relationship, and the Red Sox had a legitimate, bona fide rock star that made them, if nothing else, far more interesting.

Suddenly, the Sox had *appeal*.

"We needed a right-handed power hitter and we got one of the best right-handed power hitters in the game," a beaming Duquette said proudly on December 9, 1994, the day the Sox completed the Canseco trade. "And," he added, as if to remind followers that the Red Sox also had a business operation to worry about, "he's a fan favorite."

A few months later, after baseball had completed its soul-searching, Duquette made a series of other maneuvers all designed to make the Red Sox more competitive in the short term while preserving any chance at their long-term health. He signed a number of free agents to one-year contracts that would not require the forfeiture of compensatory draft selections, refusing to put any strain on a Boston farm system that had become barren. (By then, in his first draft with the Red Sox, Duquette had selected an array of young hopefuls that included shortstop Nomar Garciaparra and pitchers Carl Pavano and Brian Rose, all of whom would become principal players and/or bargaining chips in the years to come.) In the here and now of the impassioned and impatient Boston baseball market, Duquette added players like catcher Mike Macfarlane, starting pitcher Zane Smith, and relief pitcher Stan Belinda to a group that already included Canseco, budding first baseman Mo Vaughn, and staff ace Roger Clemens. From the scrap heap, Duquette picked up a reeling knuckleballer named Tim Wakefield and an outfielder named Troy O'Leary, replacing stale stock at the major-league level while infusing Boston's player-development system with new crops.

And Duquette did it all without giving up a single draft pick, something that would remain true during the first four years of his Red Sox administration.

Said Duquette years later, in the fall of 2007, six full baseball seasons after he had been fired by the Red Sox: "The plan that we articulated and outlined for the franchise was to sign and develop as much young pitching and talent as we could, and to support that with judicious drafts."

In the process, Duquette hoped to make the Red Sox better in the present, too, though even he could not have imagined how quickly things would come together. In 1995, the Red Sox won the American League East Division championship after finishing the strike-shortened 1994 season just one game ahead of the last-place Detroit Tigers. And though Boston was unceremoniously swept by the Cleveland Indians in the first round of the playoffs during an October in which baseball began a new playoff system that drew from three divisions rather than two, the renaissance of the Red Sox was one of the truly feel-good stories in the major leagues at a time when the game was desperately trying to rebuild its image.

In Boston, widely regarded as one of the very best baseball towns in America, fans and media were celebrating their 30-something general manager as nothing less than a genius and magician.

Soon, Dan Duquette was known as the man who resurrected the Red Sox.

And just before the start of spring training 1996, at the annual winter awards dinner hosted by the group that Red Sox lifer Johnny Pesky frequently and playfully referred to as "the carnivorous Boston press," the Boston baseball writers elected Duquette as their 1995 Major League Executive of the Year.

DUQUETTE'S DOWNFALL was that he never really played the game.

At least not in Boston.

Still, for someone who was perceived as shy and socially awkward even when he suited up for the Amherst College baseball team, Duquette, was, at various times, shrewd, crude, and entertaining. Before coming to Boston, during his stint as general manager of a Montreal Expos organization that had the unenviable task of trying to sell baseball to some of the most passionate hockey fans in the world, Duquette's relationship with reporters was healthy and functional. Once, when the Expos were at the winter meetings that effectively served as baseball's off-season fair and trade show, Duquette entered a room where Montreal writers were struggling to find anything that might serve as an appealing story for the following day's paper. (At the time, prior to the explosion of the Internet, newspapers reporter were always operating one day ahead of everyone else.) Because the cash-strapped Expos typically accomplished little at those meetings—but recognizing that the Montreal press still needed something to write—Duquette entered and gave the Expos' traveling press corps a piece of information that he believed could produce a sensational headline: EXPOS TRY TO ACQUIRE ONE-ARMED PITCHER.

Duquette told reporters that the Expos had made unsuccessful attempts to acquire Jim Abbott, a fascinating and universally admired left-handed pitcher who was born with only a stub for a right arm and who appealed to the media on two levels: first, Abbott was talented; second, he was a human-interest story that transcended the sports pages. According to one member of the Montreal media, Duquette promptly told the Montreal press that it was free to write the story, albeit on one condition: he asked the reporters to ensure that none of the information be attributed to him, because Major League Baseball had strict rules about publicly discussing players who were under contract with other teams, an offense generally known as tampering.

So, entrusted with interesting and theretofore unpublicized information, the Montreal press had its story for the day.

And if even for a short time, Duquette had the people of Montreal talking about baseball, the Expos, and an intriguing one-armed man.

Years later, when Duquette's career with the Red Sox was disintegrating, most members of the Boston media would have deemed such tales wildly far-fetched. From the time he arrived in Boston, Duquette hardly seemed like a man who was willing to work hand in hand with the press. Unlike his predecessor, the engaging and talkative Lou Gorman, Duquette regarded the Boston press as an obstacle. (In that way, he was not unlike future New England Patriots coach Bill Belichick, who saw the media largely as a menace and a distraction; the obvious difference was that Belichick won multiple championships along the way.) Duquette certainly recognized that reporters had jobs to do, but he also viewed the Boston press much differently than he viewed the reporters in Montreal. With the Expos, the team *needed* the media, craved the publicity; with the Red Sox, the press could be suffocating and detrimental. The Boston baseball media corps was one of the larger groups in the country and insanely demanding, and Duquette did not see the benefit in playing the role of a public-relations specialist for a club that did not need one—or so he thought—particularly when he had the considerable task of rebuilding a Boston baseball operation that had badly deteriorated.

Lou Gorman might have been a lovable gabber. But this was Dan Duquette's show now.

"Do I think that talking to the writers every day is good PR for the team? No. I don't think that's particularly good PR. . . . If it was, I would make common practice of it," Duquette told a *Boston Herald* reporter in January 1996, roughly two years after he had been hired. "The product that we put on the field here is a reflection of how well we do our jobs. If we're doing a good job, we're going to have an interesting and exciting team and we're going to provide a good entertainment value for the fans."

Continued Duquette: "Any business has a corporate communications [network]. If you call the governor, you don't get through to the governor. If you call a chief executive at one of the banks, you speak to the corporate communications department. In terms of the Red Sox, you can always get an answer and you can always get a quote. When we have news, we announce it in a public and constructive way."

To the Boston reporters who had covered the team for years, who were accustomed to Gorman's accommodating nature and agreeable ways, the message was clear: *There's a new sheriff in town. You're on your own.*

Unsurprisingly, then, Duquette feuded with the media throughout his tenure in Boston, though that was only part of the story. Fueled by a similar distaste for Duquette's methods, both existing and former Red Sox employees instantly had an ally in the press. And though Duquette was brought in explicitly for the purpose of rebuilding the Red Sox—like the Patrick Swayze character in *Road House*, he was hired to clean up—the *Boston Herald* and *Boston Globe* seemingly published stories on a routine basis that gave disgruntled employees and Red Sox adversaries a forum to vent about the cold, calculating, and arrogant new general manager of the Red Sox who was, at once, firing scouts and loyal, longtime employees; thumbing his nose at the establishment; dismissing the thoughts and opinions of more senior, more accomplished men; and running the Red Sox as if he were some steely-eyed chief financial officer on Wall Street and not merely the general manager of a baseball team that, by the way, had not won a World Series since the days of World War I.

During his time in Boston, for sure, Dan Duquette made more than his share of enemies.

Can you believe that man had the audacity to compare himself to the governor?

Of course, given that reality, Duquette's critics were all too eager to pounce on him beginning early in the 1996 season, when things began to go wrong. For the first time in his Boston tenure, thanks largely to the team's performance in 1995, Duquette entered a season with the burden of expectations. (Some people believed Boston could contend for the World Series championship.) Then the Red Sox came out and went an abysmal 3-15 in their first 18 games, a start so wretched that it effectively destroyed their playoff hopes before the season was four weeks old. Along the way, the relationship between Duquette and Kennedy began to crack before, ultimately, splintering beyond repair; Clemens, already regarded as the greatest pitcher in club history, was approaching free agency; the team was such a huge disappointment and there was such eagerness to issue blame—with the Red Sox, there always is—that Duquette became a punching bag, the easiest target for fans, players, and team employees to take a shot at.

Even Duquette's own words began to haunt him.

The product that we put on the field here is a reflection of how well we do our jobs.

Following the season, despite a commendable Red Sox comeback that allowed the club to finish with an 85-77 record and actually flirt with playoff contention, Kennedy was unceremoniously fired, largely because Duquette felt that his own manager was using the media against him. (This was indisputably true.) In retrospect, the relationship between manager and general manager probably was doomed from the beginning, if only because Kennedy's and Duquette's personalities were far too different for the relationship to succeed. Kennedy was reared in the accomplished Los Angeles Dodgers organization, something he was all too eager to remind people of, and he had succumbed to much of the Los Angeles culture. Kennedy's office at Fenway Park included such items as a photo of Natalie Wood, for instance, and some of Duquette's allies in the organization chuckled at the sight of Kennedy checking his hair before batting practice and alleged that Kennedy went so far as to put on makeup before doing television interviews.

Regardless of whether the latter was true, the point was clear: to Kevin Kennedy, image and appearance mattered greatly.

Duquette was much more of an introvert, someone far more concerned with the reality than the perception. If Dan Duquette had any Hollywood in him, it was only because he looked like a character from *Revenge of the Nerds* or, perhaps, like William Foster, the alienated rebel played by Michael Douglas in *Falling Down*. Duquette frequently wore his hair in a crew cut while securing his eyeglasses to the back of his head with a black elastic band, making him look more like a mechanical engineer than the man who ran the Red Sox. Beneath it all, Duquette was incredibly focused and commendably thick-skinned, though the latter characteristic was completely consistent with the rest of his personality. Dan Duquette focused on the task and nothing else, including the criticisms of him, which frequently became quite personal.

All of that taken into account, the final weeks of the 1996 season were fraught with turmoil, a development that was terribly predictable given the deteriorating relationship between the general manager and manager. Duquette believed that Kennedy's behavior completely undermined the team in the final weeks—the GM became particularly annoyed when longtime Sox outfielder Mike Greenwell, whose contract was set to expire, cleaned out his locker before the club officially was eliminated from playoff contention—and Duquette further believed that Kennedy was largely responsible for the demise of the club, both at the beginning of the season and at the end. By that point, Duquette allies believed Kennedy effectively had been turning both the media and his players against his own boss, a poor career move that subsequently might have prevented him from getting another job in the dugout and drove him to a career in, unsurprisingly, television.

When it came to the final days of the Kevin Kennedy era, Dan Duquette had reason to be outraged. After all, if the manager was backbiting the GM and promoting his own selfish interests, what kind of message did that send to the players?

In fact, even as September was playing out, Kennedy knew his days with the Red Sox were probably numbered. As part of Kennedy's original three-year contract (through 1997), the club had an option on his contract for a fourth season, 1998. The catch was that the club had to make a decision on that option by September 20, a fact that Kennedy had all too willingly shared with members of the media for the purpose of putting pressure on the organization. As the date neared, the Red Sox asked Kennedy for the right to delay that decision until after the season, as sure a sign as any that the manager's future was in jeopardy. Had the Red Sox been satisfied with the manager's performance, the Sox would proudly have issued a statement that Kennedy's contract option had been exercised, that the club expected to have stability in the manager's office through 1998.

Instead, the opposite happened.

Showing little regard for his relationship with Duquette, Kennedy turned to the media, which he often did. Once, while explaining short-stop John Valentin's uncharacteristic absence from the lineup, Kennedy hinted that Valentin had been benched because of lackluster play, though the manager was circumspect enough to avoid culpability. The next day, when Valentin found himself the subject of discussion—the Boston papers were nearly as subtle as the manager, a fact demonstrated by the *Herald* headline, "Valentin Benched"—the player erupted at a reporter, accused him of inaccurate reporting, and cited Kennedy's vague, cleverly constructed quotes as evidence that the media—and not the manager—were at fault.

When the reporter subsequently entered Kennedy's office to ask if he had misinterpreted the manager's message, Kennedy shook his head. "I was hoping that [Valentin] would see the headline and come in here to ask me about it," Kennedy said.

Which begged the question: If the manager was concerned about the play of his shortstop, why didn't Kennedy just call Valentin into his office in the first place?

Of course, by that time, Kennedy's methods were quite well known, particularly by his players. (Valentin later apologized to the reporter whom he had chastised, though Kennedy had since been fired.) In fact, from the time he arrived in Boston, Kennedy was careful to cultivate a relationship with Nick Cafardo, the beat reporter for the *Boston Globe*, the biggest paper that regularly covered the Red Sox. Most other reporters seemed of little or no use to the manager, who generally dealt with the press the same way he dealt with his players: the big-name stars got full cooperation and, perhaps, access to some privileged information; the lesser-known bodies were considered nothing more than expendable role players who would neither help nor hurt the manager's cause.

By the end of the 1996 season, Kennedy's tactics had alienated so many, particularly Duquette, that the manager had no hope of surviving. Even Cafardo, who had been switched to the New England Patriots football beat, was no longer an ally. As a result, Kennedy approached a familiar *Herald* reporter before a game against the Detroit Tigers on September 18—the manager now needed the smaller Boston newspaper as an ally—and privately admitted that the Red Sox had asked to postpone the decision on his contract option, that his fate was suddenly in question as the Red Sox prepared to play their final games of the 1996 campaign.

That very night, as luck would have it, Red Sox ace Roger Clemens took the mound at Tiger Stadium and delivered a masterpiece for the ages, striking out 20 batters in a nine-inning game for the second time in his career. To that point, no other pitcher in baseball history had accomplished the feat once, let alone twice, and Clemens's performance was the talk of the sports world as he, like fellow Sox lifer Greenwell, neared the end of his contract with the club. Because this 20-strikeout game came 10 years after the first, the effort was seen as a sign that Clemens was still capable of greatness, particularly at a time when his future with the team was in doubt. As was the case in the first 20-strikeout game—a 3–1 win over the Milwaukee Brewers on April 29, 1986—Clemens's feat was made even more remarkable by the fact that he did not walk a single batter. Moreover, the game was the 192nd victory of his Red Sox career, tying him with the immortal Cy Young for first place on the Red Sox' all-time list.

Unbeknownst to anyone at the time, the victory would also be Clemens's last in Boston.

Just the same, the news regarding Kennedy's contract option—or, more specifically, the Red Sox' unwillingness to exercise it—was big news in Boston on the morning of September 19. Precisely 11 days later—and just one day after the Red Sox played their 1996 season finale—the Red Sox announced on September 30 that Kennedy would not be retained for the 1997 season, that the team effectively was buying out the final year of the manager's contract, and that Boston would soon hire another manager, its third in the span of two calendar years and third of the Duquette era.

"I think, in part, the team had a hangover from 1995 going into 1996," Duquette said in explaining his decision to fire Kennedy. "The toughest part of managing is early in the season. You've got to get your guys together and headed in the right direction. To me, the most important part of managing is right there in spring training. It didn't help that the season ended the same way it started—without much support or leadership on the front line. To me, the manager has to look out for the team. It was abominable for me to see players cleaning out their lockers before the last game of the season. That is just not acceptable to me." Added the GM, offering even bigger reasons for Kennedy's dismissal: "I think the manager has to manage the whole roster. It takes a certain sensitivity to handle young players. It takes the same sensitivity to handle pitchers. At times, we looked like the Bad News Bears. We couldn't throw strikes. We couldn't run the bases. These are fundamental plays."

Unsurprisingly, then, Dan Duquette put his energy into replacing the politically minded Kevin Kennedy with a fundamentalist, the kind of man who would emphasize the basics of the game, who had a true love for baseball on the field, who would nurture young players and allow them to grow, who was less concerned with his image and more with the product. What Dan Duquette wanted was what many people in the game referred to as "a baseball man."

So, seven weeks after firing the egocentric Kevin Kennedy, Duquette hired the far less conniving Jimy Williams, who had most recently served as the third-base coach in Duquette's benchmark organization, the Atlanta Braves. Duquette had jumped from one end of the spectrum to the other. Williams was a no-nonsense baseball lifer who enjoyed, above all else, *instructing*, which typically endeared him to younger players who were eager to learn. Williams was not nearly as telegenic as Kennedy—nor did he care to be—and he did not care much for reporters, particularly those in television and radio, many of whom he deemed ignorant about baseball. The irony was that many media members proved Williams's point by quickly passing judgment and regarding him as something of a country bumpkin, an image perpetuated when Williams highlighted his inaugural press conference with an unforgettable line. Asked a hypothetical question about the Red Sox, Williams quickly made it clear that he would make a habit of dismissing any question that began with *if*. "If a frog had wings," said the new manager, trying to make his point, "he wouldn't bump his booty."

Predictably, the humor was lost on much of the Boston press.

Given also the manner in which the Red Sox' season had ended, Williams's hiring was met with skepticism, though much of that was a product of frustration in and around the organization. All the good that the surprisingly good 1995 season had brought, the 1996 campaign had destroyed. The general belief was that the Red Sox appeared to be going in the wrong direction again, which inevitably thrust the general manager into the eye of the proverbial storm.

So, just one year after improbably taking the Red Sox to the playoffs, Dan Duquette entered the off-season of 1996–97 faced with the considerable challenge of improving both his baseball team and his image.

The honeymoon was over.

And things would get worse before they got better.

DURING DAN Duquette's tenure with the Red Sox, the controversies frequently marked the time. From the instant Duquette was hired to the day he was fired, the Red Sox seemed defined by tumult. Never was that truer than during the off-season between the end of the 1996 season and Opening Day 1997.

Precisely 24 days after Williams was hired as Kennedy's replacement on November 19, 1996, Roger Clemens left the Red Sox to sign what would become a four-year contract with the Toronto Blue Jays for just over $31 million on, of all dates, Friday the 13th of December. And though blame issued by Bostonians was relatively split between Duquette and Clemens—many fans regarded Clemens, whom they perceived as both ignorant and greedy, with even more disdain than they viewed Duquette—the entire episode served as a line of demarcation in Red Sox history.

If Roger Clemens could leave the Red Sox, after all, then most anything else was possible.

At Fenway Park, the door now swung both ways.

"The Red Sox and our fans were fortunate to see Roger Clemens play in his prime and we had hoped to keep him in Boston during the twilight of his career," Duquette said on a conference call with reporters to address the player's departure. "We just want to let the fans know that we worked extremely hard to sign Roger Clemens. . . . We made him a substantial, competitive offer, by far the most money offered to a player in the history of the Red Sox franchise."

Continued the GM: "Unfortunately, we just couldn't get together. We were hoping [Clemens] could finish his career as a Red Sox and we also wanted him to establish a relationship beyond his playing career. We wanted him to have a status of a Ted Williams, but at the end of the day we couldn't get it done."

Countered Clemens at a press conference in Toronto that was dominated by members of the Boston media: "I knew from the first offer that Duquette put out there that it was in my heart he didn't want me back. I know [Duquette] might tell you differently, but I think he's happy today and I think I'm happy today."

So the departure of the greatest pitcher in Red Sox history played like a game of he said, she said. Depending on the perspective, one of two things had happened. Either Roger Clemens had jumped. Or Dan Duquette had pushed him.

In the end, though the Sox opened negotiations with Clemens by offering a four-year, $10 million contract packed with incentive clauses—Duquette believed Clemens had become overweight and complacent in the final years of his time in Boston—the team's final offer to Clemens was a four-year, $22 million package that was entirely guaranteed. Still, as political and nasty as the Clemens negotiations became, Duquette was not haunted by his actions as much as he was, again, by his words. *The twilight of his career.* The obvious insinuation was that Clemens was far closer to the end of his career than to the beginning, that he was past his prime, that the Red Sox and their fans had likely seen the best days of a career during which Clemens had already won three American League Cy Young Awards as the game's best pitcher and recorded two 20-strikeout games, the latter of which had come roughly three months before Clemens's departure from the Red Sox.

If Roger Clemens needed any additional motivation following his departure from the Red Sox—and, as it turned out, he did not—then Duquette surely gave it to him.*

Still, whether he intended it or not, Duquette's stance in the Clemens negotiations affected Red Sox history for years to come. By the time first baseman Mo Vaughn similarly came up for free agency at the end of the 1998 season, for instance, Duquette had already set the precedent for how he would deal with a star player. Vaughn's career in Boston was nothing if not explosive, characterized by both years of productivity on the field—he was named Most Valuable Player of the American League in 1995—and constant, public feuding with the front office. By Vaughn's final season in Boston, some Red Sox officials believed the player had become jealous and resentful of budding superstar Nomar Garciaparra, whom the club had granted a revolutionary, multiyear contract after Garciaparra's first year in the majors; Vaughn, meanwhile, believed that the Red Sox had hired private investigators to follow him in the wake of a series of off-field incidents that stemmed largely from the player's affection for strip clubs.

By the end of his celebrated career in Boston, Vaughn was a fascinating paradox of images, a pied piper to children and genuine philanthropist on the one hand, a hard-living party boy on the other. Consequently, it came as no surprise when he left the club following the 1998 season. Prior to leaving, Vaughn turned down a five-year, $65 million offer from the Red Sox, who had grown so concerned about the player's lifestyle and physical condition that they even asked the player to undergo an evaluation for alcoholism.

---

*In 11 seasons after leaving the Red Sox, through 2007, Clemens went 162-73, winning more games than all but five pitchers in baseball: Greg Maddux, Randy Johnson, Andy Pettitte, Curt Schilling, and Tom Glavine. Clemens won four more Cy Young Awards as the most outstanding pitcher in his league and climbed to eighth on baseball's all-time list for victories. After the 2007 season, however, he was named by former Senate majority leader George Mitchell in the infamous "Mitchell Report" as a player suspected of extending and enhancing his career through the use of performance-enhancing substances like steroids and human growth hormone (HGH).

True to form, Vaughn went public with the information. And in nuclear fashion. "Watch out for the smear campaign. It'll be coming soon to a theater near you," the colorful Vaughn ranted during spring training of his final season in Boston, at one point referring to Red Sox officials as "the Joint Chiefs of Staff." Added the player, who had grown increasingly frustrated with the organization's stance during fruitless contract discussions: "There are going to be a lot of things that are going to come out. Next [thing you'll know], I'm going to be selling drugs, and after that, I've been doing drugs. They're going to paint a picture of a lot of negativity throughout the last half [year] or year of my career. That's typical of the way things go around here. . . . The club is never happy with [people who speak] the truth. They just want you to show up and play, like you've got no heart, no conscience, no feelings, like you're just a machine. That's the reason I'm not signed, because I don't conform. It's not about the deal. We can't even sit in the same room together. That's just the way it is."

As much public debate as there was over Vaughn's departure, the Clemens negotiations had set the standard two years earlier. Until that point in Boston baseball history, Red Sox superstars frequently were seen as harboring greater power than the executives for whom they worked, possessors of a birthright that made them bigger than the team. Longtime Red Sox owner Thomas A. Yawkey was often blamed for what Red Sox followers frequently referred to as "the country club atmosphere," and the power that longtime Sox stars wielded was impossible to ignore. Beginning in 1939 and up until Clemens's departure following the 1996 season, Red Sox standouts generally played their entire careers in Boston, from Ted Williams (1939–60) to Carl Yastrzemski (1961–84) to Jim Rice (1974–89); many assumed Clemens would do the same. So when he left Boston after a bitter breakup, a legacy was fractured.

In the process, Duquette set the groundwork for future Sox officials—up to and beyond Theo Epstein—to firmly hold their place, with a clear and decisive message: *The inmates don't run the asylum.*

In the wake of the Clemens negotiations, Duquette quickly had other problems to worry about. Partly as a result of Clemens's departure and partly as a result of Duquette's inability to find a suitable replacement—Boston's best attempt was Steve Avery, once a promising young left-hander whose talent had mysteriously abandoned him—the Red Sox reported to spring training with little hope of making the playoffs. The team was at its spring home in Fort Myers when *Boston Globe* reporter Gordon Edes was introduced to Mike Gimbel, a wildly eccentric man whom Duquette had employed as a statistical consultant. (Duquette himself would later draw a rough comparison between Gimbel and Boo Radley, the peculiar but good-natured recluse in *To Kill a Mockingbird*.) By day, Gimbel, who lived in an apartment in which he housed a pet alligator, read water meters in Brooklyn; by night, he was one of the earliest number crunchers in a field that would come to be known as "sabermetrics," a field that tried to predict the performance of players based largely on statistical and historical data.

But years before the publication of *Moneyball*, the book that celebrated the sabermetric techniques of the low-budget Oakland A's—and years, too, before Epstein would work closely with a more respected and accepted statistician, Bill James—Mike Gimbel was looked upon as nothing more than a crackpot whom Duquette brought in to address his manager and coaching staff, all of whom were stunned. And before long, largely a result of Edes's fascinating story in which Gimbel suggested he was, in Edes's words, "the power behind the throne," word had spread through the Red Sox clubhouse, and the Boston baseball operation was seen as nothing short of a laughing-stock.

"Off the record, gentlemen?" de facto team captain Vaughn said to a group of writers at spring training during the height of the Gimbel scandal.

The reporters nodded.

"Is this the most fucked-up organization you've ever seen or what?"

All around, there was gut-busting laughter.

In reality, at least on some level, Gimbel's unveiling was more of the political process at work, though by then Duquette had fewer and fewer allies. The GM believed that Edes had been turned onto Gimbel by Kevin Malone, the man who replaced Duquette as general manager of the Expos when Duquette jumped to Boston. Malone had served as an assistant under Duquette in Montreal, where Gimbel was similarly consulted, and he knew quite well that Gimbel's eccentricities would not play well publicly in a Boston market that was terribly uptight to begin with. By the time the story hit the streets as the lead in the *Globe* sports section, the reaction among media and Duquette's critics was predictable: *No wonder the Red Sox haven't won a World Series since 1918.*

By the time the 1997 season ended, Duquette could be forgiven if he was happy to see it go. While the Red Sox went 78-84 to finish with their only losing record of the Duquette era—excluding Duquette's stepson season of 1994, of course—the general manager's image took a terrible beating. First there was the Clemens departure, which left the Red Sox without a leader to their pitching staff. Then there was the discovery of Gimbel, whose involvement in the Red Sox operation dealt a serious blow to the team's credibility. And finally, there was the public-relations mess that stemmed from a domestic dispute involving Red Sox left fielder Wilfredo Cordero, a player whom Duquette had coveted and acquired via a trade with the Montreal Expos prior to the 1996 season, only to see Cordero and the Red Sox organization tainted by a publicized arrest for domestic dispute at a time when American awareness of such matters was heightened in the wake of the O. J. Simpson murder trial.

Immediately after the Red Sox completed the 1997 season, the Red Sox released Cordero from their active roster, concluding what amounted to a 12-month period during which Duquette fired his manager; lost his best pitcher to free agency; cut loose a player whom he had all but salivated over; and saw his image, reputation, and credibility dealt a potentially fatal blow.

On the surface, especially for Dan Duquette, 1997 seemed a damning year.

But on much deeper levels, particularly relating to the long-term future of the Red Sox, it was one of Duquette's best.

THE DUKE'S LEGACY

ONE OF THE BEAUTIES OF BASEBALL IS THAT THERE IS ALWAYS something to play for, be it in the short term or the long. Relative to other sports, the game possesses a continuity that is impossible to ignore. Because the baseball season typically runs from February (when players report to spring training) through late October (when the World Series ends), the years frequently run together. As a result, long stretches of time can pass before the most significant moments in a team's history are realized.

In Boston, the 1997 season was one of those moments.

In the midst of a season during which the Red Sox were, at their best, both troubled and mediocre, Dan Duquette continued going about the business of rebuilding the Red Sox, even if nobody cared to notice. The most tangible evidence of Boston's future was the play of rookie shortstop Nomar Garciaparra, Duquette's first draft pick, whose ascension to star status in the major leagues was nothing short of meteoric. In his first season as the Red Sox shortstop, the dynamic Garciaparra batted .306 with 209 hits, 122 runs scored, 30 home runs, 44 doubles, 11 triples, 98 RBIs, and 22 stolen bases. Garciaparra was a landslide winner for the American League Rookie of the Year Award and finished eighth in the league's Most Valuable Player Award balloting, a considerable accomplishment for a rookie player on a losing team.

Quite simply, amid all the controversy that highlighted the 1997 Red

Sox season, Nomar Garciaparra had one of the greatest rookie seasons in baseball history.

Still, beyond the play of the new Red Sox shortstop, the team was struggling. During a May stretch in which the Red Sox lost seven straight and 11 of 12, the team dipped below the .500 mark and never again got its head above water. Duquette knew that there was little chance of the Red Sox righting the ship, largely because he knew the club was short on pitching. Up to that point in his Red Sox career, in fact, Duquette had gone on record as saying that the first six to eight weeks of a baseball season served as a good length of time for a general manager to assess his team accurately, a method that again would become far more popular (and accepted) when revolutionary Oakland A's general manager Billy Beane raised the organization from ruin in the late 1990s. Regardless, Duquette was not expecting any miracle turnarounds in June—and he didn't get one—which made his role and responsibilities clear as the 1997 baseball season entered its middle months.

Dan Duquette was playing for the future. Even if he wasn't about to say so.

Thus, at a time of the season when baseball teams inevitably fall into two groups—buyers and sellers—Duquette knew that the Red Sox were actually in a position to help themselves. Because the pressure to win is so great in professional sports—and because in baseball, in particular, winning is so difficult—teams frequently pay steep prices in trading for veteran talent that might be able to help them during the second half of a season. The Red Sox themselves had learned that very lesson when, while in contention for the 1990 American League East Division championship, they traded a minor-league third baseman named Jeff Bagwell to the Houston Astros for a veteran right-handed relief pitcher named Larry Andersen. Though Andersen helped the Red Sox immensely—he had a sterling 1.23 ERA in 15 games with the team—the Red Sox ultimately lost Andersen to free agency following a season in which the Oakland A's swept them in the minimum four games of the American League Championship Series.

So while Larry Andersen helped, the Red Sox fell well short of a world title. And when the price for Andersen proved steeper than anyone might have guessed, the Sox appeared actually to take a step backward.

Still, while the trade scarred the Red Sox and their fans forever—Bagwell went on to have a Hall of Fame–caliber career with the Astros during which he hit 449 home runs—Duquette frequently went out of his way to defend his predecessor, Gorman, for making the trade. The baseball season was long and unpredictable, after all—only one team per year could call itself a champion—and Duquette believed it was a general manager's obligation to do everything necessary to win a world title when the opportunity presented itself. (Many executives shared this same feeling.) In fact, when the rebuilt 1995 Red Sox surprised many with a strong early-season start, Duquette lived up to his word and fortified the team for the second half of the season by acquiring relief pitcher Rick Aguilera from the Minnesota Twins for a right-handed minor-league pitcher named Frankie Rodriguez, one of the Red Sox' more highly regarded prospects at that time. But now, in 1997, the proverbial shoe was on the other foot. Duquette had a few veteran players to sell, and he knew there might be a team willing to pay handsomely for them.

Given the departure of Clemens and the Red Sox' resulting difficulties, Boston's needs were obvious: pitching. Still, prospects Pavano and Rose (both drafted with Garciaparra) were having stellar seasons in the minor leagues, and Duquette believed that both pitchers might be ready to make contributions to the major-league team as early as 2008. That possibility allowed Duquette to focus on another position, catcher, which had become a troublesome spot for the Sox (as it is annually for many teams) during the 1997 season. Veteran Mike Stanley had seen his catching skills begin to erode while in the second year of a three-year contract, forcing him to play more time at first base and less behind the plate. And because Duquette was not entirely sold on the younger Scott Hatteberg, the general manager hoped to trade Stanley or, perhaps, embattled closer Heathcliff Slocumb before the annual July 31 trading deadline for someone who might give the Sox some long-term stability behind the plate.

So, with his sights fixed on obtaining a catcher, Duquette began discussions with a number of other executives, including then–Seattle Mariners general manager Woody Woodward, whose club seemed, at least on the surface, to be a good trading partner for the Red Sox. (Baseball officials frequently call potential dealing mates "a match" or "a fit.") At the time, Woodward's Mariners were a team blessed with explosive offensive talent like Ken Griffey Jr., Jay Buhner, and Edgar Martinez, as well as a wildly gifted young shortstop, Alex Rodriguez, all of whom routinely took the field behind a strong starting rotation headed by Randy Johnson. In fact, only a year earlier, Duquette and Woodward had made a similar deadline trade in which the reeling Red Sox acquired outfielder Darren Bragg for pitcher Jamie Moyer, a veteran left-hander who already was having a huge impact in Seattle and would go on to have a marvelous career with the Mariners.

Yet, as the 1997 deadline approached, the Mariners were still in search of an elusive world title despite a stocked roster and a celebrated manager, Lou Piniella, who was known to lose his patience in explosive fashion. That summer, a self-destructive relief corps had caused Piniella even more agita than usual, so Woodward had set out to rebuild almost the entire bullpen, a considerable goal that nonetheless seemed attainable largely because Woodward had two young players that had value to other clubs.

The first was outfielder Jose Cruz Jr., an immensely gifted prospect whom the Mariners could sacrifice given the depth of their offensive talent.

The other was a minor-league catcher named Jason Varitek.

For Duquette, Varitek was an intriguing prospect, the kind of player

THE DUKE'S LEGACY | 43

who could make the Red Sox and Mariners "a fit." Though the Mariners probably had no interest in catcher–first baseman Stanley, Duquette knew that the Mariners might have a use for Slocumb. Varitek, for his part, had been a two-time College Player of the Year at Georgia Tech University in 1993 and 1994, though he had since earned far more attention thanks to the actions of his agent, Scott Boras. Drafted in the first round by the Minnesota Twins as a junior in 1993, Varitek held out in hopes of a bigger contract and ultimately reentered the draft a year later. Subsequently selected by the Mariners in 1994—again in the first round—Varitek again held out and finally signed late, failing to enter the team's player-development system until 1995. When Varitek's progress was slow, many blamed agent Boras for derailing the career of a star player.

Said Sox outfielder Bragg when rumors first surfaced about the Red Sox' interest in Varitek, with whom Bragg played at both Georgia Tech and in the Seattle system: "Slow bat, stone hands."

And he was right.

Still, while Varitek had been a bust to that point in his career, Duquette saw an opportunity for the player to blossom. Working with younger players was one of manager Jimy Williams's strengths, and both manager and GM believed in one of baseball's oldest adages: You never give up on talent. Williams believed that every player had at least some value, that the ones who succeeded did so because they were given an opportunity. Had Kevin Kennedy still been the Red Sox manager during the 1997 season, there is no telling whether Duquette would have attempted to trade for Varitek—and pitcher Derek Lowe—at all or, if he had, whether Varitek and Lowe would have developed into productive major-league players, as they later did. But at that time in Red Sox history, Boston had both a need for young talent and a manager capable of nurturing it, a random convergence of elements and personalities that so frequently results in success.

For Jason Varitek and Derek Lowe, Boston had the chance to be everything Seattle was not: the right place, at the right time, with the right people.

In Seattle, the opposite was true. Frustrated by Varitek's lack of development—and blessed with a 28-year-old catcher, Dan Wilson, who he believed would continue to serve as the Seattle backstop for years to come—Woodward was open to the idea of trading Varitek for Slocumb, though the Red Sox wanted more in the deal. Boston ultimately settled on Derek Lowe, a tall right-handed pitcher whom Duquette privately would admit to knowing very little about, other than that Lowe was coveted by the Detroit Tigers, whose baseball operation was then under the control of general manager Randy Smith.

"Derek Lowe was from Michigan," Duquette said years later, recounting the deal. "Randy Smith was the Tigers GM then and he was trying to acquire a local player. We knew that if Lowe didn't work out, we could always trade him [to Detroit]."

To general managers, even potential bit parts can be commodities based on one of the laws of baseball management: If a player has value to someone else, he has value to you.

So, with the Mariners fighting for a playoff spot and the Red Sox looking to rebuild their future, Duquette and Woodward made a trade for the second straight season in the hours approaching baseball's annual July 31 trading deadline: Slocumb to the Mariners for Varitek and Lowe. The deal came at the 11th hour on a night that Slocumb blew a game against the Kansas City Royals, after which Slocumb stood at his locker and answered questions from reporters about the defeat and his potential departure. (Slocumb was sure that reporters knew he had already been traded when, in fact, they did not.) Shortly after most Sox players (including Slocumb) had left the ballpark, Sox manager Jimy Williams was getting on an elevator when a reporter delivered the message that Duquette was trying to reach his manager with the news that the Red Sox had just made a trade, a piece of information that Williams quickly accepted before scurrying out the door to speak with his boss.

The Slocumb deal concluded a busy day for Woodward, who was at the center of a flurry of baseball activity. In another trade, Woodward sent outfielder Cruz to the Toronto Blue Jays for relievers Mike Timlin and Paul Spoljaric, giving the Mariners—and their itchy-trigger-fingered manager, Piniella—three veteran relievers that the team hoped would stabilize and solidify its bullpen in the quest for a world championship.

In Boston, meanwhile, the trade was celebrated as, at worst, a classic case of addition by subtraction thanks to the departure of the remarkably good-natured (off the field) and terribly erratic (on the field) Slocumb, whose career in Boston had consisted of a series of high-wire acts. As for Jason Varitek and Derek Lowe, nobody in Boston had any idea that the Red Sox had just pulled off the kind of trade that would have the hardball value of the Lufthansa Heist.

"Let's face it," Duquette said proudly more than 10 years after making the deal. "Jason Varitek has been the most stable influence on the [Red Sox] for the last decade."

But at the time, the Red Sox did not know what they had just obtained.

WITH REGARD to Pedro Martinez, on the other hand, the Red Sox knew exactly what they were getting.

Especially Dan Duquette.

And so following a 1997 season in which Red Sox pitchers finished with a collective 5.29 ERA that ranked an abysmal 12th among the 14 American League teams—the Sox ranked 25th among the 28 clubs in all of baseball—the general manager of the Red Sox set out with a single goal in mind: an ace. As much promise as the Red Sox saw in young pitchers like Pavano and Rose, Duquette also knew that the transition to the major leagues usually took years, especially for pitchers. While someone like Garciaparra had immediately established himself in the majors with what some were calling the single greatest rookie season in baseball history, Duquette recognized that it was naive to think a pitcher could be so effective, so early. Throughout both major leagues, there was a collection of aces—from Greg Maddux to Tom Glavine to Clemens—and all of them had something in common beyond their greatness. They had all had difficulty at the beginning. They had all had to endure some growing pains.

Coming off the disappointments that were, in varying degrees, 1996 and 1997, Duquette seemed to recognize that he was at a crossroads in his career as a Red Sox executive. Boston was an impatient market to begin with, and the 1997 season, in particular, had been frustrating on many fronts. For the fourth time in six years, the Red Sox were coming off a losing season. Duquette had traded away Slocumb at the July 31 trading deadline and first baseman Mike Stanley less than two weeks later, the latter in a deal with the Sox' longtime rival, the New York Yankees, that brought back a journeyman reliever, Jim Mecir, and pitching prospect Tony Armas Jr. Things were so bad in Boston that even someone like the dignified Stanley beamed upon learning of his return to the Yankees, for whom he had played the best years of his career before joining the Red Sox as a free agent.

Getting out of Boston was akin to being paroled. "You don't have to smile so much," a somber Mo Vaughn told Stanley while embracing his (former) teammate in the hallway outside the manager's office at Fenway Park.

Three months later, Duquette headed the Red Sox contingent that arrived at the lush Princess Hotel in Scottsdale, Arizona, for the annual general managers' meetings, an event that typically kicked off each baseball off-season in earnest. In this year, especially, there was much work to be done. Because baseball was planning to add two teams for the 1998 season—the Tampa Bay Devil Rays and Arizona Diamondbacks—the game was undergoing significant changes. Divisions were being realigned, and one team, the Milwaukee Brewers, was being asked to change leagues altogether, going from the American League to the National League. And because both the Devil Rays and the Diamondbacks needed to have their rosters stocked with major-league-caliber talent, the 28 existing clubs in baseball needed to sacrifice some of their players in an expansion draft during which the Devil Rays and Diamondbacks would build their rosters from lists of players that other teams could not protect.

In other ways, too, the off-season of 1997–98 presented a different challenge. Because of the expansion draft, baseball's entire winter calendar had to be shifted. Though the bulk of activity by teams—trades and free-agent signings—did not traditionally take place until late November and December, the expansion draft necessitated more roster shuffling than usual. Prior to the draft, teams were able to protect only 15 players from being selected by Arizona or Tampa, which created a myriad of issues: some clubs had too much veteran talent to protect and subsequently sought to make trades; others, like the Red Sox, had an abundance of younger players and risked losing youth. One week before the draft, which was to be held at the Phoenix Civic Plaza, officials from Major League Baseball put a freeze on all trades so as to prevent roster manipulation.

With all of that in mind, Duquette arrived at the meetings intent on speaking with Jim Beattie, the man who now ran the baseball operation of Duquette's former club, the Montreal Expos, an organization in a perpetual state of crisis. Unable to generate significant interest and revenue in the Montreal market, the Expos were being forced to explore the idea of trading their best pitcher, 26-year-old right-hander Pedro Martinez, who was coming off a spectacular season during which he won the National League Cy Young Award while going 17-8 with a 1.90 ERA and 305 strikeouts. The simple truth was that the Expos could no longer afford Martinez, who was already earning an estimated $3.6 million per season. In the short term, Martinez was eligible for a salary-arbitration process that might double his salary for 1998; in the long term, his contract with Montreal was due to expire at the end of the '98 campaign.

So, faced with the prospect of losing Martinez in a year (and getting nothing in return for him) or trading him now (and getting something back), the Expos let it be known that they were essentially putting their best player up for auction.

In baseball, at that time, there was a distinct and expanding gap between the rich and the poor, the haves and the have-nots. "I'm just trying to get as good a set of [prospects] as I can, guys with good ceilings," admitted Beattie. "I'm just trying to get good players for Pedro. If I end up with one good player and with some others who have good shots, I'd feel good, to be honest with you."

As it turned out, Dan Duquette had the one good player Jim Beattie wanted.

Though Carl Pavano would never quite live up to the potential that many major-league scouts saw in him, he was, in November 1997, the baseball equivalent of a young Grace Kelly: he had it all. Pavano was 6-foot-5 and 230 pounds, and he had yet to celebrate his 22nd birthday. He was coming off consecutive minor-league seasons during which he went a combined 27-11 with a 2.80 ERA, the most recent at Triple-A Pawtucket of the International League, which meant he was ready to make the jump to the major leagues. A team could control Pavano's salary for the first three years of his career and own his rights for three additional seasons, which made him everything a team like the Expos would want.

Pavano was young. He was strong. And he was talented.

Most of all, he was cheap.

For all of Duquette's talk about rebuilding the Boston farm system, Duquette recognized, too, that Martinez was the ace on which he could build his pitching staff for years to come. The failures of 1996 and 1997 had put some pressure on the club to win immediately, but even so, Duquette felt Martinez was anything but a gamble. The general manager kept telling himself: *He's only 26.* It might be three or four years before Pavano became what Martinez already was—if he became it at all—and by then Martinez would already have pitched several seasons in Boston, assuming things went the way Duquette wanted them to. The primary question was whether the Red Sox could sign Martinez to a contract extension that would keep the pitcher in Boston for longer than a season, and major-league rules prohibited the Red Sox from discussing a contract with Martinez or his representatives (veteran agents Jim Bronner and Bob Gilhooley) as long as the pitcher wore the uniform of another team.

Even Beattie acknowledged that any trade for Martinez was a gamble, largely because the pitcher wanted to be assured of joining a playoff contender after leaving the depressing state of affairs in Montreal. "I think there's a lot you'd have to do to sell the guy on your team because the guy is going to have a lot of opportunities if he becomes a free agent next year," Beattie acknowledged, issuing a statement that might actually have hurt his bargaining position. "I think what you need to do as a team is feel confident you're going to put a winning team out there and feel you're going to sign him."

While Duquette had serious questions concerning the Red Sox' ability to sign Martinez, he also had an affection for Martinez that went well beyond his desire to rebuild the Red Sox. In fact, Duquette had acquired Martinez once before, while with the Expos, in a trade that sent speedy second baseman Delino DeShields to the Los Angeles Dodgers. (That trade, too, proved to be a steal.) The Dodgers had signed both Martinez and his older brother, Ramon, as free agents out of the Dominican Republic, but Ramon Martinez was taller, 6-foot-4, and had thrice won 15 or more games in a season. Dodger manager Tommy Lasorda believed that Pedro Martinez lacked the size and durability necessary to be an effective starting pitcher in the major leagues, so the Dodgers traded what they thought was a relief pitcher, at best, for a top-of-the-order hitter who batted .292 in 1992 and would finish with 463 career stolen bases.

In Montreal, of course, Pedro Martinez flourished, and it was there that Duquette learned of Martinez's colorful personality, his burning desire to win, the sizable chip on Martinez's shoulder that drove the pitcher to be as good as big brother Ramon and to disprove, among others, the great Tommy Lasorda.

Given Martinez's remarkable talents, the interest in him was considerable. Any team with young players and a big payroll was a candidate to trade for Martinez, though there was just one club, the Cleveland Indians, that could present a real threat to the Red Sox. The Indians were coming off a season in which they lost to the Florida Marlins in the seventh game of the World Series, and a pitcher like Martinez could easily make the Indians the team to beat—for years to come—in all of baseball. The primary question was whether the Indians would be willing to give up a young right-handed pitcher named Jaret Wright, who had enjoyed a stellar October and been a force for the team throughout the playoffs. Wright was just 20, the son of a former major-league pitcher, Clyde Wright, who had never quite lived up to his potential. Against the New York Yankees in the American League Division Series and against the Marlins in the World Series, Jaret Wright went a combined 3-0 with a 3.42 ERA and 22 strikeouts in 23.2 innings, demonstrating a fearlessness that opened eyes throughout the baseball world. Wright was young and cocky, and he had the kind of exploding fastball that could completely overpower hitters, allowing him to win games even if he used no other pitches from his repertoire.

In Jaret Wright, the Cleveland Indians believed they had a force for years to come, the kind of pitcher who could be every bit as good as Pedro Martinez and who could give the Indians the bull they had lacked in a fruitless championship pursuit that had been ongoing for four years.

Given all of the factors with Martinez—that he was six years older than Wright, that he could become a free agent after just one year—Indians general manager John Hart took a decidedly different view than Duquette. With his team seemingly so close to a championship, with Wright seemingly having proven that he could handle big games, Hart decided that Pedro Martinez wasn't worth the risk. Had the Indians decided otherwise, it is impossible to determine just how much baseball history might have changed.

But John Hart didn't want to make the trade.

Meanwhile, Duquette had already decided that he would give up Pavano or Rose, the two young pitchers around whom the Red Sox were marketing their future. Pavano and Rose were watched with such scrutiny during the regular season, in fact, that some veteran Sox players grew tired of hearing their names. At the big-league level, after all, the Red Sox were losing more than they were winning, and veteran players recognized that valuable time was passing by. Vaughn and infielder John Valentin were among the players in the prime of their careers at the time, and neither was thrilled about the prospect of introducing young pitchers into a market like Boston at a stage when more development was necessary.

At one point, with the Sox on the West Coast preparing to play the Anaheim Angels, a frustrated Valentin thought about the prospect of returning for the 1998 season behind a pair of rookie pitchers, knowing it would take a virtual miracle for the Red Sox to compete. "First grade [all over again]," Valentin said with a shake of his head.

Duquette, too, knew that he might be able to integrate one rookie pitcher into the starting rotation the following season, but two was another matter. So after meeting with Beattie over lunch at the start of the meetings, Duquette continued to have discussions with his Montreal counterpart throughout their stay in Scottsdale. On November 16, during a late-afternoon briefing with reporters who were concerned about making their deadlines on the East Coast, Duquette admitted that he was continuing to speak with the Expos, but gave little indication that the club was on the verge of completing one of the biggest trades in franchise history. "That's a team that we'd like to continue to pursue," an unusually playful Duquette said of the Expos. "They're asking for our first- and second-born sons. I've got to call my wife. She might be willing to give up the firstborn."

The message was clear: the Expos can have Pavano or Rose, but they can't have both.

By that night, after the first-edition newspaper deadlines had passed on the East Coast, word in Scottsdale began to spread: the Expos had whittled the field and were now negotiating with just one team to finalize a deal for Martinez. Teams from Colorado, New York, Los Angeles, and—yes—Cleveland were believed to be out of the running, and that left just one team that was a fit with Montreal: the Red Sox. Duquette was working in his hotel room when he received a call from a *Herald* reporter who wanted to know if the Sox had a deal in place for Martinez, the man whom many regarded as perhaps the best pitcher in baseball.

"We need to improve our pitching," Duquette told the *Herald*.

"So you're getting Pedro?" replied the reporter.

"You tell me," Duquette answered, quite seriously. "The *Globe* just called and said we're getting Robb Nen."

Indeed, Duquette was telling the truth. Throughout the meetings, in fact, Duquette had consistently said that a team like the Red Sox could rebuild its pitching staff in a variety of ways, from the front or from the back. One was to acquire a starter like Martinez; another was to acquire a closer like Nen, who had just helped the Marlins to the World Series title. Because the Red Sox had a pitcher like Tom Gordon, whom they believed could help the club as a starter or a reliever, Duquette believed he had the flexibility to explore an array of options when the team arrived at the general managers' meetings. Still, Martinez could contribute three or four times as many innings as Nen during the course of a full season, and it was possible that Duquette was merely using Nen as leverage in his talks with the Expos. *If your demands get ridiculous*, Duquette could always tell Beattie, *I can make a different deal.*

Several hours later, long after an unflinching Duquette had hung up his phone with reporters from Boston's two major dailies, the *Herald* and the *Globe* hit the streets of Boston on the morning of November 17, 1997, in what will be remembered as one of the great sports news days in the history of the city. While the *Globe* claimed that the Red Sox had, in fact, reached a deal in principle for Marlins closer Nen, the *Herald* indicated that a trade for Martinez was imminent. Major League Baseball's freeze on trades precluded the club from making any announcement until almost 48 hours later, following the expansion draft on the night of

November 18. And it was after 10 p.m. on that night, Phoenix time, when Duquette and Red Sox manager Jimy Williams sat in front of a crowded conference function room at the Phoenix Civic Plaza and revealed that the Red Sox had acquired Martinez from the Expos in exchange for Pavano and a player to be named.

At that instant, a Red Sox year that effectively began with the departure of Roger Clemens and included the Mike Gimbel affair, the Wil Cordero controvesy, and a fourth-place finish concluded in spectacular fashion.

For Duquette, it was as if all of his sins were washed away.

"He's pure competitor. I think what you're getting here is Roger Clemens in a smaller frame," Red Sox pitcher Butch Henry, who had played with Martinez in Montreal, said when apprised of the deal. "He's 100 percent into the game. Anytime he's on the mound, he wants to win and gives you 120 percent. To me, he's a heck of a competitor and has a heck of an arm. I never got to play with Roger, but from everything everybody's told me, he wanted to win. I think that's what you're getting with Pedro."

Continued Henry, who was also brought to Boston by Duquette: "I think Dan has outdone himself with this one. If they can tie Pedro down to a long-term deal, that's one of the best deals they've done, aside from drafting Nomar."

Said a proud Duquette when asked about the Martinez acquisition: "It sends a message to the rest of baseball that the Red Sox are back in business."

Still, for Duquette, the work was not yet complete: there was still the matter of signing Martinez to a long-term contract, a potential wrinkle that was now prompting even greater worry. Before the conclusion of the expansion draft, even before the Red Sox had announced the trade, the Associated Press moved a story citing unnamed sources (believed to be agents Bronner and Gilhooley) that Martinez would not sign a contract extension with the Red Sox under any circumstances. Duquette deemed the report "disconcerting," though there was always the chance the agents were posturing so as to secure for their client one of the richest deals in baseball history.

Regardless, this much was known: in his heart of hearts, Martinez had told some of those close to him, he wanted to play for Cleveland, and he had little or no interest in Boston. Earlier in the 1997 season, in fact, Martinez had been part of the All-Star team that represented the National League at Cleveland's Jacobs Field in July, and the pitcher had left the event impressed. The Indians were in the midst of a truly great run, and Jacobs Field was annually the site of October baseball, making Cleveland (of all places) a truly grand stage. The Indians were also enjoying a streak of consecutive home sellouts that would ultimately be the longest in baseball history, and as much as anything else, Martinez wanted to go to a place where he would be *noticed*. He wanted to go to a place where he *mattered*. After pitching in the obscurity of the Montreal market and in the shadow of his older brother, and after enduring the skepticism of Tommy Lasorda, Pedro Martinez was like the midwestern farm girl who wanted to pack her bags and make the trip to Hollywood.

He wanted to be a *star*.

Duquette knew all of this when he completed the trade with Beattie and the Expos, but he also knew that Martinez could be extremely temperamental, and that the pitcher would thrive in a Boston market that was one of the most passionate baseball cities in America. *If Pedro Martinez doesn't want to play baseball in Boston*, Duquette said to himself, *it's only because he doesn't understand what baseball in Boston is about.* Certainly, Duquette believed, Martinez would need some convincing—and in more ways than one—but there wasn't a baseball player on the planet who believed that Cleveland and Boston were remotely comparable when it came to a passion for baseball. And while Boston was a difficult place to play when the team was losing, as Valentin once pointed out, the opposite was also true: there was no better place to play when the Red Sox were winning.

For Duquette, beyond the politics and posturing, the omens continued to be good. Despite losing one young pitcher (Jeff Suppan) in the expansion draft, the Red Sox escaped the entire week in Arizona with astonishing success. The only other Red Sox player taken from Boston in the expansion draft was relief pitcher Jim Mecir, the same veteran right-hander whom Duquette had acquired from the New York Yankees in the Mike Stanley trade. Mecir had been injured at the end of the regular season and never actually pitched for the Red Sox, so Duquette deemed the loss insignificant. The general manager all but broke out into laughter when discussing the departure of Mecir, who was nothing more than a throw-in in the Stanley deal and, thus, entirely expendable. "Jimmy, we hardly knew ye," Duquette guffawed. "Our fans won't be disappointed, because they never got a chance to see him pitch. Our staff won't be disappointed either. Nobody met him but me."

The next morning, Duquette planted himself in a first-class seat on an America West flight bound for Boston and succumbed to the fatigue caused by his prosperous trip out west. He had reason to rest easy. Though the Red Sox had yet to identify him, the player who would be accompanying Pavano to Montreal in the Martinez deal was none other than Tony Armas Jr., the pitcher whom Duquette had acquired, along with Mecir, from the Yankees in the Stanley trade during August. How was that for poetic justice! For decades, the Yankees had haunted the Red Sox, beginning with the day that former Sox owner Harry Frazee sold the Yankees the inimitable Babe Ruth. Now the Yankees were helping the Red Sox through the expansion draft, all while facilitating a trade that would change the history between the teams for years to come.

And so at the end of the week, less than four months after trading an ineffective closer (Slocumb) for Jason Varitek and Derek Lowe, Duquette traded Pavano and Stanley for the best young pitcher in baseball, even if Pedro Martinez was not yet obligated to pitch for the Red Sox for more than one year.

A few hours later, by the time Duquette's flight touched down in Boston, the general manager of the Red Sox was being celebrated again.

The entire 1997 baseball season was nothing but a memory now. Duquette was standing in the baggage-claim area at Boston's Logan Airport when, flanked by Sox publicist Kevin Shea, he encountered the *Herald* reporter who had called him on the night of the Martinez deal. In the reporter's hand was a copy of that day's issue, proclaiming Duquette and the Red Sox the indisputable winners of the general managers' meetings.

"You did well on this trip," Shea told the reporter as a weary Duquette pulled his suitcase from the conveyor belt.

The reply was obvious. "So did you."

Precisely 24 days later, in the Diamond Club at Fenway Park on Friday, December 12, 1997, the Red Sox conducted a major press conference to announce that they had signed their new ace, Pedro Martinez, to a six-year, $75 million contract that was the richest in baseball history. The deal contained a Red Sox option for a seventh season that would bring the total value of the package to a stunning $90 million over seven years, an average of just under $13 million per season. Duquette and the passionate baseball followers of Boston noted that the deal was formalized precisely 52 weeks—exactly 364 days—after Roger Clemens had sat in a conference room on the ground level of the SkyDome and announced that he was leaving the Red Sox to join the Toronto Blue Jays. Dan Duquette had needed less than a year to replace Clemens with the man who would become the next great ace in Red Sox history.

"They treated me like a first-class man," a beaming Martinez said of the Red Sox upon signing the biggest contract in baseball history. "I wanted to go to a team that was going to contend right away. I saw the effect Dan was doing in bringing me over and trying to [re-]sign Mo Vaughn. I think it's great and I think it sends a message to the fans that we're trying to win it."

With those words, for one of the rare moments in their tragicomic history, the Boston Red Sox seemed to be in perfect harmony.

Dan Duquette got his man.

Pedro Martinez was a star.

The Red Sox were indeed back in business.

FOR ALL of the theories about the best way to build a successful base-ball team, this much has always remained true: There is nothing more valuable than an ace. In baseball, a pitcher is the only man to touch the ball on every play during which his team is on the field. And so a truly great starting pitcher, a truly dominating one, can influence the out-come of any game in which he participates, even if he ventures on the field for a mere 30–35 games per season.

During his first five seasons in Boston, from 1998 to 2002, Pedro Martinez went 87-24, producing an average of 17–18 wins per season against an average of fewer than five defeats, a winning percentage of .784, which bordered on the godlike. During those same seasons, the Red Sox went a collective 101-40 in any game that Martinez threw even a single pitch. Contrasted with the team's performance when Martinez did *not* participate—the Red Sox were an extremely mediocre 345-323, an average of roughly 69–66 per season during his first five years in Boston—the statistics indicated a most obvious truth: without Pedro Martinez, the Red Sox of 1998–2002 were as average as they were in 1997; with him, they were a championship contender.

At the time he negotiated Martinez's seven-year, $90-million con-tract, Duquette was so certain of Martinez's potential impact on the Red Sox that he was quite literally willing to bet on it. Part of Martinez's first (and only) contract with the Red Sox included a provision by which Martinez could demand a trade if the Red Sox failed to qualify for the postseason during the first three years of the contract, a clause that quickly became moot. With Martinez posting a 19-8 record during his first season in Boston, the 1998 Red Sox qualified for the playoffs; a year later, the Sox qualified for the postseason again. And though Boston would not reach the playoffs again during Duquette's tenure as general manager, Martinez pitched three more seasons for the club—through 2004—after Duquette was fired as general manager during the spring of 2002.

"I knew that if he signed with us, we had a pitcher who would be 15 games over .500 every year—and that would attract other players, too," Duquette said when asked why he agreed to a loophole that might have allowed Martinez a chance to escape. "In his mind, it was a competitive issue. He wanted the chance to compete and I was confident we would be able to. With him, we had a good chance to be over 90 wins [a season], and if you get there, you have a chance to be in the playoffs." Added the GM, offering further explanation as to why he agreed to the clause: "[Martinez] deserved an opportunity to go somewhere else if we didn't live up to our part of the equation."

As it turned out, Pedro Martinez outlasted Dan Duquette.

Indeed, for all that happened to the Red Sox over the final five years of Dan Duquette's career as general manager, Martinez remained a constant. Without him, there is no telling how many times the Red Sox might have disintegrated. In 1999 and 2000, Martinez was so dominant that he won two American League Cy Young Awards and finished second in the balloting for the AL Most Valuable Player Award, an honor typically dominated by positional players. No single game better demonstrated his value than a truly historic performance on September 10, 1999, when even the fans of the rival New York Yankees took special note of Martinez's greatness and did a most unusual thing during the final moments of a 3–1 Red Sox victory at Yankee Stadium.

As an opposing pitcher completed a masterful domination of the beloved Yankees, a capacity crowd stood.

And applauded.

In that game, with the New York Yankees in the midst of a truly historic run during which they would win three straight World Series and four in five years (1996, 1998–2000), Martinez struck out 17 and allowed just one hit. He retired the final 22 batters he faced and threw just two pitches from the stretch—*two*—in what remains arguably the greatest game ever pitched against the storied Yankees on the hallowed ground of New York's home field.

"This is as good as it gets. I won't lie. I had nine perfect innings one time [for Montreal, against San Diego on June 3, 1995] and this is just as good, and probably more dominating, especially coming against New York," Martinez admitted. "It makes me more confident that I can beat anybody."

Said Red Sox manager Jimy Williams, a baseball lifer with tremendous respect for the game who rarely overstated anything: "I've never seen a guy pitch like that."

For Duquette, over the final four seasons of the general manager's career in Boston, Martinez proved to be more than just an ace; he was a heat shield behind which the controversial general manager could always find refuge. Not long after a historic 1999 season during which Martinez went 23-4 with a 2.07 ERA and a team record 313 strikeouts, Duquette acquired troubled center fielder Carl Everett from the Houston Astros for a package of prospects that included shortstop Adam Everett, then a highly regarded prospect and former first-round pick. Duquette made the deal after fruitlessly trying to sign center fielder Bernie Williams away from the Yankees, who swept in at the last minute and retained Williams's services only because megalomaniacal owner George Steinbrenner refused to let Williams go to the hated Red Sox. Both the Yankees and the Red Sox were coming off an October during which New York defeated Boston in five games of the American League Championship Series, but there was a sentiment throughout baseball that the Red Sox were making up ground on the Yankees, that Boston was closing the gap, that the Yankees suddenly had cause to be looking over their shoulder.

For Duquette, even in defeat, the 1999 ALCS against the Yankees was gratifying on a number of levels. Though the Red Sox won just one game in the series, the team had defeated the Cleveland Indians in the previous round to win Boston's first postseason baseball series since

1986, a span covering 13 years. The Red Sox actually fell behind the Indians in the first round of the playoffs, two games to none, before orchestrating a dramatic comeback that culminated with a Game 5 win in Cleveland. And though Martinez had been injured during Game 1, the Red Sox' secret weapon came out of the bullpen to pitch in relief in Game 5—against the same Indians club that might have had his services, remember—and completely shut down the vaunted Cleveland attack. While the victory established Martinez's place as a truly great competitor, it similarly announced the end of Cleveland's reign through the mid- and late 1990s; not long after blowing the series, the frustrated Indians fired manager Mike Hargrove and began disassembling a club that might have been a dynasty.

Instead, the Indians ended up just another talented team that went unfulfilled, much like the Red Sox of so many years past.

Five days after Martinez eliminated the Indians, the Red Sox returned home from New York for Game 3 of the AL Championship Series facing a 2–0 series deficit against the more-talented Yankees, though there was reason for optimism. With Martinez due to start the game against predecessor Roger Clemens—the *Herald* billed the game as the "Fight of the Century," with a front page that was laid out like a fight card—there was a belief that the Red Sox could still make a series of it. With Duquette watching from his private box at Fenway, Martinez completely flustered the Yankees while Clemens was shelled, leading to a 13–1 Red Sox victory that, for a day at least, made everything right in the world of Boston baseball.

In fact, several hours after the Boston victory, cars driving the streets near Boston's North Station were still honking joyously, celebrating the Red Sox' victory and the demise of the team's former ace. Parents who brought their children to the circus at the nearby Fleet Center emerged from the arena to ask passersby about the results at Fenway Park, then pumped their fists as they walked their children to the parking garage.

In Boston, that is what it meant to beat the Yankees, to avenge Clemens's departure, to celebrate the power of Pedro.

The Yankees won the next two games, of course, then won the World Series by wiping out the Atlanta Braves in the minimum four games. In claiming their second straight World Series title and third in four years, the Yankees won 11 of 12 postseason games, losing only to Martinez in truly historic fashion. All of that only magnified the point that Martinez was the one force in baseball for which even the great Yankees had no answer, the kind of pitcher who was so gifted that he would lead a team to a championship all by himself. Though the Red Sox had lost the other four games of the series against the Yankees, Boston had competed quite well, only to be victimized by some poor umpiring. Nonetheless, Duquette believed that he had to upgrade the team's offense in one position above all others—center field—and that it was the Yankees' advantage at that position, in particular, that ultimately delivered New York to the World Series.

So, frustrated in his attempt to lure Williams from the Yankees, Duquette brought in the multitalented Carl Everett with the hope that he could be the final piece in delivering a World Series trophy to Boston.

Instead, Carl Everett proved to be the proverbial straw that broke the camel's back.

In retrospect, had things gone differently, there is no telling how Everett might have adapted to Boston, whether the plan could have worked. But by the time Everett came to the Red Sox, Boston had already bade farewell to Mo Vaughn, who had left the team via free agency. And while Vaughn was not missed on the field in nearly the fashion that Clemens was—the 1999 season was the first following Vaughn's departure, and the Red Sox *improved*—the Red Sox certainly missed him in their clubhouse. Vaughn had a thunderous voice, and he was the dominating presence behind whom all Red Sox players lined up. Had Vaughn been there to rein in the unpredictable and rebellious Carl Everett, there is no telling whether Everett's stormy tenure in Boston might have lasted far longer than it did.

Of course, there was also the possibility that Carl Everett was simply a time bomb that could not be defused.

Whatever the explanation, Everett's first half season in Boston was a smashing success, one that sent him to the All-Star Game as a worthy representative of the franchise; after that, his Red Sox career went steadily downhill. Everett had a frightening meltdown and confronted umpire Ron Kulpa in a nationally televised game shortly after the All-Star break, and alienated most everyone in the Boston organization over the next year and a half. He turned off teammates—"Crazy Carl," more than one teammate dubbed him—and openly undermined his manager, the impatient Williams. Once, when the Red Sox were in Oakland during a losing streak, Williams called a team meeting before the game to address the team's overall attitude. Everett stood during the session and openly chastised his manager—a sin akin to dressing down one's boss in a board meeting—and prompted a procession from the clubhouse during which more than one Red Sox player was shaking his head.

"You know what?" one Sox player said while standing at the batting cage before a game later that day. "Carl Everett is a fuckin' asshole."

Had that incident been the sole transgression during Everett's stint in Boston, nothing would have come of it; but by then, the proverbial horse had left the barn. Everett arrived in Boston with a spotty reputation to begin with—he was seen as having anger-management issues—and Boston got its first glimpse of his inner rage in the second half of his inaugural Red Sox season, when Everett head-butted umpire Ron Kulpa during a disagreement at home plate. As Everett literally kicked and screamed while being dragged off the field, observers were given a window into the soul of a man whose career was subsequently marked by similar eruptions. There was a time, for instance, when Everett and manager Jimy Williams, behind the closed door of the manager's office, could be heard shouting profanities at each other in a confrontation initiated by the player. There was another when Everett and fellow outfielder Darren Lewis had to be separated in the Boston clubhouse when Everett was repeatedly late for the treatment of an injury with the Red Sox in the midst of a playoff race. ("You're disrespecting me," Lewis told him.) And there were those countless occasions when Everett forced his wild theories on anyone who would listen—among them was the notion that dinosaurs never existed because they were not mentioned in the Bible—which gave teammates a very clear view of Everett's rigidity.

Carl Everett believed that he owed *nothing* to *anyone*, which, of course, went against everything any team has ever stood for. On a team, after all, *everybody* owes *something* to *everyone*. Failing to meet a responsibility is regarded as letting down the group. In a locker room or club-house where players were encouraged to set aside their differences and to play, despite injuries, *for the good of the team*, teammates saw Carl Everett as the kind of guy who made no attempt to meet them in the middle, who had an answer for everything, who showed no urgency in getting treatment for injuries because to do so, on some absurd level, was seen as selling out.

"It's unbelievable," one Sox player said. "I mean, the fucking guy has an opinion on *everything*. And he's never wrong."

For Williams, Everett was the worst thing that could have happened to him. A former utility player in the major leagues who took nothing for granted, Williams was the complete opposite of his predecessor, the egocentric Kennedy. While Kennedy used the media to his benefit, Williams *withheld* information from the media to his own detriment. While Kennedy gravitated toward the superstars like Jose Canseco, Williams gravitated toward the role players like Mike Benjamin. And while Kennedy took credit for most things and blame for little—his players frequently pointed that out behind his back—Williams frequently downplayed his contributions, even in 1999, when he was named American League Manager of the Year. "I'm not trying to be right," Williams would frequently say during his Sox career. "I'm trying to *do* right."

Nonetheless, thanks largely to the cancerous effect of Carl Everett, the Red Sox began disintegrating during the latter stages of a 2000 season in which *Sports Illustrated* had made Boston its preseason pick to win the

World Series. Consequently, the bond between Duquette and yet another manager (in this case, Williams) disintegrated too quickly for it to be salvaged. The entire series of events once again highlighted the brittle nature of success in Boston, where the relationship between a manager and a general manager was put through unusual strains and pressures, the kind that would destroy most any marriage.

In Williams's case, he, like everyone, came to the Red Sox with some baggage. In his only previous stint as a manager—with the Toronto Blue Jays—Williams lived through two experiences that affected him greatly. The first came when Toronto officials reportedly asked him to bypass pitcher Dennis Lamp so that the pitcher would not make the necessary game appearances to trigger an incentive in his contract; the second was the team's failure to back him in a dispute with a player, the temperamental George Bell. In both instances, Williams rightly felt that the front office drew a line between itself and the manager, leaving Williams on an island, undercutting his credibility and authority with the remaining players on the team. It was a mistake for which he never forgave some Toronto officials, and it left an exposed nerve deep in his soul.

When Carl Everett came along, it was probably just a matter of time before something touched that painful nerve in the manager of the Red Sox. In fact, during his first year as Red Sox manager (1997), Williams showed signs of his scars, of his stubbornness, of the things on which he absolutely, positively would not bend. Like Lamp with Toronto, pitcher Steve Avery had an incentive clause by which the second year of his contract (1998) would have become guaranteed if Avery made a minimum number of starts. In an eerie case of history repeating, Sox officials advised Williams to move Avery to the bullpen, something Williams steadfastly opposed. Less than one year after being billed as a front-office suck-up in the wake of the Kevin Kennedy fiasco, a manager Duquette could control, Williams sent Steve Avery to the mound as a starter, and made it clear to anyone who cared to notice.

I'm not trying to be right. I'm trying to do right.

A year later, with Avery helping, the 1998 Red Sox made the playoffs; a year after that, with Williams declared the AL Manager of the Year, the Red Sox won a playoff series. The Red Sox were going *forward* again, and one of the primary reasons was a manager who made decisions based on principle, who operated with conviction in his beliefs.

But once Everett arrived and things began to unravel, Williams lost control of the team. Turned off by veteran players who felt they were *owed* things, Williams quickly lost clubhouse support when his unwillingness to play politics began to backfire. On the one hand, Williams wanted the front office to butt out when it came to Avery's contract, when it came time to decide whether Avery should pitch again; on the other, he wanted the front office to intervene when Everett became insubordinate. Carl Everett was driving a wedge between the manager and the general manager of the Red Sox: the former wanted nothing to do with him, and the latter had forfeited a first-round draft pick (and a multiyear, multimillion-dollar contract) to get him.

Despite Boston's disappointing finish in 2000—the team went a relatively mediocre 85-77—there was cause for optimism entering the 2001 season. Following the 2000 campaign and having once again lost out to the Yankees in his primary pursuit of the off-season—New York had signed pitcher Mike Mussina to a six-year contract valued at roughly $90 million—Duquette nonetheless had completed the greatest free-agent signing in Red Sox history, luring outfielder Manny Ramirez from the Cleveland Indians with a record eight-year, $160 million contract that was second in baseball history only to the 10-year, $252 million deal awarded then-shortstop Alex Rodriguez by the Texas Rangers that same winter. Though Red Sox owner John Harrington was preparing to sell the team at the time, Duquette saw Ramirez as an asset that would increase the value of the franchise, particularly at a time when the New England Sports Network (or NESN, the cable station in which the Red Sox held an 80 percent ownership stake) was about to enter a previously unmatched number of households thanks to a new provider agreement. Ramirez was a truly prolific run producer—the kind of powerful right-handed hitter who would take on Fenway Park's famed left-field wall, the "Green Monster"—and his acquisition was a landmark event. To that point in Red Sox history, the Sox were known far more for *losing* marquee players to free agency than for *acquiring* them, a fact most recently evidenced by the departures of Clemens and Vaughn. But this time, just three years after executing the trade for Pedro Martinez, Duquette once again landed a very big fish, leaving the Cleveland Indians (and an eight-year offer worth between $135 and $140 million) holding the bag.

In that way, swooping in with a pile of money, the Red Sox did to the Indians precisely what the Yankees had so frequently done to the Red Sox. And at a time when the Sox were preparing to put their house on the market, they did not merely slap on a coat of new paint. They put on an addition.

"If you take a look at what the Cubs did [during the 2006–7 off-season], that's a pretty fair comparison," Duquette said years later, during November 2007. "I really don't see it as any different. They were dressing up the team for sale. They felt they enhanced their team by signing [outfielder Alfonso] Soriano to a [$136 million] contract.

"NESN was changing their base structure and they were going to be introduced into new households, and it was important for the club to have marquee players," Duquette said. "When the television station was changing its format so that we could attract additional customers, that was our focus. And, of course, the team was for sale. If we could give the fans marquee players, we felt that they would come out and support us."

Consequently—and adding further pressure and tension to a situation already supersaturated—the 2001 Red Sox entered the season with great expectations. The Sox got off to a strong start, winning 14 of their first 20 games, before settling into a slow but steady pace through May. When June arrived, so did a rash of injuries. Already playing without wonder-boy shortstop Garciaparra, who had undergone wrist surgery early in the spring, the Red Sox lost both Martinez and iron-man catcher Varitek to major injuries. Williams somehow kept the team in playoff contention into the middle of August, when the Red Sox caved in under their own selfishness. Veteran players like Dante Bichette, whom Williams had aggressively relegated to part-time status in favor of the younger and hungrier Scott Hatteberg, criticized Williams behind the manager's back when the Red Sox should have been focused on their opponents.

On August 16, following a 6–4 victory over the Seattle Mariners that left Boston's record at 66-53 with roughly six weeks to play, Williams was fired and replaced by his pitching coach, Joe Kerrigan, whose stint as manager of the Red Sox would prove nothing short of disastrous.

In the final six weeks, the 2001 Red Sox season was in a state of a revolt. During a time when America was forever altered by the terrorist attacks on New York and Washington, D.C., the Red Sox acted like petulant, self-absorbed children. During one private workout, Martinez ripped off his jersey and all but tossed it at his manager before storming off the field. Lowe, who had blossomed into an effective reliever and was one of Kerrigan's primary successes, was not speaking with Kerrigan after the manager demoted him in the Boston bullpen. (According to Lowe, the two had just had a discussion in which Kerrigan assured the pitcher that his job as closer was safe.) And then there was the behavior of Ramirez, whose considerable talent was balanced by his astonishing immaturity.

Manny Ramirez was a follower more than a leader, and the 2001 Boston clubhouse was the worst possible environment for him to begin his Red Sox career. At the end of the season, during which the Red Sox lost nine straight and a mind-numbing 13 of 14, Kerrigan left his seat on the team bus during a road trip and asked Ramirez to turn down his boom box, a request that was consistent with club policy. According to one onlooker, Ramirez dressed down his manager—the general message was "Go fuck yourself"—and Kerrigan promptly returned to his seat, castrated by his own cleanup hitter. Said one observer who witness the entire, sorry episode: "At that point, Joe should have kicked [Ramirez] off the fucking bus."

Of course, Kerrigan did no such thing.

Not long after the season ended—the Red Sox had to win their final five meaningless games to finish with an underachieving 82-79 record—Duquette went about the business of trying to rebuild the team, its image, *his* image. In the span of seven years—from the end of the 1994 season to the end of the 2001 season—Duquette had now worked with four managers: Butch Hobson (whom Duquette had inherited), Kevin Kennedy, Jimy Williams, and now Joe Kerrigan. The middle two, Kennedy and Williams, were polar opposites, men who approached their Boston experiences from entirely different directions; Duquette could not work with either of them. Duquette's turning to Kerrigan was a desperate move that reflected an array of flaws in the Boston organization. During his time as a major-league coach, Kerrigan was looked upon by players as nothing short of a know-it-all; those who wore the same uniform believed he talked to the media too much. During Kerrigan's stint as a coach in Montreal, it was said that Expos outfielder Moises Alou once confronted Kerrigan about an anonymous quote that appeared in a national column, suggesting that Alou's skills were "eroding." Alou believed Kerrigan was the source of the claim. And regardless of whether the player was right, the conclusion was obvious: the players didn't trust him.

Kerrigan's inability to manage a club—or least the 2001 Red Sox—revealed just how far out of touch Duquette had become with the happenings in his own clubhouse. Duquette had underestimated the negative effect that Carl Everett had on the entire roster and foolishly supported Everett when conflicts with Williams escalated. He completely misread Kerrigan's potential as a successor. And he had amassed a collection of talent instead of building a *team*, a fact that became terribly apparent when veteran players (like Bichette) grumbled about reduced roles with the team vying for the playoffs.

Nonetheless, with all of the injuries the Red Sox had absorbed during the middle of the season, the truth is that the Red Sox were far better off than many might have guessed. Certainly, they were far better off than they had been when Duquette took over the team in January 1994.

Even if it didn't necessarily feel that way.

ON THE day that Johnny Damon signed with the Red Sox, Dan Duquette's tenure as general manager of the Red Sox effectively came to a close. Earlier that day, in the very same room, the Red Sox had introduced the trio of John Henry, Tom Werner, and Larry Lucchino, the men who would become the next caretakers of the Red Sox. With principal owner Henry leading the way, the new owners and operators of the Red Sox (Lucchino was to be team president and had nothing invested in ownership, at least at the time) paid in excess of $700 million for the Red Sox, Fenway Park, and the blossoming New England Sports Network.

Hours later, after the room had cleared out and filled up again, Sox assistant general manager Mike Port stood quietly in the back of the room. "It's like a split doubleheader in here," mused Port, the possessor of a lovably dry wit, noting the day's comings and goings.

In many ways, the days leading up to the Damon signing were a microcosm of the Duquette era. On the one hand, Duquette was continuing to make moves that would aid the franchise for years to come; on the other, he was embroiled in controversy. In 2001, baseball's annual winter meetings were held at the Sheraton Boston, right in Duquette's backyard, just a short walk from Duquette's office at Fenway Park. Duquette entered those meetings with a pair of primary objectives—to rid the Sox of the divisive Everett and improve the team's speed—and he did both, trading Everett (and more important, the remaining money on his contract) to the Texas Rangers for a marginal (at best) left-hander named Darren Oliver.

But even as Duquette was cleaning up a mess, the media focused on his lame-duck status. "Dead Duke Walking," said the back-page head-line on the *Herald*, Boston's tabloid equivalent to the *New York Post*.

To that point, Henry, Werner, and Lucchino had given no indication that they intended to replace Duquette as general manager, having chosen a far more diplomatic approach; still, in Boston, it certainly felt as if everyone just *knew*. Duquette had failed so miserably in public relations, and the 2001 season had been such a disaster—on the field and off—that the idea of a new management team bringing in a new general manager seemed like a forgone conclusion.

And ultimately, it was.

"I'm confident I made mistakes with the Red Sox," Duquette admitted years later. "I made a personal inventory of what those mistakes were and how I could have made different choices. But you know, if you look at my body of work [in Boston], there were a couple of things we did. We turned them into playoff contenders and we rebuilt the farm system, and we made the Red Sox a more diverse international brand. Are there things I would have done differently? Sure. There's a bunch of 'em. But that's water under the bridge at this point."

Indeed, for all the criticism during Duquette's tenure, certain things were indisputable: The Red Sox entering the 2002 season were a better team—and organization—than they had been only seven or eight years before. Duquette had signed Ramirez and Damon to major contracts, ending years of Red Sox futility on the free-agent market. He had traded for Varitek and Lowe. And in acquiring the incomparable Martinez, Duquette had indeed made the Red Sox a considerable presence in the Dominican Republic, a baseball hotbed in which the Red Sox had been all but nonexistent during their entire history.

Duquette also brought the Red Sox' international scouting efforts to other baseball-producing nations, like Venezuela. And at a time when the game was extending into the Far East, Duquette acquired pitchers from both Korea and Japan—in the latter case, Hideo Nomo began his Red

Sox career by pitching a no-hitter—planting the organization's first seeds in those markets as well.

In the process, Duquette changed the long-standing reputation of a Red Sox franchise that had been known for bigotry under the longtime ownership line of Tom Yawkey; Boston had been the last major-league club to integrate after Jackie Robinson broke baseball's color barrier in 1947. (The Red Sox did not do so until 12 years later, in 1959, when Pumpsie Green became the first African American player in franchise history.)

"The most important part of the philosophy was to expand our scouting network on an international basis and to bring diversity to the ballclub," Duquette said. "We got involved in the Dominican, in Venezuela, in Japan, and in Korea. We put our emphasis on signing and developing young pitchers, even though we knew that we would probably have to trade those players before they were ready because of the interest of our fan base and the need to field a competitive team year in and year out."

Consequently, through it all and despite allegations to the contrary, the Red Sox improved their farm system to the point where, even in 2007, the impact was still being felt. When the Red Sox traded for ace Curt Schilling following the 2003 season, for instance, they did so primarily with players drafted or signed under Duquette. The same was true when the Sox acquired ace Josh Beckett from the Florida Marlins in 2005. Kevin Youkilis, one of the key contributors to the 2007 championship team, was drafted under Duquette.

So, as much as the Red Sox and the fans might have blamed him when Duquette was fired during the spring of 2002, the same accusers overlooked some critical evidence. To this day, Duquette's fingerprints are on significant parts of the franchise. "I've seen some sabermetric studies that said between two-thirds and three-quarters of that major-league roster were players signed or acquired during the previous ownership," Duquette said following the 2007 season. "We made a contribution," he added. "We weren't on the scene when they won, but we made a contribution—and we left a good collection of players in their minor-league system."

Still, Dan Duquette left the beloved Red Sox franchise he adored as a boy without the thing he wanted most.

A championship ring.

THE START OF A NEW ERA

FROM THE BEGINNING, BEFORE THE RED SOX OFFICIALLY CHANGED hands, Boston was as wary as it was welcoming.

For as much as Boston was regarded as a major American city, it had something in common with every small town in the United States: politics. There were the people who ran Boston and the people who catered to them, and never was that truer than during the sale of the Red Sox. By the time the smoke cleared and left John Henry, Tom Werner, and Larry Lucchino holding the keys to Fenway Park, the Red Sox had endured such a maddening and dirty political process that the Massachusetts attorney general, Tom Reilly, had announced an investigation into the sale of the club. Because the Red Sox were regarded as a local institution, there was tremendous support in Boston for the team to be entrusted to local owners, specifically a group headed by Joe O'Donnell, a Boston native who had made much of his money as a concessionaire. O'Donnell was the people's choice—or at least the choice of *the right people*—and his subsequent loss to Henry, Werner, and Lucchino was met with predictable resistance. Columnists from the *Herald* and the *Globe* deemed the sale process a bag job by baseball commissioner Bud Selig, who was accused of hand-picking the new owners of the Red Sox at a time when baseball was in another economic crisis. Said a Selig ally years later, after Henry, Werner, and Lucchino had delivered two World Series titles to Boston: "Do you think Tom Reilly ever called Bud and said, 'Hey, I'm sorry. You made the right choice'?"

Of course, the question needed no answer.

The response was predictable the day that Henry, Werner, and Lucchino first met the Boston media in precisely the same room—the Diamond Club—where Dan Duquette would later announce the signing of Johnny Damon. Henry, Werner, and Lucchino were all from small-market clubs—the Florida Marlins for Henry, the San Diego Padres for Werner and Lucchino—and there was a feeling among Boston baseball followers that the three would bring small-market philosophies to Boston. At the time, baseball commissioner Selig was arguing for the implementation of revenue sharing and a payroll luxury tax—the latter was the closest baseball could get to a salary cap—and that only fueled speculation that Henry, Werner, and Lucchino were the personal choice of the commissioner. After all, the Red Sox were a big-market team, capable of outspending almost any club but the Yankees. If Selig could get officials from Boston in his corner, he could significantly shift the balance of power toward a more balanced economic structure in baseball. In that way, the Red Sox could be a swing vote.

At the outset, Henry, Werner, and Lucchino did nothing to suggest that such perceptions of them were inaccurate. During the 2001 season, just prior to the unveiling of the new Red Sox owners, the club had increased its payroll by more than $100 million, a number significantly inflated by the signing of outfielder Manny Ramirez. The Red Sox were spending like never before. And even though the rival New York Yankees had just lost the World Series to the Arizona Diamondbacks in the maximum seven games, New York had still won four World Series during a six-year span while reaching the World Series in every year but 1997. The general belief was that the Yankees weren't going anywhere, so the Red Sox had to spend to keep up. "The Boston Red Sox certainly have the revenue to compete with anyone, and revenue drives payroll," Henry said when asked how much he intended to invest in the team during what served as his victory speech. "We have the revenue to be competitive, and we're going to give the Yankees a run for their money starting [in 2002]."

But Henry suggested the Red Sox would "maximize the effect of every dollar" and "put emphasis on the player-development system," words that raised a flag with regard to the Red Sox' future. At the time, the Oakland A's were revolutionizing baseball management philosophy with what forever came to be known as "Moneyball," named after the Michael Lewis book written about the creative manner in which the A's were winning. In implementing "Moneyball," revolutionary A's general manager Billy Beane had been building wildly successful teams with a significantly smaller payroll than teams like the Yankees and Red Sox, largely by placing set values on specific skills. In the process, Beane's theories were making the A's—not the Yankees—the model for all teams in major-league baseball. Even though Oakland had failed to win a World Series during Beane's tenure—to that point, in fact, the A's had not even won a playoff series—Beane was winning despite spending far less than most other teams, which delivered the simplest message to the 29 teams in baseball trying to keep up with the free-spending Yankees: *It can be done. You have hope.*

But for the 2002 season, Henry, Werner, and Lucchino had their hands tied. Because the formal transference of the Red Sox would take time, the new owners of the club would have little control over the team for the coming year. Just as Dan Duquette regarded the 1994 Red Sox as a stepchild, so would Henry, Werner, and Lucchino regard the Red Sox of 2002. Because the new owners of the club were not identified until the days just before Christmas, Duquette had already completed much of the major work on the team's projected roster for the subsequent year. Johnny Damon belonged to the Red Sox, whether John Henry liked it or not, and the new owners had little choice but to play the hand they were dealt.

Meanwhile, Henry, Werner, and Lucchino officially embarked on a fact-finding mission, gathering the kind of information that Lucchino (who had a law degree) would frequently refer to in another fashion throughout his career as Red Sox president: due diligence.

NOT LONG after being identified as the new caretakers of the Red Sox, the group headed by owner-elect Henry began meeting individually with members of the Boston media, a group that had learned to harbor resentment and ill will toward the entire Red Sox organization. Since the club's miracle season of 1967, the Red Sox had learned that they had a blindly loyal fan base that kept returning, year after year, despite the extended torture that was the absence of a championship. The club subsequently spent little time on media relations—with the Red Sox, the term was an oxymoron—mostly because the Red Sox felt they did not need to. The fans always seemed to show up, no matter what, so the Red Sox saw the media as an unnecessary evil, an adversary more than an ally.

Consequently, after years of being denied access and, in many cases, the dignity of a mere response, the Boston media generally learned to regard the Red Sox with disdain, taking any and every opportunity to criticize the organization.

For decades, the Red Sox effectively thumbed their nose at the Boston press.

In response, the media ripped.

Seeing a golden opportunity to extend the reach of a franchise that had theretofore been a regional phenomenon, the new owners of the Red Sox promptly seized upon the chance to make peace with most reporters, many of whom regarded the sale of the Red Sox as the end of a dictatorship. On the whole, the Boston media were all too eager to eat up what the new guys were selling. In a scene reminiscent of the final minutes of *The Godfather*, new Sox owner Henry (playing the role of Michael Corleone) sat behind the desk in a suite of a downtown Boston hotel as members of the media were ushered in, one at a time, essentially to kiss the ring of the new man who had ultimate control of the Red Sox. Reporters had been given specific appointment times—one every 15 minutes—and Henry questioned each about specific wants and needs, about how the relationship between the team and the media could improve and grow as the Red Sox entered a new era in their history.

For a Boston media corps that had a chronic inferiority complex, the change was almost too good to be true. In the reign of the tight-lipped Dan Duquette, the reporters covering the Red Sox had felt as if they could not get answers to the most basic questions. Now, they were being told they had a *say* in how things were done.

Before long, as reporters were promised, the changes in and around Fenway Park were impossible to ignore for a press corps that saw the new owners of the Red Sox as a breath of fresh air. Before the arrival of Henry, Werner, and Lucchino, for instance, Red Sox employees and members of the media dined in separate rooms in an area behind the Fenway Park press box, separated by a partition that some members of the media playfully referred to as the "Berlin Wall." The idea was that the previous owners and operators of the Red Sox did not want their employees mingling with the media for fear that such fraternization would result in sordid relationships, at least in the eyes of those who ran the club. The environment was one of mistrust, breeding caution and cynicism. Reporters were treated as a threat and, collectively, eyed as an institution that could only bring harm to the Red Sox and what they were trying to accomplish.

Of course, the media regarded the Red Sox as foolish and politically inept, particularly when the club suffered one spectacular failure after the next. Consequently, at those moments, the Red Sox had no goodwill to fall back on.

Then along came Henry, Werner, and Lucchino, who not only tore down the "Berlin wall," but gave reporters their most valuable asset: *time*. Relationships were not merely cultivated, but encouraged. The dining room menu and general press box conditions were improved. Henry, Werner, and Lucchino were happy to be the new owners of the Red Sox, and the large majority of the Boston media were happy to have them, if only because it made life better for the press. On a most personal and selfish level, whether the Red Sox would be a better baseball team was largely irrelevant to members of the media, particularly a Boston group that could be at least as self-serving and self-important as any group in the country. Reporters wanted their access. They wanted their stories. And no matter what happened on the field, the media generally were satisfied as long as they had their needs fulfilled, as long as bureau chiefs or assignment editors weren't crawling up their backs wanting to know why their competitors had more information.

The change in Red Sox ownership leveled the playing field again, which most reporters saw as a good thing. The few relationships that had existed during Duquette's perceived tyranny—and there had been very few—were long gone. With the new owners of the Red Sox, all reporters believed they had a chance again, a fact that shrewd men like Henry, Werner, and Lucchino could easily exploit.

By the time the Red Sox began spring training 2002, most everyone in Boston knew that there were major changes coming. Through various channels, including Lucchino's personal press aide, Charles Steinberg, the dismissal of Duquette came to be seen as a foregone conclusion, with the firing of manager Joe Kerrigan not far behind. Neither step was a surprise. In fact, Lucchino had actually polled some reporters on whether they believed Kerrigan was a capable manager, a fact that terribly blurred the line between the people who make the news and the people who report it. Lucchino undoubtedly thought he was conducting more due diligence to find out everything he could about his new manager, whose brief stint at the end of the 2001 season had been nothing short of a train wreck. But to the discriminating reporter, the process crossed the border of propriety and had a feeling of dirtiness that was impossible to wash away. At the end of the day, the Red Sox had a team to run—in spite of any public or media sentiment—and the press had its stories to report. So why, in God's name, would the Red Sox ask *a reporter* for input on the fate of the team's manager?

Of course, given the informational embargo that had existed at Fenway Park for far too long, most reporters did not take the time to look the proverbial gift horse in the mouth. They had traveled much too far for that. In the blink of an eye, the Red Sox had seemingly gone from an organization that failed to return phone calls to one that could not stop talking, and that kind of turnaround was good for the media business. Reporters were not bought literally but figuratively, primarily at the cost of information and human decency. Once, when an inevitable disagreement later arose between the new Red Sox owners and a member of the media, one lobbyist for the Boston organization took the media tampering to a new level. The Sox loyalist pointed out that media relations had improved considerably during the reign of the new owners, emphasizing that reporters now were afforded common courtesies like a continental breakfast and use of the bathroom facilities when none had previously existed. "You get doughnuts every morning now, don't you?" the loyalist asked with a straight face. In the media mind, the comment was akin to Marie Antoinette's legendary and snide remark, "Let them eat cake."

On February 28, 2002, slightly more than two months after Henry and Company were identified as the next owners of the Red Sox and the dollars-to-doughnuts future of Dan Duquette was both frosted and boxed, the sale was completed: Dan Duquette was fired as general manager. Less than a week later, Kerrigan got the ax too, a swift purge that effectively beheaded the Boston baseball operation. Eight years had passed since Duquette had taken over as general manager of the Red Sox in 1994, a year that similarly included a change in Red Sox managers. Now the Sox had new owners, no manager, and no GM, though longtime Duquette assistant Mike Port had been named interim general manager for the purpose of getting the Sox through the regular season.

Still, with only four weeks to go before Opening Day and lots of new friends in the Boston media, John Henry, Tom Werner, and Larry Lucchino had a major hole to fill.

They needed a manager.

UNDER THE circumstances, Grady Little was the obvious choice. A former Red Sox bench coach under recently deposed manager Jimy Williams, Kerrigan's predecessor, Little was serving as the bench coach of the Cleveland Indians when the Red Sox came calling. Sox officials considered a handful of candidates at the time—from the venerable Felipe Alou to the crusty Tom Kelly—but most every discussion concerning the identity of the next Red Sox manager stopped the instant Little's name was mentioned. *That's the guy.* As bench coach for Williams, Little was easygoing and extremely well liked, the kind of man most people could feel comfortable talking to. A North Carolina native and onetime cotton farmer, Little spoke in a slow, deliberate drawl, and a conversation with him usually included a playful wisecrack about his wife, Debi. Little had spent most of his baseball career as a minor-league manager with the Atlanta Braves—Duquette's benchmark organization—and it was that affiliation, in part, that had prompted Duquette to push Little as Williams's bench coach in the first place.

Grady Little came from a place where winning was expected.

Nonetheless, as the relationship between Duquette and Williams began to disintegrate, Little became a casualty of the feud. When the Red Sox made consecutive playoff appearances in 1998–99—the first time since 1915–16 that they had done so—Little sought a pay raise, but Duquette allegedly denied him, presumably to spite Williams. At the time, the manager was seeking greater control of his coaching staff—specifically, Williams wanted to replace first-base coach Dave Jauss, a Duquette ally—and Duquette essentially made the concession on one condition: Little had to go too. For a year, anyway, the Red Sox coaching staff was thrust into a transitional state, largely because the manager and general manager of the team were struggling for power within the walls of the home clubhouse.

The message to everyone around the club was clear: You take my guy, I'll take yours.

Little and Jauss were truly victims, pawns in the struggle between Williams and Duquette. As it turned out, the break might have been the best thing to happen to either. Temporarily demoted to the role of advance scout, Jauss excelled in that area and quickly established a reputation for being thorough and knowledgeable, praise he otherwise might never have received. Prior to that point in his career, Jauss had been regarded by many almost exclusively as a Duquette informant, another set of eyes and ears in the clubhouse to keep the GM in touch with the inner workings of his club. Rightly or wrongly, the perception stemmed from the fact that Duquette and Jauss had built a friendship during their time together at Amherst College. So Jauss was in an impossible position in the Boston clubhouse.

Quite simply, the manager did not seem to trust him. Neither did the players and, to a large degree, the media. But over the years, following Duquette's dismissal and through his own efforts, Jauss established himself as a respected major-league coach who would one day end up as the bench coach for one of the most storied and accomplished teams in professional sports, the Los Angeles Dodgers.

The man who hired him was none other than Grady Little.

But back in the spring of 2002, Little was serving as bench coach of the Cleveland Indians when the new owners of the Red Sox fired Joe Kerrigan, whose brief tenure as manager was doomed from the start. After having Ramirez undermine his authority on the famous bus ride at the end of the preceding season, Kerrigan tried to visit the player during the off-season; Ramirez turned him away. By the time the Red Sox showed up for spring training amid the pending change in ownership, Ramirez was convinced that Kerrigan had leaked information to the media regarding the player's failure to pay his 2001 clubhouse dues, a sum totaling about $5,000. The amount was trivial for a player who had just signed a $160 million contract, making Ramirez look irresponsible and selfish, particularly to his teammates. No matter how much they made, all players were required to pay their clubhouse dues, which afforded them certain comforts. A large amount of the money was spent on buffets both before and after games—players typically referred to this as "the spread"—and the fees were paid to the clubhouse manager, whose responsibility it was to manage the funds.

In fact, Kerrigan had had nothing to do with the leak concerning Ramirez's negligence, but that was largely irrelevant—Manny Ramirez didn't trust Joe Kerrigan enough to talk to him, and Ramirez was about to begin just the second year of an eight-year contract. Ramirez's inherent distrust of Kerrigan raised a greater question with regard to Kerrigan's reputation with some of the Spanish-speaking players on the club, specifically Pedro Martinez, the most respected Latin player in the Boston clubhouse. Ramirez and Kerrigan seemingly did not have enough of a history for their relationship to deteriorate so rapidly, so many believed that Ramirez's distaste for Kerrigan had to be coming from someplace else. Many believed that Pedro Martinez was in Ramirez's ear.

Whatever the source of Ramirez's feelings, he was not Kerrigan's sole problem. At the end of the day, though Kerrigan was a good-natured sort, he frequently could not keep himself from talking too much. During the previous winter meetings in Boston, for instance, Kerrigan had told some reporters that the framework for a potential trade with the San Diego Padres for troublesome outfielder Carl Everett was put in place on a hotel napkin while he and San Diego general manager Kevin Towers sat at the lobby bar in the early morning hours. (It was the kind of "old-time" baseball story that Kerrigan loved to tell.) Regardless of the fact that Everett ended up in Texas, the scene painted Kerrigan in an unflattering light, highlighting why some players felt Kerrigan could not be trusted: in their minds, Joe Kerrigan liked the spotlight a little too much. After all, it was the GM's job to make trades.

By contrast, Grady Little was a relatively unassuming sort who, among other things, shared with players a general distaste for Kerrigan. Consequently, he was in a no-lose situation. When Sox president Larry Lucchino made the announcement that Little would be the team's next manager and introduced him in the home clubhouse at City of Palms Park—the team's spring stadium in Fort Myers, Florida—the players erupted with such a thunderous roar that they could be heard, through closed doors, from the hallway outside the room. The scene concluded what had been a terribly unusual spring, from the change in ownership to the firing of the general manager to the removal and replacement of Kerrigan, the last playing out in roughly a week. Along the way, most everyone was nervously looking at the clock as if making a desperate dash to the airport. Opening Day was only a few weeks away.

The Sox were very fortunate to get Little. Despite the general belief that the baseball season begins every April, the truth is that it does not; it begins each fall. Immediately after the World Series, teams go about the business of rebuilding their rosters and coaching staffs, raising ticket prices, making stadium renovations. During the winter, when most baseball stadiums in America remain empty, teams break ground on reconstruction. By the time spring training begins, particularly with regard to managers and coaches, most teams operate under the assumption that what's yours is yours, what's mine is mine. In the case of someone like Little, the Red Sox were required to ask for permission to interview Little because he was under contract with the Cleveland Indians. Cleveland officials could justifiably have denied the Red Sox the chance to speak with their bench coach by giving Boston a simple response: "You should have thought about this last fall."

Of course, the Red Sox' circumstances were unique. During the winter, the team had been sold. The formal process of the sale was not completed until after the start of spring training, handcuffing the new operators of the Red Sox until just before the start of the season. And though new Sox owners could have waited before making wholesale changes—under similar circumstances, another ownership group might have used the first year as an evaluation period—Henry, Werner, and Lucchino saw no point in wasting any time, taking an aggressive and hands-on approach to the franchise despite having a very limited window in which to operate.

So when the Cleveland Indians graciously granted permission for the Red Sox to interview Grady Little, the Red Sox acted swiftly, and decisively brought closure to a tumultuous period that had begun with the ugly end to 2001. Gone, now, was the bitterness of the preceding season, which had ended in tactless fashion. Gone were the frustrated veteran sluggers of 2001, replaced by a younger and more athletic team that featured, among others, Johnny Damon. Gone was the baggage of relationships gone sour. Gone were the old regime and the old way of life, which had begun to smother the Red Sox after their last postseason appearance in 1999.

"At the end of the day, we chose Grady Little to be the manager because Grady did it the old-fashioned way: he earned it," Sox president Larry Lucchino said upon introducing the then-52-year-old Little as the team's new manager. "We believe he'll be an exceptional manager in the short term and in the long term."

Said Little: "I've waited a long time for this opportunity, and to be able to get an opportunity like this in Boston is second to none."

Suddenly, in Boston, there was once again the anticipation of a rapidly approaching baseball season.

OFFERED A new beginning, the early Red Sox of 2002 played like a team liberated from its past.

After going 6-21 during a disastrous stretch at the end of the ill-fated 2001 campaign, Boston completely reversed the flow the following April. Though the Sox lost to the Toronto Blue Jays, 12–11, on Opening Day, Boston stormed from the gate and built a 40-17 record by the early part of June. During one remarkable stretch from April 15 to May 15, the Sox won 21 of 26—a 21-5 record that was nearly the mirror reflection of their 6-21 stretch from the previous season—and emerged as the lead horse in all of major-league baseball. The Red Sox were so downright dominating that people were drawing comparisons to the 2001 Seattle Mariners, a team that won a jaw-dropping 116 games before losing to the New York Yankees (who else?) in the American League

Championship Series. Through 57 games, the Red Sox were playing at a clip that would produce 114 victories over a 162-game schedule.

Though the Red Sox had failed badly at the end of the 2001 season, their 2002 resurgence fell short of qualifying as a complete surprise. The 2001 Red Sox had talent, after all—from Pedro Martinez to Nomar Garciaparra to Jason Varitek to Manny Ramirez—but the first three of those players had suffered significant, season-ending injuries, while Ramirez had struggled through the transition of his first season in Boston, leading many to wonder whether he should have left Cleveland at all and whether agent Jeff Moorad had pushed the player to Boston solely in pursuit of the almighty dollar. All of that, coupled with the internal organizational strife surrounding the sale of the club and the poor relationship between Dan Duquette and Jimy Williams—as well as the renegade behavior of Carl Everett—had destroyed what was, on paper, a very talented team.

Still, for all of the changes that took place in Boston between 2001 and 2002, the team's early-season success centered on two pitchers: Pedro Martinez and Derek Lowe. The Martinez of spring training had described himself as being "in Wonderland" in the wake of an off-season shoulder rehabilitation that led many to ask whether he would again reclaim his dominance of 1999 and 2000. (He would.) Lowe was beginning his first full season as a starter after a disastrous 2001 season spent mostly as the Boston closer. Ultimately, Lowe's failures out of the bullpen in 2001 prompted then-GM Duquette to acquire right-hander Ugueth Urbina in a trade with the Montreal Expos, who chose to trade away a talented pitcher—as was the case with Martinez during the off-season between 1997 and 1998—simply because they could no longer afford him. So the Red Sox got Urbina, and Lowe got banished to baseball Siberia, a forgotten and disgruntled man.

While Lowe was furious at Kerrigan at the time—according to the pitcher, the manager had assured him that Urbina's arrival would not affect Lowe's place as closer—the move proved incredibly beneficial to the pitcher. Though Lowe had begun his big-league career as a starter, the Red Sox had moved him to the bullpen when Lowe went 0-7 in his first 10 starts as a member of the organization. Lowe quickly became a productive reliever and effective setup man, and his metamorphosis from caterpillar to butterfly culminated during the 2000 season, when he finished tied with Detroit Tigers right-hander Todd Jones with an American League–leading 42 saves, making him every bit as valuable as Jason Varitek in the heist that was the 1997 Heathcliff Slocumb trade.

A year later, in 2001, Lowe went belly up. The arrival of Urbina inspired the Sox to try making Lowe a starter again, and Lowe very quietly finished the season by going 1-0 in three starts. In 16 innings, Lowe struck out 15 and walked only two while not allowing a home run. His ERA during the span was a minute 1.13.

Nonetheless, baseball being baseball, no one was expecting Lowe to continue that kind of performance when he showed up for spring training looking noticeably bigger and stronger, the result of an off-season workout program designed to improve his durability. Most every player in baseball has a good run, and Lowe's performance at the end of 2001 came when the Red Sox were playing meaningless games. The simple truth is that almost no one but Lowe paid much attention to Lowe's strong finish, which the pitcher used as a springboard to his off-season. Deep down, after all, Lowe wanted to be a starter more than he wanted to be a reliever. Though he was blessed with an incredibly resilient arm that allowed him to pitch frequently out of the bullpen, the emotional demands of closing wore on him. Lowe was "goofy," as former Sox starter Steve Avery once described him, and his personality was much more suited for the responsibilities of a starter, who did not have to throw every pitch feeling as if the outcome of the game depended on it.

Consequently, when the 2002 season began, nobody embraced freedom from the 2001 season quite like Lowe. Lowe went 4-1 with a 2.04 ERA in April, 4-1 with a 1.88 ERA in May. By the time baseball reached the All-Star break in the middle of July, Lowe was 12-4 with a 2.36 ERA, earning him the prestigious right to serve as the American League starting pitcher in the All-Star Game. While Martinez was getting his legs under him in the early part of the season, Lowe was positively brilliant. He established his place as a significant force on April 27, 2002, when he became the first Red Sox pitcher since Dave Morehead (1965) to throw a no-hitter at Fenway Park, in a 10–0 wipeout of the Tampa Bay Devil Rays.

"I remember last year I would get up in the bullpen to go to the restroom and [the fans] would boo me," Lowe said after the performance. "That sticks with a person, so [later in the year], I would slither along the bullpen wall so they wouldn't see me. You don't forget those things. Never in my wildest dreams did I think something like this could happen. It's almost surreal. You almost don't think it's you. I still don't feel like I did what I did, as amazing as it sounds. You just don't think something like this could happen."

Infused with a healthy dose of confidence, Lowe never looked back. Though he faded just a touch in September, the 2002 season would prove to be the best of his big-league career. Lowe finished 21-8 with a 2.58 ERA that garnered him a third-place finishing in the AL Cy Young Award balloting, setting the stage for the truly historic performances that would come later in his career. With Lowe, confidence was critical. While most every major leaguer has bouts with self-doubt during his career, Lowe fought a never-ending war. One bad start could lead to two, which could lead to three, which could lead to four. Nobody on the team rode the tide—in or out—quite like him. Above all else, Lowe was terribly *human*, a fact that endeared him to both teammates and media alike. He was likable. He was worth rooting for. He sometimes just had trouble believing he was as good as he was. But in 2002, at least, Derek Lowe had no reason to doubt himself, and no one else had a reason either.

With Lowe out in front, Martinez overcame a poor performance on Opening Day and steadily regained form, albeit without the same kind of dominating fastball he'd had at his peak, when he could regularly register 95 or 96 miles per hour on stadium radar guns. Still, the end result was the same. Aided by a Red Sox offense that provided him with ample run support at the few times he needed it, Martinez did not suffer his first loss until June 8; by then, he had seven victories. Martinez was 11-2 with a 2.72 ERA by the All-Star break, at which point he was just starting to hit his stride. During the second half of the season, with his confidence and arm strength fully restored, Martinez went 9-2 with a 1.61 ERA and 98 strikeouts in 83.2 innings, an average of 10.5 strikeouts per nine innings pitched. Opposing hitters batted just .189 against him, a fact that led Martinez to a controversial second-place finish in the AL Cy Young Award balloting, behind Oakland A's left-hander and 25-game winner Barry Zito.

And one place ahead of Derek Lowe.

Back in June, no one was aware that Lowe and Martinez were both on their way to 20-win seasons, that they would become the first Red Sox teammates to win 20 games in the same season since Mel Parnell (25-7) and Ellis Kinder (23-6) in 1949. But the early signs were good. While Martinez was slowly reclaiming his place at the top of his profession, Lowe was moving into a much more exclusive neighborhood. Fifty-seven games into the season, it appeared as if the Red Sox had two aces, not one, and that could only serve the club well as the Sox sought to return to the playoffs for the first time since 1999.

While everyone in baseball was chasing the Red Sox, things at Fenway Park were looking up.

FOR THOSE who believed in such things, the omens quickly turned ominous for the 2002 Red Sox. Between the start of July and the end of September, the Sox mourned the deaths of three major personalities from the history of their franchise, beginning with the great Ted Williams. In the subsequent months, former Red Sox general manager Dick O'Connell and broadcaster Ned Martin also passed away, distributing grief evenly at fabled Fenway Park. One Red Sox player. One Red Sox administrator. One member of the media.

The death of the incomparable Williams prompted an extended mourning period and stripped the Red Sox of the greatest player in their history, a title that was promptly passed on to Carl Yastrzemski. Arguably the greatest hitter of all time, Williams, who served his country as a Marine Corps pilot during World War II and the Korean War, died, oddly enough, on Fourth of July weekend. The news came less than five months after Williams made a rare and celebrated public appearance at the annual induction ceremonies at his Hitters' Hall of Fame—then in Hernando, Florida—an event that brought tears to a sizable crowd that included many of Williams's friends and former teammates.

By the end of the baseball season, following the deaths of O'Connell and Martin—the former among the greatest general managers in team history, the latter who came to be known as "the voice of the Red Sox" during a career in radio and television—it was as if the Red Sox had postponed the new era in their history to grieve for what they had lost.

On the field, despite the efforts of a new Sox management team that included a highly touted young executive named Theo Epstein, the Red Sox began to wilt. Despite the performances of Martinez and Lowe, a radioactive Red Sox relief corps cost the team games that were having a damning effect. Lowe's transition from the bullpen to the starting rotation had left the club without a reliable setup man, and the state of the bullpen only grew worse when plump, lovable reliever Rich Garces—a fan favorite for his body type—saw his career go *poof* in an unforeseen run of ineffectiveness. Red Sox hitters seemed demoralized by the bullpen's inability to protect leads—or, for that matter, to minimize deficits—and before long, the Red Sox seemed incapable of winning a game in which they were trailing through the middle innings.

Meanwhile, in the front office, the likable and dignified Port was starting to get frustrated, largely because his role as interim general manager had left him without the power he had anticipated. In fact, while relying on young aides like Epstein as much as (or more than) he did on Port, Lucchino oversaw the entire baseball operation at a most pivotal time of year. The Red Sox were in contention and the trading deadline was approaching, and Lucchino recognized that the club needed to be aggressive, to make a maneuver that would fortify it for the final two months of the regular season. To do anything less would send a bad message to fans, who were now watching their new owners and management team with even greater interest than usual to see whether the new operators of the Red Sox intended to run a profitable business or to build a better baseball team.

To his credit, Port remained loyal to the club to the end—even after the Sox bypassed him in their formal GM search—though there was nonetheless strife in a Boston organization that was undergoing transition. The team had new owners, after all. Some Sox employees would be retained and others would go, all of which was to be expected. In some ways (minus the new ownership), the changes taking place in Red Sox management bore an eerie resemblance to those that had taken place under Duquette more than eight years earlier, though the inner politics of the Red Sox did not play out in the media in nearly as ugly a fashion at they had under Duquette. In this case, members of the media had something to gain from a Red Sox management staff that seemed willing to cooperate, to steer them in the right direction, to provide them with information. Those were benefits they had never enjoyed under Duquette. So, for every Sox employee who was stripped of power or terminated, relatively little was written or reported, primarily because the changes were all seen as a cost of doing business.

This time, the media had something to lose.

Regardless, Lucchino's nature was to be aggressive, and the Red Sox sought the kinds of trades and player acquisitions that could help them in both the short term and the long. The club struck quickly, acquiring left-handed reliever Alan Embree from the San Diego Padres in a late-June trade that seemed to give the Red Sox a rare commodity: a power left-handed relief pitcher who could succeed against both left-handed and right-handed hitters. Several other teams were believed to be in contention for Embree, whose arrival in Boston inspired immediate speculation that Lucchino and Epstein were capitalizing on their prior careers with the Padres, whose general manager (Kevin Towers) had served as both Lucchino's understudy and Epstein's mentor. Just as Dan Duquette dealt with Montreal, it seemed, Lucchino and Epstein were dealing with San Diego.

"We tried to get a jump on the trade market and get the player we wanted as early as possible," said Epstein. "There are a number of reasons to do a trade like this in June rather than July."

The primary reason, of course, was that the Red Sox had a glaring need.

But how could it hurt if the Sox deprived their competitors of a valuable commodity in the process?

Just the same, Red Sox officials were careful to set the bar low, something that most executives in the game chose to do as the trading deadline approached. The chance to make any trades was impossible to assess—particularly if the deal was to be of any impact—and the better approach was always to keep the expectations of fans and media to a minimum. In Boston, there was enough media and fan pressure to make a deal any time the Red Sox were in contention, and the interest was even greater now that the Red Sox had a new owner, new executives, new decision makers who would determine who stayed and who went, off the field and on.

New Sox officials had already stressed the need to rebuild Boston's minor-league and player-development systems, areas that had seemingly grown barren during the final years under Duquette. Boston's farm system was now regarded as among the worst in baseball, though there were far more resources available that anyone might have guessed. In the Embree deal, for instance, the Red Sox had parted with a pitching prospect named Brad Baker, an early-round selection during Duquette's tenure. The trick frequently was to find the teams that had interest in your players—beauty, as always, rested in the eye of the beholder—which suggested that there was always a deal to be made. It was really just a question of whether two teams wanted to make a trade.

Nonetheless, the new operators of the Red Sox stressed the need to collect bushels of young talent because a surplus could only benefit the Red Sox in the long run. Those players could be kept or traded, all with an eye toward improving the Red Sox at the major-league level. Along the way, competition from within would only heighten player development and weed out the lesser players, which would allow the Red Sox the best of both worlds if they could evaluate their players properly. Boston could keep some prospects and trade others, maintaining a mix of veteran and young talent.

But as always, caution was preached. "We have been looking at deals already, but any deal has to make sense for the long term as well as for the short term," said owner Henry. "We have traded away too many prospects historically. You cannot rebuild a minor-league organization by trading your top prospects to rent a player. I believe we already have the second-highest salary structure in baseball. I also believe the team and organization are happy with the chemistry we presently have, but our baseball people continue to talk with other teams. Every team has wants and just about every team wants to reduce payroll. That hasn't led to anything thus far." Added the owner: "Don't expect any blockbusters."

In between the lines, Henry's message was clear: We're not going to rape this organization of young talent the way the previous administration did. Part of the reason a trade is going to be difficult is because the last ownership and management team didn't develop and keep enough young players.

Nevertheless, with Embree already added to the bullpen, Lucchino and the Red Sox set their sights on what appeared to have become a worrisome area: the Boston offense. The Red Sox were having difficulty scoring runs in the late innings of close games, particularly when they were behind, which raised questions about the versatility of their offense. There were a handful of spots in the Boston lineup where the Red Sox lacked production—first base and second base were the most notable—so the club set out to find an offensive player who could help them in an assortment of offensive areas, from power to speed. Because free-swinging second baseman Rey Sanchez had been playing excellent defense—and because, too, first base was regarded as a much more productive offensive position—the Sox had accepted the notion that they could more effectively upgrade at one position than another. So they focused on first base, a position where the team was getting relatively little from the tandem of Tony Clark and Brian Daubach, the latter a find under Duquette but whom new Sox officials considered insufficient.

Still, the question was obvious: Where were the Red Sox going to get an impact offensive player in the middle of the season, with allegedly no prospects to trade?

Relentless as ever, Lucchino instructed his baseball people to persist, which proved critical when news of two players' potential availability began to leak from, of all places, Dan Duquette's training (and trading) ground in Montreal: outfielder Cliff Floyd was available, and so, perhaps, was pitcher Bartolo Colon. The news sparked immediate interest throughout baseball partly because Floyd and Colon were regarded as potential impact acquisitions, partly for a reason that had nothing to do with their talent. In recent weeks, the surprising Expos had *acquired* both Colon and Floyd in hopes of fortifying a run for the playoffs, a maneuver that opened eyes throughout the major leagues. At the time, the Montreal franchise was in such dire straits that Major League Baseball had assumed operation of the club until a new owner could be found, and it was widely assumed that MLB officials were running a bare-bones operation, one that would cut costs and play conservatively. Now, with Colon and Floyd in Montreal, the opposite appeared to be true. The Expos, the team without an owner, were trying to *win*.

Montreal's aggressiveness raised eyebrows throughout baseball, though officials at MLB offices were doing their best to run the Expos in a manner that was as consistent as possible with the workings of the other 29 major-league clubs. Major League Baseball had hired the team's general manager, respected former Texas Rangers assistant Omar Minaya, wisely using the Expos as a way to get executive experience for a worthy minority candidate. Major League Baseball required all clubs to interview a minimum number of minority candidates anytime a position became available, particularly one with such a great profile as general manager. So MLB gave the keys to Minaya, who later parlayed the Expos job into a position as general manager of the New York Mets, for whom one of his biggest acquisitions was a player quite familiar to the Red Sox: Pedro Martinez.

At the time, though, most assumed that the Expos had neither the resources nor the financial flexibility to add high-salaried players like Floyd and Colon, the latter in a blockbuster deal that would ultimately prove key to the resurgence of the Cleveland Indians. (The package of minor leaguers sent to Cleveland included pitcher Cliff Lee, center fielder Grady Sizemore, and second baseman Brandon Phillips, all of whom became productive major leaguers; Sizemore became an All-Star.) Yet, Minaya acquired both players within several weeks of each other—Colon at the end of June, Floyd at the end of July—to reinforce a Montreal club that had been one of the baseball's biggest surprises during the first three months of the 2002 season. Not long before Minaya had become general manager of the Expos, he had been a Texas assistant GM *under Melvin*, and the two had enjoyed a healthy relationship. Recognizing that the link between the two could prove invaluable, Lucchino sent Melvin essentially to camp out at Expos team offices during the days leading up to the trading deadline, and his instructions to Melvin were simple: If Minaya decides to trade either Colon or Floyd, Lucchino told Melvin, do everything you can to make sure he sends the player to us.

So, after the Red Sox sale that many still regarded as commissioner Bud Selig's "bag job," the news of Floyd being traded to Boston for Korean pitchers Sun-Woo Kim and Seung Song was not received especially well throughout the rest of major-league baseball, particularly in New York. Remember, the Expos were being run by Major League

Baseball, a fact that resulted in an indisputable conflict of interest. Coming on the heels of the sale to Henry, Werner, and Lucchino, there was a rapidly spreading opinion in the game that Selig did not merely want his people in place in Boston, but also wanted them to win. Conspiracy theories only intensified when the Sox also acquired right-handed reliever Bobby Howry (from the Chicago White Sox) before the trading deadline, meaning the club had executed three deals in one month—two for relief pitchers, one for the multitalented Floyd. MLB appeared to be helping Red Sox officials, who were doing their job quite well to begin with.

But the perception of favoritism could not have been further from the truth. The reality was that the Red Sox now had a cast of executives who were every bit as aggressive and competitive as those officials who ran the New York Yankees, a fact that would further prove itself over time.

But then, no one knew quite what to make of it. "It really started the week before. I called Omar and said, 'If you have a bad week, would you consider trading Colon or Floyd?' He said they wouldn't trade Colon, but they'd consider Floyd," said Melvin, recounting how Lucchino took the aggressive and uncharacteristic step of sending him to Montreal. "But it really started heating up three or four days ago. We were in on [talks for Texas left-handed starter Kenny Rogers] a little bit and after a couple of conference calls, there was a decision to aggressively go after Floyd." Added Melvin: "There was no doubt that them sending me up to Montreal helped out. I think I smothered [the Expos] in their offices a little bit."

The Floyd deal took place on the same night that ace Pedro Martinez was brilliantly pitching the club to an all-important victory over the Anaheim Angels, the team immediately ahead of the Sox in the wild-card race. For all of the whining coming out of New York, the Red Sox' extended lethargy had allowed New York to overtake Boston and build a five-game lead in the American League East. As a result, the Red Sox had their sights set on the Angels, a team that had overcome a poor start to play exceptional baseball over an 80-game stretch during which the club went 54-26. Martinez, in particular, took the news of the deal quite well, partly because he had played with Floyd previously and knew the depth of the player's talents, partly because he was pitching as well as he had at any point in his Red Sox career.

As incredible as it seemed, the Red Sox had improved by leaps and bounds in one night—and everybody knew it. Said Martinez: "Right now, I have a pretty good team that has been behind me the whole year. Now with Floyd, I'm going to be even better."

Despite the flurry of trades made at the deadline—in all, the deals for Embree, Howry, and Floyd required the Sox to part with six minor-league players—Red Sox officials gave almost no credit to Duquette, who clearly had left them with a great deal more to work with than anyone guessed at the time. In fact, when Sox officials were asked about their ability to make three trades—especially one as big as the Floyd deal—with a supposedly barren minor-league system, they all but thumbed their nose at Duquette while going to great lengths to pat themselves on the back. But, Boston was so caught up in the excitement of having a new, friendly, and cooperative ownership group that nobody cared to notice. "We were able to make the deal *despite* our minor-league system," one new Sox official said when asked about the perception that Duquette had left them empty-handed.

Said a Duquette ally years later: "Those guys have a way of rewriting history."

Indeed, had Sox officials given much thought to the matter, they would have realized that, in some ways, the Floyd deal put them between the proverbial rock and hard place. If the talent traded away was not a credit to Duquette, after all, then the Sox were admitting that they had fleeced Minaya, with whom Melvin shared a good relationship. Beyond that, the Sox would later request to interview Minaya for their own general manager's opening after the season, a request Minaya turned down because he believed Boston was merely patronizing him in order to meet its obligation to interview at least one minority candidate.

In the end, the Sox ensured that they would sacrifice at least part of the credit for the Floyd deal. Either they made the deal with Duquette's players, or they ripped off a man whom they later wanted to interview.

Whatever the case, the Sox clearly had no use for the players whom they were trading, though that hardly made them different from any new ownership or management team in the history of professional sports. One of the players included in the Floyd deal, young right-hander Kim, had been celebrated by the Sox as a major international signing that would enhance the club's position in Korea. In fact, Kim had pitched at Fenway Park as a member of a Korean traveling team and decided that he wanted to pitch for the Red Sox, with whom he eventually signed. Privately, Duquette had indicated that he would resist trading the player, because he knew that Kim wanted to pitch for the Red Sox and at Fenway Park, and he had given Kim his word that he would make every effort to keep him in the Boston organization.

But now, with Dan Duquette gone, the new owners of the Red Sox had no such promises to live up to. And when they saw the chance to trade Kim for a potentially dynamic talent like Cliff Floyd, they did not give the move a second thought.

IN THE recent evolution of the Red Sox, the 2002 season proved to be the forgotten middle child.

Despite the acquisitions of Floyd, Embree, and Howry, despite having two 20-game winners and seven All-Stars, despite two players with 100 RBIs and two more with 100 runs scored, and despite a closer with 40 saves . . . the Red Sox missed the playoffs. Boston outscored its opponents by more runs than any other American League team except the New York Yankees and Anaheim Angels, yet the club still somehow managed to miss qualifying for the postseason by a sizable six games.

After going a sizzling 40-17 in their first 57 contests, the Red Sox went an illogical and inconceivable 53-52 over their final 105 games, a period during which the Sox added players. Yet, despite adding players only one year after injuries had stripped them of so many key contributors, the Red Sox ended up in the same place when the baseball postseason began: on the outside looking in. "I don't know what else to tell you," colorful veteran right-hander John Burkett said at the peak of Red Sox frustration. "There's only so many things you can say, especially with my vocabulary."

Along the way, while being baptized into the ways of Red Sox suffering, the new operators of the Red Sox were afforded a glimpse into the personalities of their players, many of whom they were evaluating for the first time. Among them was wonder-boy shortstop Nomar Garciaparra, the Duquette prodigy whose first four major-league seasons had produced astonishing results. After winning the American League Rookie of the Year Award in 1997 and finishing second in the Most Valuable Player Award balloting in 1998, Garciaparra won consecutive batting titles in 1999 and 2000, becoming the first right-handed hitter to do so in the American League since Joe DiMaggio. (Former Sox manager Jimy Williams once said that he saw similarities between the two players.) After Garciaparra's 2001 campaign had been cut short due to wrist surgery, he came back in 2002 to bat .310 with 24 home runs, 101 runs scored, 197 hits, 85 extra-base hits, and a team-leading 120 RBIs. Though Garciaparra wasn't quite the same destructive force he had been—he batted .357 and .372 in winning batting championships—he once again looked much like the dynamic, slashing shortstop whom most baseball evaluators were lumping into a group with Alex Rodriguez and New York Yankees great Derek Jeter, a trio sometimes referred to as baseball's Holy Trinity.

But Garciaparra also possessed an outlook that was, at times, dark and disturbingly pessimistic, a characteristic that undoubtedly resulted from the immense pressure he routinely placed on himself. "Good place to play, right?" a sarcastic Garciaparra said after a late-season loss to Baltimore that moved the Sox one step closer to being eliminated from postseason contention. "A lot of positive vibes around here. It's great."

On this occasion, Garciaparra's soul had been exposed following a rare baserunning blunder that stifled a Red Sox rally. Boston had trimmed a 6–1 deficit to 6–3 when Garciaparra—usually an exceptional base runner—was picked off second base to end the Red Sox threat. Garciaparra did not help matters by cryptically suggesting that third-base coach Mike Cubbage was at least partially at fault. Questioned by reporters after the game, Garciaparra said he "didn't hear anything" before being picked off, suggesting that Cubbage had failed to shout a warning as Orioles second baseman Jerry Hairston Jr. sneaked in to apply the tag. Garciaparra was furious at reporters the following day— "Are you turning into one of them now?" he asked one *Herald* reporter, convinced the media were out to get him—making it clear to almost everyone that Nomar Garciaparra did not take failure well. In Boston, that trait was potentially lethal.

Before the Red Sox season ended, Boston fans did not wave goodbye before hearing a parting word from long-deposed manager Joe Kerrigan, a passionate sports fan who made his home in his native Philadelphia. Kerrigan had begun doing some work as a television analyst for Comcast with the hope of returning to the majors as a coach (he would soon become the pitching coach of his hometown Philadelphia Phillies), and he was keeping a close eye on the Red Sox, for obvious reasons. Kerrigan had kept a low profile since his dismissal early in spring training, and most people assumed that he was merely trying to cause controversy when he made remarks that generally went ignored in the Boston market. "I've had a chance to sit and watch games from behind the plate [at Veterans Stadium] with the scouts. That's how I've been able to keep up with what's going on," Kerrigan said. "The scouts say that the Red Sox are going to cut $20–$25 million from their payroll [by next season] and they're trying to trade Manny [Ramirez]. That's what the scouts say."

Trade Manny Ramirez? Utterly ridiculous, most assumed.

Before they did anything, the Red Sox had to find a new general manager.

FIVE OUTS AWAY

HAVING FAILED IN THEIR INAUGURAL QUEST FOR A WORLD CHAM-
pionship, the new owners OF the Red Sox began their first off-season
with a predictable endeavor.

They went Beane stalking.

Though the Anaheim Angels went on to win the World Series with a
seven-game Series victory over Barry Bonds and the National League
champion San Francisco Giants, there remained little doubt in baseball
as to the identity of the game's next great general manager: Billy Beane.
The general manager of the Oakland A's, Beane had begun to spawn an
entirely new generation of baseball executives with his "Moneyball"
philosophy, which was having dramatic results in Oakland. Though
most recently the A's had been eliminated by the Minnesota Twins in
the first round of the playoffs, there was little disputing Oakland's dominance during the four-year period beginning in 1999. During that time,
despite having failed to win even a single playoff series, the A's had
won as many regular season games (383) as the New York Yankees;
only the Atlanta Braves (387) had won more. But because both the Yankees and Braves had considerably higher payrolls, Beane was getting
credit for doing more with less, which was indisputably true. As a result
of Oakland's efficiency, Beane's assistants were getting the kind of attention typically showered upon NFL assistant coaches whose team had
just won a Super Bowl.

More than anything, what opponents were interested in was the *system*.

In 2002, especially, Beane's operation was running at peak efficiency. Oakland won a whopping 103 games during the regular season, tied with the Yankees for the most in the major leagues. And though Oakland had been upset by the Twins in the first round of the playoffs, Beane's explanations for his team's postseason failures were taking hold with the quantitative analysts—otherwise known as sabermetricians—who were beginning to take over in front offices everywhere. The logic was simple: Major-league baseball was a game played over the course of a 162-game schedule, during which executives like Beane tried to chart (and, subsequently, forecast) player performance. Most every player had streaks and slumps because the length of the season made it nearly impossible to be consistent. But if a team showed *patience*, if it scouted its players properly and let them perform, the odds were that most every player would end up at or near a base line projection given his past performance, age, and other variables.

The playoffs were a different matter. Getting there was one thing; succeeding was another. Because playoffs series were so short—best of five or seven games—performance was more difficult to predict. The human element became a far greater factor. There also existed the element that many acknowledged but most underestimated—luck—and Beane believed that it took less skill to win in the playoffs than it did to get there. Generally speaking, he was right.

Back when the Red Sox were up for sale, Beane's name had been bandied about in Boston as if it were a foregone conclusion that he would be the next general manager of the Red Sox. Oakland's success, coupled with the Red Sox' inability to keep up with the free-spending Yankees, suggested that the Red Sox needed to be more efficient with their spending. Many believed it was the only way the Sox could compete with and, ultimately, defeat New York. Even some of the groups who ended up losing the auction were believed to be eyeing Beane as their general manager, making Beane's arrival in Boston almost as certain as Duquette's departure.

But between the perception and the reality, there was one significant problem: Beane had a long-term contract with the Oakland A's.

Never one to be deterred by something so trivial as a contract—in this day and age in professional sports, such deals are not worth the paper they are printed on—Sox president Larry Lucchino set out to find the club's next general manager, a process that would prove to be exhaustive. A graduate of Princeton University and Yale Law School—Lucchino's aide, Charles Steinberg, was fond of reminding people that Lucchino had been an understudy of renowned Washington attorney Edward Bennett Williams—Lucchino believed in, above all else, the *process*. He turned over rocks. He looked under sofa cushions. He made sure any and every angle was covered before arriving at a decision, which was undoubtedly part of the reason he asked sportswriters for their opinions on whether someone like Joe Kerrigan could manage the Red Sox. Even when he felt he could learn nothing, Lucchino frequently asked the question anyway, largely to eliminate the possibility of surprises.

So, though the Oakland A's initially resisted Red Sox requests to interview Beane—in such instances, it was understood that the team already employing a potential candidate should be asked for permission, which was akin to a marriage blessing—Lucchino took his time and dragged out the process. He poked around about other candidates, some of them young assistants, like Epstein, with other organizations. He consulted people within the Boston organization, including Epstein, about their opinions on some of their peers with other teams, and he took it all into account, building a case file, while every so often knocking on Oakland's door: *Um, can Billy come out and play now?*

From the start, Oakland owner Steve Schott had resisted Red Sox attempts to interview his sought-after GM, though Lucchino, as was his wont, remained unrelenting. (At one point, Lucchino called Oakland's unwillingness to release Beane "predictive rather than definitive," and insisted that he had yet to receive a flat-out denial.) Whatever the case, the Red Sox continued to drag out the process while Lucchino warded off reporters, many of whom were growing impatient as another Red Sox off-season neared and with the team's baseball operation standing as a headless body.

Along the way there were some curious developments, some that reflected on Lucchino's desire to manipulate the situation, some that did not. Doug Melvin, the longtime Lucchino ally who had played such a critical role in the Cliff Floyd trade, accepted a job to become the general manager of the Milwaukee Brewers. The Milwaukee job was seen at the time as a dead-end opportunity, the kind of job that would lead to an inevitable firing because the smallness of the market made it so difficult to succeed. (Despite Beane's success in Oakland, small-market clubs were still seen as having little chance to win.) Because the Red Sox job was open, many found it curious that Melvin did not stay to take his chances on the Boston operation; many interpreted his move as showing an unwillingness to work so closely with Lucchino on a daily, long-term basis.

Not so, said Melvin. In fact, after being entrusted with the Floyd deal, Melvin felt as if he owed Lucchino an enormous debt of gratitude. "I said to Larry when I took the [Red Sox] job that if they were still looking for a general manager when the season ended, I would like to be considered for it," Melvin said. "But I also told him that if something else came along, I'd like the opportunity to explore it. Larry and I had the understanding that he would not stand in my way. With the Red Sox not yet having made a decision, I couldn't take the chance." Added Melvin: "The [acquisition] of Floyd probably energized me to want to get back into this even more."

As for the other "candidates" on Lucchino's list, the large majority of them never stood a chance. Among those believed to have been eyed as the successor to Dan Duquette (and, of course, to interim GM Mike Port) were Sox special assistant Lee Thomas, Philadelphia Phillies assistant GM Mike Arbuckle, New York Mets assistant GM Jim Duquette (Dan's cousin), Cincinnati Reds director of player personnel Leland

Maddox, Seattle Mariners general manager Pat Gillick, and former Chicago White Sox general manager Ron Schueler. Lucchino also let it be known that the Sox asked for permission to interview Montreal Expos general manager Omar Minaya—the same GM that Sox operators had boasted about fleecing in the Floyd deal—primarily to make it clear to Major League Baseball officials that the Sox were taking the time to interview minority candidates, too.

Sensing that the Red Sox had no real interest in him, Minaya declined the opportunity to interview for the job, a fact that the new Sox owners could not leak to the media quickly enough in order to perpetuate their image as a new and progressive organization. In fact, Lucchino essentially instructed Sox media-relations people to be forthcoming with the news about Minaya, telling some of the club's spokespeople that reporters should be *encouraged* to call Lucchino with questions about Minaya. So when reporters subsequently called Lucchino, the response was predictable: *Well, since you asked . . .*

In the courtroom, such charades might be regarded as jury tampering, but in baseball, they were regarded as media relations. After all, the Red Sox *wanted* it out there that they had asked for permission to interview Minaya and that he had turned them down, because it would relieve them of their responsibility to interview a minority candidate when the man they wanted, Billy Beane, was still trying to extricate himself from his contract in Oakland. And so, not long after some reporters called Lucchino thinking they had stumbled on a small scoop, the Associated Press transmitted a wire story indicating that Minaya was out of the running, completing the team's media operation for the day.

Finally, with baseball's free-agent season about to begin, the Red Sox made one final push to free Beane, whose bosses finally relented. Through club president Mike Crowley, Oakland owner Steve Schott gave Beane permission to interview for the Red Sox opening, though the Red Sox would have to grant the A's compensation if Boston were to secure Beane to a deal. In Boston, the deal essentially amounted to a trade for the next general manager. By then, New England sports fans had become well versed on the subject; in recent years, the New England Patriots had both been granted and been charged compensation for head coaches Bill Parcells and Bill Belichick, respectively, and the latter had recently led New England to a stunning victory over the heavily favored St. Louis Rams in Super Bowl XXXVI in January 2002. Whatever the cost was for Belichick—four draft picks—New England sports fans felt the coach was well worth it, and all professional sports were reaching an age where management was viewed as a critical element in success given the economic factors that were now dominating sports.

Even in baseball, it seemed compensation packages were becoming the norm. Immediately after the 2002 season, the Tampa Bay Devil Rays were forced to send All-Star outfielder Randy Winn to the Seattle Mariners as compensation for Lou Piniella, a fiery manager who the Rays hoped would lead their young team for years to come.

However, to those on the outside, any discussion about Beane or compensation remained completely speculative, if only because Red Sox officials did not want it known that they now had the chance to sweep their man off his feet. (This time, no Sox spokespeople were encouraging reporters to call Lucchino.) Still, word of Oakland's decision began to filter throughout baseball, which was no better than any other industry when it came to keeping secrets. An executive from a team unconnected to the Beane negotiations subsequently informed a *Boston Herald* reporter that the A's had granted permission—"You may want to look into that a little more," said the executive—so the reporter promptly called the usually accommodating Lucchino. Undoubtedly feeling the stress as the Beane matter was finally coming to a head, Lucchino snapped. "I'm *fucking* tired of answering *fucking* rumors," snarled Lucchino, whose phone had persistently rung with wild assertions through the process. "So my comment from now on is 'No *fucking* comment.'"

Believing that he had been fed false—or, perhaps, premature—

information from the unnamed executive, the *Herald* reporter hung up the phone, convinced that the information he had presented to Lucchino was untrue. In a place like Boston, after all, the abundance of media could sometimes lead to a feeding frenzy, and there were always wild rumors circulating. Many concerned things like extramarital affairs in the clubhouse, steroid use, theories that a player was traded because he slept with a teammate's wife. The large majority of them were untrue, so the reporter replayed the conversation in his head, focusing on one word. *Rumors.* Larry Lucchino had called it a *rumor*.

The following day, November 9, 2002, in the sports pages of the *New York Times* (which also had a 17 percent ownership stake in the Red Sox), the story first appeared publicly: the A's had relented. Predictably miffed, the *Herald* reporter expressed displeasure about the entire matter to Steinberg, who frequently served as Lucchino's liaison with the press. In fact, even before Lucchino had arrived, Steinberg had taken the time to warn some reporters about Lucchino's sometimes abrasive nature—"Don't misinterpret his passion," Steinberg stressed—and in this case, Steinberg felt the need to set up a lunch meeting between Lucchino and the reporter for fear that the matter had gotten the new Red Sox president and the newspaper off to a bad start. (During an introductory meeting with *Herald* officials earlier in the year, Lucchino and Sox representatives had literally brought a hatchet, which they vowed to bury, playfully recognizing the paper's frosty relationship with the previous administration.) Lucchino later defended his response to the reporter on the night of his expletive-filled blast, saying that a rumor is by definition something that may be true; such semantics dissatisfied the reporter. To reporters, after all, rumors have a negative connotation. Despite deteriorating standards in journalism, reporters don't try to print *rumors*. They try to avoid becoming *rumor*mongers. If the word *rumor* had a literal meaning, there was an implied meaning that contradicted it.

Of course, to someone like Lucchino, the slightest bit of gray area created an uncertainty, a potential to negotiate, a loophole to exploit. In law, after all, everything was based on *interpretation*. And if the precise definition of a rumor allowed Larry Lucchino the escape hatch he needed from being branded a deceitful liar, the president of the Red Sox was inclined to use it, no matter the effect on his reputation.

And so, as much as Larry Lucchino was regarded as an operator as shrewd as former Celtics coach and executive Red Auerbach—the crafty Auerbach, too, was renowned for finding loopholes—the effect on his reputation was damning.

In many circles, he was seen as someone who could not be trusted.

Regardless, through Lucchino's persistence and relentlessness, Billy Beane was granted the right to interview for the job of Red Sox general manager. Throughout baseball, it was widely assumed that Boston had just found its next general manager, the man who would take on the great New York Yankees empire with far more money than he had in Oakland and a revolutionary new approach. All that was left to be determined was precisely how much Beane would cost the Red Sox in terms of salary and player compensation. "I wouldn't eliminate anything at this point—a trade, cash. There's all types of forms of compensation and we're going to look at all of them if it comes to that," said Crowley, the Oakland team president. "You are always looking at [comparable scenarios] and there have been a number of comps when it comes to both managers and head coaches that have moved to other organizations."

While speculation in Boston centered on promising left-handed pitcher Casey Fossum and third baseman Shea Hillenbrand as compensation for Beane, the Red Sox and the executive agreed on a five-year, $13 million contract that would make Beane the highest-paid general manager in baseball; the average annual salary of $2.6 million would be significantly greater than that of even Atlanta Braves general manager John Schuerholz, widely considered the best GM in the game. Because Beane had a daughter living on the West Coast—the Oakland GM was divorced and, thus, separated from the child—the Red Sox agreed to let

Beane run the Boston operation from the West Coast for the first two years of his contract. The Red Sox had given Billy Beane the world, it seemed, and all that remained was for Beane to formally bring matters to a close.

Billy Beane was about to take over a position that many deemed a dream job—the role of Red Sox general manager. He prepared to put his signature on his new $13 million contract.

And then he backed out.

IF IT was possible to be such a thing, Theo Epstein was an experienced 28 years old. Few executives ever have come into the game with as much fanfare. While working his way through the San Diego Padres organization after beginning his career as an intern with the Baltimore Orioles, Epstein caught the eye of everyone from Lucchino and Steinberg to San Diego Padres general manager Kevin Towers. All of them recognized in Epstein an intelligence and poise beyond his years, as well as a willingness to learn. At the urging of Lucchino, Epstein went to law school. At the urging of Towers, Epstein sat in the stands and learned the skills of a scout, on whose evaluations almost every baseball decision was made. In the San Diego area, where Billy Beane's daughter resided, the people who ran the San Diego Padres—on the field and off—were building the perfect beast.

To that point in Boston's search for a new general manager, Lucchino had resisted calling Epstein a candidate, though many believed otherwise. If Epstein was not named the general manager of the Red Sox this time, they thought, he would be named GM at another. From the moment Epstein had arrived in Boston after relocating with the San Diego operation that Lucchino had transferred, there was little doubt that he was doing so with the understanding that he would someday assume the big chair.

But few really expected for that time to come so quickly.

Even Epstein had expressed his personal preferences to Lucchino during the interview process, and his suggestion to Lucchino was not Beane, but Toronto Blue Jays general manager J. P. Ricciardi. A former assistant to Beane, Ricciardi was respected throughout baseball as a tremendous evaluator with exceptional people skills, the latter of which made him an easy man to like. Beane frequently was perceived as arrogant, often rigid, and impossibly demanding, and some characterizations in *Moneyball* did as much to hurt Beane's image as to help it. During the previous year's winter meetings in Boston, at least one Boston reporter saw Beane chastise an employee working behind the front desk of the host hotel, the Sheraton Boston, because a fax belonging to someone else had incorrectly been delivered to Beane's room. The idea of Lucchino and Beane working together prompted many in baseball to believe that the tandem would be far too combustible to last for long. Most believed that Lucchino and Beane were simply too much alike, two insanely driven, fiercely competitive men who could explode over seemingly trivial matters. Larry Lucchino and Billy Beane both wanted to win, to be sure; but what would happen if they disagreed?

In Ricciardi, Epstein believed, the Red Sox would have the best of both worlds: a knowledgeable, progressive baseball executive with a far more engaging disposition. Ricciardi knew baseball. He knew people. And he had an uncanny knack for getting along with just about everyone while sharing with Epstein something else: Massachusetts roots.

A native of West Boylston, Ricciardi had been hired as general manager of the Blue Jays only a year earlier, on November 14, 2001. Immediately, he impressed Toronto ownership by dramatically paring the club's payroll while bringing the Jays back to respectability with trades like the one that delivered Toronto an infielder named Eric Hinske, who had just won the American League Rookie of the Year Award. As a result, even before the Red Sox had been given permission to speak to Beane, Boston's interest in Ricciardi quickly inspired Jays officials to extend Ricciardi's contract and keep him in Toronto, where

Jays officials sought to rebuild a deteriorating organization that had once ruled the baseball world. As recently as 1992–93, Toronto had won consecutive World Series championships. But baseball's historic work stoppage of 1994–95—the same one during which Dan Duquette began reshaping the Red Sox—had dealt the game a major blow, and the Jays were among the teams hardest hit. Toronto's attendance dropped dramatically. The team started losing money. Like the Montreal Expos, Toronto played in a hockey-crazed land that regarded baseball as something of distraction during the summer months, and the Jays had grown into a stagnant franchise (even after adding Roger Clemens) by the time Ricciardi took control. Further, because Toronto and Boston played in the same division—the American League East— losing Ricciardi would have doubly affected the Jays by aiding one of their chief rivals.

So Ricciardi was beyond Boston's reach. By the time Beane bowed out, Lucchino had ruled out several other candidates, while additional ones had yanked themselves from contention. All of that only intensified the focus on Epstein, the ruler in waiting, who many believed was prepared to take over his own franchise. Among Epstein's biggest proponents were Lucchino and Towers, the latter of whom by Lucchino had also been hired.

Once J. P. Ricciardi and Billy Beane were out of the running, Larry Lucchino did not see a clear cut favorite in a field that included the requisite number of retreads and also-rans. If he was going to go with someone new, he was going to go with his own guy.

On Monday, November 25, 2002—just three days before Thanksgiving—the Red Sox introduced Theo Nathan Epstein as the youngest general manager in baseball history. Looking like a boy dressed for his college interview, Epstein addressed the challenge of running the Red Sox, of rebuilding Boston's farm system and player-development operation, of making the Red Sox a perennial contender, like the Atlanta Braves. Like Duquette before him, Epstein was a Boston-area native, though he grew up in Brookline, all but in the shadow of fabled Fenway Park. Epstein spoke of turning the Red Sox into "a scouting and player-development machine," the kind of self-sustaining operation that would give the Red Sox a chance to contend for World Series titles year after year after year.

Theo Epstein wasn't interested in winning just one championship. He wanted several.

But then, Dan Duquette had said almost exactly the same things in January 1994.

"It's a big job. It's a big responsibility," Duquette said in 2002 when asked about the challenge facing Epstein. "It's much bigger than I expected it to be because, in Boston, you can sign players and draft players, but nothing matters unless you win a championship. That's what everybody's looking for. . . . I just felt very proud to be associated with the Red Sox and very proud about the opportunity to work with the hometown team, but it's a big job and a big challenge." Added the former Sox GM: "[Epstein] must be thrilled to have this opportunity and to have it at this point in his career. . . . They have a good nucleus intact on the ballclub. I wish him a lot of luck."

Offered Epstein on the day that served as his inauguration: "I think we're very close [to winning a championship]. The way I look at it, we won 93 games last year, we were unlucky [in one-run games] and we're going to get better. So how bad off can we be?"

In the days that surrounded Epstein's hiring, Lucchino and Henry further fortified a Boston baseball operation with two other acquisitions that spanned the full spectrum of baseball theory. Lucchino and Henry agreed to hire Bill Lajoie, a longtime, respected baseball evaluator who had been part of successful operations with both the Detroit Tigers and the Atlanta Braves; and they hired Bill James, the author and statistical analyst who had introduced revolutionary concepts to baseball through his well-known *Baseball Abstract*. If Lajoie was the classic, crusty old baseball man complete with a straw hat and a cigar, James was the prototypical stat geek, armed with reference books and a brilliant mathematical mind, the preeminent baseball scientist of his time.

By that point in Red Sox history, given the success of "Moneyball" and in the wake of the Mike Gimbel fiasco that had helped smear Duquette's legacy, Boston had become far more receptive to new ways of thinking, regardless of whether Gimbel and James deserved to be mentioned in the same sentence. "Meaning no disrespect, if you guys hadn't brought it up, it would never occur to me to compare myself to Mike Gimbel," James said, quite aware of the perception that Gimbel was a crackpot. "I'll try to help the Red Sox think in organized ways and make good decisions. I think of myself as a part of this organization and I'll try to make myself as involved in it as I possibly can." Added the analyst, noting that part of Gimbel's theories involved analyzing players solely by their data and *not* by any visual aids: "Evaluating a player without ever seeing the player is sort of like being a movie reviewer without ever going to the movies. I suppose you could do it, but I don't know why you would want to."

By the time Epstein and Lajoie were hired—the latter was to serve as Epstein's mentor and adviser—the Red Sox had all but completely rebuilt a baseball operation that had two distinct branches, the old school and the new school, both supervised by a young general manager who had been exposed to both during his developmental years. Years later, the entire process would reflect especially well on Lucchino, who was nothing if not thorough throughout the entire process, bringing in a range of voices and opinions that would allow the Red Sox to look at the game from all angles, in a variety of lights. Further, the hiring of Epstein, in particular, made it quite clear that Lucchino dared to be bold, that he was unafraid to tap into the promise of youth, something he had routinely done with office and administrative staff in San Diego. Now he was doing the same in the baseball operation of the Boston Red Sox, a team that had gone decades without a world title and that frequently seemed misguided and poorly managed.

Clearly, Larry Lucchino knew what he was doing. The only question was whether he could stay out of the way.

DESPITE THE perception, the baseball season does not begin each spring. It begins in the fall. In the aftermath of the World Series, teams go about building their roster for the subsequent season. The off-season is frequently when championships are won and lost, because that is when teams make the decisions that affect the outcome on the field.

In his first off-season as general manager of the Red Sox, Theo Epstein sought to address the three primary weaknesses of the 2002 Red Sox: the bullpen, first base, and second base. Though Rey Sanchez had been a defensive wizard as the team's second baseman, Epstein deemed him a terribly inefficient offensive player because Sanchez rarely walked. So while Sanchez finished 2002 with a solid .286 average, he walked just 17 times in 357 at-bats, leaving him with a poor on-base percentage of .318. Epstein was among the many who believed that second base had become an offensive positive—Duquette shared the same belief, which is why he had traded for headache-in-the-making Wilfredo Cordero following the 1995 season—and so Epstein wasted little time trying to make improvements. Within days, Epstein pulled off a pair of trades that brought second baseman Todd Walker and first baseman Jeremy Giambi to the Red Sox, almost instantly improving Boston's offense from the right side of the infield.

Giambi, like Walker, came with certain holes—specifically, defense—but he was a very disciplined hitter coming off his best professional season, and Epstein saw the chance to add substantial depth to the Boston lineup. "He's an on-base machine," Epstein said of Giambi, who drew 79 walks in 313 at-bats with the Philadelphia Phillies during the 2002 season. "You can count on him for close to a .400 on-base percentage."

While Epstein's latter remark again prompted instant comparisons to Duquette—the former GM once justified signing infielder Jose Offerman to an outsize contract by suggesting the player replaced the departed Mo Vaughn's "on-base capability"—it was other remarks that came back to haunt him some. The younger brother of new New York Yankees first baseman Jason Giambi, Jeremy Giambi was regarded as a part-time player, at best, by the large majority of baseball officials. Yet Epstein suggested that Giambi was "a big part of our solution at first base," which seemed an ambitious statement about a player with a reputation for being an atrocious fielder. Regardless, the early moves by the Red Sox reflected a definitive approach build in the mold of "Moneyball," with the Sox placing great emphasis on a player's ability to get on base.

Given Epstein's age and newfound celebrity, early criticism was inevitable. Showing the kind of aggressiveness that would later come to define the new management and administration of the organization, Epstein and his baseball-operations staff made a Cuban defector, pitcher Jose Contreras, one of their primary pursuits during the offseason. The 6-foot-4, 245-pound Contreras had developed a reputation in Cuba as a bull, a fearless competitor who could shoulder a tremendous workload on any pitching staff. The New York Yankees also had expressed an interest in Contreras, who had established residence in Nicaragua in the wake of his defection and was expected to command a considerable sum for an international free agent. And when negotiations were due to reach their apex, the Sox and Yankees were among the teams who sent representatives to Nicaragua to interview with the player and his agent, Jaime Torres.

While the Yankees ultimately signed the player to a four-year, $32 million contract, the fallout from the event revealed far more of what Epstein would encounter during his stint as Sox GM. On the night before Contreras committed to the Yankees, Sox officials socialized with the player and shared cigars, a night so enjoyable that the Red Sox believed they were close to landing the player. When Contreras subsequently broke the news that he was going to Boston's chief rival, Epstein was said to have responded with shock. ("If you want more money, we have more money," he allegedly told Contreras.) In the days that followed, Yankees officials leaked information that the Red Sox had bought a block of hotel rooms so that New York officials could not get close to Contreras, then told certain media members that an angry Epstein trashed his hotel room when the Sox lost out.

While Epstein privately and publicly denied all of the assertions, the larger point was this: the Yankees already were mounting a campaign against him, trying to manipulate the press, attempting to exploit Epstein's inexperience. All was fair in love and war, after all, and everyone was quite aware that the Red Sox and Yankees did not exchange cards on Valentine's Day.

Amid the gamesmanship, Epstein continued going about his business. Though the Red Sox needed a closer, Epstein did not find any of the potential off-season options appealing, so he opted instead to sign a versatile reliever, Ramiro Mendoza, to a multiyear contract. Mendoza's arrival gave the Sox three middle relievers and/or setup men in the wake of the midseason trades for Alan Embree and Bobby Howry, and Epstein believed one of the three might be able to close. He further stocked the Red Sox infield by acquiring an unheralded and versatile switch-hitter named Bill Mueller, the kind of fundamentally sound player who had always caught the eye of, among others, former Sox manager Jimy Williams while in the National League. Mueller was that rare player who bridged the gap between the old and new schools of baseball—the scouts and the sabermetricians—with an array of skills and abilities that made him what baseball evaluators like to call a *winning player*.

Still, for all that Theo Epstein had accomplished and taken on in his first five weeks as general manager of the Red Sox, his best work was yet to come. Shortly after the New Year, at a time when the off-season typically turned into a flea market—all of the big buys were long gone—Epstein took special note when another relatively unheralded player, Kevin Millar, showed up on the waiver wire. Millar was one of many first basemen and corner infielders available by trade or free agency during that off-season, so his current team, the Florida Marlins, had approached him about the possibility of playing in Japan. Marlins officials felt they could afford to keep Millar, given his status with the club as a part-time player, but they also felt he was too good to release, a scenario that would have earned them nothing in return. So Marlins officials cut a deal with a Japanese team, the Chunichi Dragons, to sell Millar's rights to them for $1.2 million, a deal that also benefited the player. As a result of going to Japan, Millar was granted a two-year, $6.2 million contract that was far more than a player like him had ever dreamed of making, and so all parties had something to again.

The Marlins got money that served their small-market baseball operation.

The Dragons got a new and potentially productive player.

Millar got the kind of contract that would give him and his family some long-term security.

Nonetheless, Epstein had an interest in Millar, whom he had scouted in the minor leagues when Millar was in the Marlins' player-development system and Epstein was working for the Padres. Epstein just wasn't sure how to get him. Though baseball rules allowed Epstein to claim Millar off waivers, he also knew that to do so would be a violation of baseball etiquette, at least according to how teams had begun to operate. Player traffic between the United States and Japan had increased tremendously in recent years—in the Pacific Northwest, Seattle Mariners outfielder Ichiro Suzuki hit the major leagues like a meteor in 2001—and teams had allowed one another a certain latitude when it came to international deals. In the case of a player like Millar, who was being put on waivers so that a club could send him *to* Japan, major-league teams operated with the understanding that the player would not be claimed, allowing him to take his talents overseas. The implied message: If you don't get in the middle of our deal, we won't get in the middle of yours.

Just the same, having completed his law degree and worked under Lucchino, Epstein wondered what would happen if he *did* put in a claim. Red Sox officials discussed the matter before going ahead with the controversial maneuver, which caused a predictable logjam. Suddenly, Kevin Miller had an option to play in the United States, *for the Red Sox*, who were willing to sign him to a multiyear contract that rivaled that of the Chunichi Dragons. Quickly, Millar and his agents, twin brothers Sam and Seth Levinson, seemed to concoct a wild story about how Millar had developed cold feet about playing overseas in the wake of America's military presence in Iraq. Millar went so far as to bring his father, a former Vietnam medic, to a meeting with Dragons officials in New York, where the father made a plea to the Japanese team representatives that his son remain in the United States. Dragons officials nonetheless remained steadfast in their belief that Millar was obligated to honor his contract, which prompted the Major League Baseball Players Association (at the urging of Millar and his agents) to threaten the cancellation of scheduled regular games in Tokyo between the Oakland A's and Suzuki's team, the Mariners. In the end, the Dragons and the governing body of Japanese baseball finally relented, allowing Millar out of his contract on the condition that the Marlins return their $1.2 million. (Chunichi subsequently used most of that amount on major-league outfielder, Alex Ochoa.)

Now, with Millar on waivers, it was up to the Red Sox to make up the $1.2 million to the Marlins. Epstein negotiated a deal in which the Sox paid Florida $1.5 million—the sum included $300,000 in tickets for underprivileged youth, half of which was paid by Millar—during a process in which the Red Sox spoke of making all parties "whole." The entire process—from the moment Millar was placed on waivers to the moment he finally became official property of the Red Sox—took almost six weeks, then perceived as an absurd amount of time for a player many saw in part-time duty, as a classic role player. The Millar saga showed just how far the Red Sox were willing to go—and what they were willing to do—to get what they wanted.

If the team's reputation throughout baseball suffered some as a result, the Red Sox chalked it up to the cost of doing business. "It wasn't the most comfortable feeling in the world being two months in [as Red Sox general manager] and doing something that would seriously ruffle some feathers," Epstein admitted to the *Herald*. "So we did some research on how this would play out and there was no scenario in which anyone would remain worse off. We didn't want to hurt anyone else. We wanted to do something good for us. Once we were able to reconcile those things, we did it."

As for Millar, he ended up with a two-year, $5.3 million contract with an option for a third season, and a new lease on his baseball life. Undrafted by major-league teams, Millar had made a name for himself competing in an independent league before the Marlins signed him to a minor-league contract. By the time he got the major leagues, he was regarded as a good hitter without a position, the latter of which clearly was not an issue to Red Sox officials, who greatly valued Millar's hitting skills. (With the Marlins, however, Millar's defensive deficiencies were exposed because the National League operates without a designated hitter.) At worst, Epstein believed, the Sox could work Millar into a rotation at the corner infield positions with, among others, Jeremy Giambi, Shea Hillenbrand, and Bill Mueller. The point was to give the Red Sox *options* at a position where they had underachieved during the previous seasons, particularly after the team allowed the injury-prone Floyd to depart via free agency.

Additionally, Epstein felt there was a side benefit: the surplus of players should allow the Sox the flexibility to trade for a relief pitcher—specifically a closer—in case the group built around Embree, Howry, and Mendoza did not pan out.

For Millar, despite the competition, coming to Boston was a dream come true. He was the bluest of the blue collars, and his rags-to-riches career had made him truly appreciate life in the major leagues. Millar was the opposite of the stereotypically pampered and spoiled professional athlete; he just wanted to play. Almost immediately after the

Red Sox unraveled the red tape surrounding Millar's escape from Japan, Millar hopped into his pickup truck in Beaumont, Texas, and drove across the southeastern United States, through the night, to join his new Red Sox teammates.

While many players had dreaded coming to Boston and the Red Sox, Millar couldn't wait to get there. "I think this team's developing a makeup," said Millar, who already had friendships with Sox new-comer Walker as well as incumbents Trot Nixon and Nomar Garcia-parra before arriving in camp. "Hopefully we can brings the mullets back and grow the hair out. These guys are baseball players." Added the personable first baseman: "I'm vocal. I'll say what's on my mind. I have *fun*. I'm a big fan of team chemistry. I think that's one thing you can't buy."

Indeed, while the Red Sox were without a closer, there was little question that Millar was right. Unlike so many of past teams that saw the Boston uniform as a burden, the 2003 Red Sox had *personality*. They had a carefree attitude that was critical for playing in Boston, where the absence of a championship had made the baseball season such a bur-den that most every Sox team forgot the simplest fact: they were playing a game.

Still, by the time Millar got to camp—even with a two-year contract—the situation at the corner infield positions had further clut-tered. Not long before the start of camp, Epstein had picked up yet an-other candidate for first base or designated hitter, a theretofore underachieving slugger from the Minnesota Twins named David Ortiz. Like Millar, the affable Ortiz was seen as a vital clubhouse presence in Minnesota; but the Twins felt that Ortiz's salary had outgrown his per-formance. So Twins general Manager Terry Ryan decided to release Ortiz, whom Minnesota had unsuccessfully tried to trade. The Red Sox and Yankees were among those clubs interested in the player, and Ortiz's agent, Fernando Cuza, had tried to push Ortiz on the Sox while representing another client, relief pitcher Mendoza. In the end, partly because the far more talented Jason Giambi was in New York, Ortiz decided that his best chance to play regularly was in Boston, leading him to sign a one-year, $1.25 million deal with Red Sox.

As with Millar, Epstein had followed Ortiz when Ortiz was in the Minnesota minor-league system and Epstein was working for the Padres. Because the salary risk was minimal—a $1.25 million base was roughly half the major-league average at the time—Epstein saw little downside in rolling the dice for a player that the Red Sox believed could be, in a best-case scenario, well, serviceable.

As it turned out, David Ortiz proved to be a winning lottery ticket.

"It was just luck and good timing," Epstein admitted years later in Ortiz's memoirs, *Big Papi: My Story of Big Dreams and Big Hits*. "The way we assessed the needs of the team, we needed at least a couple of corner bats. It was a good market to be aggressive on the lower- or mid-term players, so we let Cliff Floyd go and decided to spread the money around a little bit."

Indeed, for slightly more than half the long-term dollars that Floyd received in a four-year, $26 million contract with the New York Mets, Epstein had added Millar ($5.3 million), Mueller ($4.5 million), Walker ($3.5 million), Giambi ($2 million), and Ortiz ($1.25 million) to a team that had won 93 games. Additionally, he had added relief pitchers Ramiro Mendoza, Chad Fox, and Mike Timlin, effectively treating Boston players as stocks and diversifying the team's portfolio. Along the way, Epstein had challenged baseball's conventional way of doing business during the Millar saga and rekindled a smoldering rivalry with the Yankees, whom most everyone continued to regard as the favorites to win the World Series, despite New York's failures during each of the past two seasons.

Now 29, Theo Epstein had been the general manager of the Red Sox for less than three months.

TO THIS day, in the clash that inevitably takes place between the old and new schools of baseball philosophy, the noise is naturally loudest in a small, self-contained area: the bullpen.

The early part of the 2003 season proved a learning experience to Epstein, Bill James, and anyone else involved with the management of the Red Sox. Given their terribly apparent need for a closer—and the absence of a desirable one on the market—the Red Sox elected to open the 2003 season with an experiment that failed as spectacularly as the *Hindenburg*: the infamous approach of closer by committee. The concept, supported by statistician James, was simple: while many teams saved their closer until the ninth inning of a game, a close look at any game often revealed that the most important outs were recorded (or not) an inning or two earlier, usually by an inferior pitcher. To James, this made no sense. Wouldn't it be more efficient to use the closer during a crisis in the seventh or eighth innings, then leave a potentially easier ninth for someone else?

In theory, it made perfect sense.

But there were flaws in the viewpoint. First, the importance of any outs in any given game could be determined only after the game had been completed; only then, after all, did anyone possess the benefit of hindsight. Second, major-league relievers were helpless creatures of habit who liked to know *precisely* what their job was; the structure eased their anxiety. While it was easy to suggest that four or five relievers could sit in a bullpen together with each responding at a moment's notice, the uncertainty often had an unsettling effect. As the final innings of the game approached, as situations unfolded, relievers nervously waited to see whose name would be called when the game was typically most delicate.

As it turned out, at the most sensitive points of early-season games, the 2003 Red Sox were playing musical chairs.

Had the Red Sox had a different cast of relievers or, for that matter, a different manager, the plan might have worked. But in Grady Little, the Red Sox had a skipper who had spent most of his managerial career in the minor leagues, carrying out the directives of officials at the major-league level. And in their bullpen, the Red Sox had a cast of setup men who had all failed in closing games at one point or another during their careers. Even the most accomplished, Timlin, had developed a reputation for being a pitcher incapable of handling ninth-inning pressure, something the Seattle Mariners learned after acquiring him at the 1997 trading deadline that delivered Jason Varitek and Derek Lowe to Boston for a similar soul, Heathcliff Slocumb.

As the year began, the question was obvious: Who is going to close?

"I don't know," one Sox player privately admitted as newcomer Timlin stood a distance away. "But we know *he* can't do it."

Just the same, Epstein was willing to take a chance, though it didn't take long for the experiment to blow up in his face. On Opening Day 2003, despite a brilliant performance by Pedro Martinez and a 4–1 lead entering the bottom of the ninth inning against the wretched Tampa Bay Devil Rays, the Red Sox spiraled to a 6–4 defeat that ended with a three-run home run by Tampa outfielder Carl Crawford in the ninth. Embree and Fox were the primary culprits. Thus the Red Sox began 2003 with the same song they sang to conclude 2002: "The Bullpen Fucked Us Again."

"We've got 161 more of these," said Fox, who served up the homer to Crawford. "If you think I'm going to lay down or Alan is going to lay down, you're sadly mistaken."

Said Embree: "It's Day 1 and we have a long way to go. If we were to panic and scrap this, it would be a waste of an off-season."

Concluded Little: "We just didn't get the pitches made. It doesn't matter when they pitch in a ball game. If the situation comes up again [today], you might see the same guys out there. I don't know."

Of course, that was precisely the point. The Red Sox had no order, rhyme, or reason to how they planned to use their relief pitchers. *Nobody* knew.

Nonetheless, the Red Sox persisted, and before long they were winning games thanks to the kind of offense everyone expected. Despite the continued difficulties of their bullpen, the Red Sox went 18-9 in their first 27 games, ending April by averaging just under six runs per game. It would be an omen of things to come. Month after month, despite changes in the weather, and no matter the chaos taking place in their bullpen, the Red Sox continued to hit. By the end of the season, while setting a major-league record for slugging percentage—breaking the mark held by the otherworldly 1927 New York Yankees team that included, among others, Lou Gehrig and Babe Ruth—the Red Sox scored 159 runs in April, 163 in May, 190 in June, 151 in July, 158 in August, and 140 in September. They would finish with 961 runs scored, a figure that led the major leagues and translated into 5.9 runs per game.

Even when Red Sox pitchers failed, it seemed, undeterred Sox hitters would rally to win as if spiting both the passionless 2002 team that preceded them and the idealistic ideas of their management.

Of all the things the Sox offense accomplished in 2003, none was more impressive than what they did on the night of June 27 in a game against the Florida Marlins. Facing Marlins right-hander Carl Pavano—yes, the same can't-miss prospect Dan Duquette traded for Pedro Martinez following the 1997 season—the Red Sox put on a fireworks demonstration that went down in history. In defeating the Marlins 25–8, the Red Sox scored an absolutely incredible 14 runs in the first inning, including *a major-league-record 10 before the Marlins recorded an out*. They finished with 28 hits to tie a team record, and their 25 runs were the second most in the history of the franchise. Said Millar, who went 3-for-4 in a game that also featured five hits from Johnny Damon and four each from Mueller and Walker: "I've never seen anything like that. It was amazing."

No one was about to argue.

By that point, while having fully developed the "makeup" that Kevin Millar had correctly identified as far back as spring training, the Red Sox had also taken steps to address their biggest questions: the shortage of reliable relief pitchers and the surplus of corner infielders. Frustrated by the continued ineptitude of his bullpen, Epstein had pulled the trigger on a May 29 trade in which he acquired right-hander Byung-Hyun Kim from the Arizona Diamondbacks for free-swinging third baseman Shea Hillenbrand, a player who did not fit the club's new offensive philosophy. Possessing all but an allergy to the walk, Hillenbrand was the kind of player whom Red Sox officials regarded as terribly overrated, someone whose statistics grossly inflated his actual contribution; in their minds, Hillenbrand was frequently an easy out. Further, Sox officials regarded Hillenbrand as both ignorant and boorish, which left them feeling as though he contributed little to the club off the field, too. So Epstein traded for Kim in a rare one-for-one swap of players who had been named to the most recent All-Star Game and that served the short-term needs of both clubs.

Nonetheless, Kim came with questions. Two years earlier, as a member of the Diamondbacks, Kim had failed spectacularly against the New York Yankees in the World Series, blowing a pair of games and posting a 13.50 ERA in his only two appearances. Right there, with television cameras chronicling his every move—think Jim Carrey in the *The Truman Show*—Kim appeared to be having a nervous breakdown so debilitating that Arizona manager Bob Brenly was forced to bypass him for the final games, using Randy Johnson to close out the seventh and final game of the Series after Johnson had started Game 6. (Ironic as it was, the Yankees' steely-eyed closer, Mariano Rivera, blew Game 7 for New York.)

By the time the Red Sox came calling, Kim had rebounded from the disaster to post a 2.04 ERA and 36 saves in 2002 before being moved into the Arizona starting rotation. The Red Sox' long-term plans for Kim similarly involved moving him into their rotation—in fact, partly as a condition of the deal, the Red Sox agreed to a two-year, $10 million contract extension that they failed to announce until after the season—but Boston's immediate need was for Kim to stabilize their bullpen, which he promptly did. At least for a while.

The infield situation had sorted itself out far more nicely. Partly as a result of Hillenbrand's departure—and partly as a result of injury and to the general ineptitude of Giambi—Ortiz and Mueller had settled into regular roles, the former as the designated hitter, the latter as the third baseman. (Millar played first regularly.) Afforded the opportunity to play every day, Ortiz began producing almost immediately, benefiting greatly from both a working relationship with Manny Ramirez (who helped school Ortiz on the finer points of hitting) and the undying support of fellow Dominican Republic native Pedro Martinez. In fact, frustrated by a lack of playing time early in the season, Ortiz had gone so far as to call his agents about the possibility of being traded from Boston, but Red Sox officials assured the player that his time would come when they made a deal for a relief pitcher. As it turned out, the acquisition of Byung-Hyun Kim proved of immeasurable value to the Red Sox simply because it created playing time for Ortiz.

Of course, the cries of Martinez didn't hurt either, particularly after Little benched Ortiz for a June 21 game at Philadelphia for what Little perceived as a slight. "Somebody complained that David left [the previous game early], but the game was over [when Ortiz departed]," Martinez recalled in *Big Papi*. "The next day [on June 21, a game pitched by Martinez], I got really upset. David was supposed to be in the lineup and [Little's reason for benching Ortiz] was an excuse that Grady gave me. I snapped. I said, 'Grady, don't give me any of that bullshit.' He looked at me and said, 'Hey, don't blame me. It's not up to me.' And I said, 'Well, you're going to play him when I pitch. You're going to start playing him in my games.' "

Though Ortiz appeared in that June 21 game only as a pinch hitter—he struck out—Martinez's claims were nonetheless revealing on two levels. First, Little essentially was admitting that the decision to play Giambi was being made by his superiors. Second, Epstein was obviously intent on giving Giambi every opportunity to succeed after deeming him "a big part of our solution at first base."

Eight days later, the situation resolved itself; Jeremy Giambi was placed on the disabled list with a wrist injury. Ortiz had long since begun thundering away at opposing pitchers, giving the Red Sox yet another productive bat in the middle of their lineup. During the off-season, Epstein had acquired Millar, Mueller, and Ortiz with the hope that one of them might be able to produce for the Red Sox on a regular basis, and the situation had developed far better than even the general manager could have imagined. All three players were having a profound impact on the Boston lineup, and the Red Sox looked to be very much in contention for a playoff spot as the season reached its homestretch. As the calendar turned to August and then September, the Red Sox had October on their minds.

WITH THE Red Sox continuing their seemingly never-ending pursuit of the holy grail, Theo Epstein kept his foot on the accelerator. Boston made deals with the Pittsburgh Pirates just before the July 31 trading deadline for both starting pitcher Jeff Suppan and left-handed reliever Scott Sauerbeck, and he also picked up right-handed reliever Scott Williamson from the Cincinnati Reds. The large majority of players traded away by the Red Sox were minor leaguers drafted or developed under Dan Duquette.

While the acquisition of Williamson was of particular interest—Howry had been injured early in the year and Fox was released on July 30—his arrival quickly grew in importance. Despite a fabulous July during which he allowed just two runs in 18.2 innings—a sparkling 0.96 ERA—Byung-Hyun Kim began to belly up in August. By the end of the month, Kim had posted a 5.74 ERA in 15 appearances, showing the kind of vulnerability that had defined the Red Sox bullpen for most of two seasons.

Theo Epstein wasn't the only one ready to beat his head against the wall. All of New England shared the same feeling. *Here we go again.*

Yet, for all of the flaws the Red Sox continued to reveal, the team plodded through August with a 15-14 record thanks to the tireless spirit and productivity of the Boston lineup. Everyone from Epstein to manager Little acknowledged that the Red Sox could not make the playoffs—or, more important, win a championship—unless the team's pitchers showed dramatic improvement, but the Boston lineup seemed intent on winning regardless. The Red Sox opened September by winning five straight and eight of 10, including a pair of victories at Yankee

Stadium by a combined score of 20–3. By the end of the regular season, Boston and New York would have played 19 games during which the Red Sox scored 109 runs, an average of 5.7 runs per game that was consistent with Boston's production against the rest of major-league baseball. And though the Yankees won 10 of those meeting as well as a sixth straight American League East Division championship, the Red Sox actually outscored New York, 109–94, while delivering a critical message to the Yankees, their pitchers, and their fans: *We can beat you.*

Still, as reassuring as the Boston attitude and offense were, the bullpen remained problematic. The Red Sox were in control of the wild-card race thanks largely to a four-game home sweep over the Seattle Mariners in late August—the series would prove critical when the Red Sox ultimately secured the final American League playoff spot by a mere two games—but there was still uneasiness as the Red Sox moved closer to clinching. Suppan and Sauerbeck had been big disappointments from the Pittsburgh deal, and Williamson, too, was struggling. Mendoza had long since bottomed out, and there was a feeling that no matter whom the Red Sox sent to the mound in the late innings, the team would have to endure a high-wire act. For two years, every game had felt like a drama.

By the time the Sox got to late September, the season had become a frantic race to the finish. The Sox were playing a three-game series in Cleveland when a *Herald* reporter walked into the visiting manager's office intending to speak with Little and encountered Epstein standing in the room, alone, with a blank look on his face. Epstein had not been the general manager of the team for even a year to that point, yet the demands of the job were clearly taking their toll. Epstein looked simultaneously tired, nervous, and even scared, emotions undoubtedly familiar to any executive who had ever assembled a team. Oakland general manager Billy Beane, for instance, was far more experienced and just as competitive as Epstein, and he often chose to run on a treadmill while his team was on the field because he found the experience too agonizing. Even Duquette, whom most reporters viewed as bloodless and robotic, succumbed to the emotional torture of the job. Once, while outfielder Troy O'Leary was botching a relatively routine play in the outfield, a reporter passing by Duquette's private box heard the general manager scream his frustration from the top of his lungs: *"Fucking O'Leary!"*

Now, for the first time, Epstein was showing the effects of a long season while further proving a long-standing truth: there is simply no substitute for experience. Epstein had been involved in baseball so long, it was easy to forget sometimes that *he was only 29*, which meant that Epstein lacked perspective. He was not married. He had no children. His entire life—inside and outside of the ballpark—was built around his job, an unhealthy imbalance that almost everyone has experienced at one point or another. But Epstein's job happened to be general manager of the Red Sox, a venerable institution with an often unreasonable and traumatized fan base susceptible to panic, and there was little question concerning Epstein's state of mind in Cleveland. The heat was getting to the kid.

Fans and reporters often speak of a player's ability to deal with pressure, but at least the player has a hand in the outcome; for executives, it is different. Epstein had begun working tirelessly as the general manager of the Red Sox the previous November, making a series of maneuvers designed to take Boston to the next level. He acquired Walker, Mueller, Millar, and Ortiz. He signed Mendoza, picked up just about any other available reliever with a decent arm, and even picked up another starter in Suppan. Yet there was the distinct possibility now that it would lead to nothing, that the Red Sox would win fewer than the 93 games they had won during 2002, that Epstein would have to go back to square one as soon as the season ended and begin rebuilding the Red Sox again. For all the work that Epstein had put in, he simply could not control the events on the field.

Four days after leaving Cleveland—the Sox took two of three from the Indians—the Red Sox bludgeoned the Baltimore Orioles by a 14–3 score to clinch the American League wild-card berth, giving Boston a place in the playoffs for the first time since 1999. Red Sox players and fans partook in a boisterous celebration at Fenway Park, where the Red Sox collectively had batted a preposterous .316 while posting a 53-28 record.

"I like our chances against anybody," said Red Sox veteran pitcher Tim Wakefield, who had been with the Red Sox longer than any other player on the team. "We have a special team. I like our chances because our foot is in the door and that's all we asked for coming out of spring training."

Said elated owner John Henry: "I am declaring New England to be a no-fret zone. Let's enjoy the postseason. If we get behind by a run, or behind by a game, let's not fret, because this is what it's about."

Said manager Little, perfectly capturing the spirit of his club: "We continued to battle all season long. We had some earth-shattering losses, but we came out the next day like nothing happened. That's what makes this team special."

Indeed, by becoming one of eight teams to make the playoffs, the Red Sox had distinguished themselves from many of their peers and predecessors. The journey had been long and arduous. And as Boston rejoiced at the reality of fall baseball at Fenway Park, Theo Epstein celebrated with his players in the home clubhouse at Fenway Park.

The Red Sox were going back to the playoffs.

And awaiting them there were Billy Beane and the Oakland A's.

THE PROBLEM with the playoffs, as Billy Beane has argued, is that luck becomes a greater factor. The sample size is so small and there are so many variables that the best team does not always win. In the short term, after a 162-game regular season, the performance of players is impossible to predict. Over the next 16 days, the Red Sox learned both the drawbacks and the benefits of that reality.

In the strictest baseball sense, the Red Sox and A's were a fascinating matchup of strengths. In making their fourth straight playoff appearance, the A's led the American League in pitching with a 3.63 team ERA. The Red Sox were a mediocre eighth at 4.48. Meanwhile, the Boston offense led the American League with 961 runs, while Oakland ranked ninth at a mere 761, a fact that pitted strength against strength as baseball began its postseason tournament. The question was simple: Oakland's pitching or Boston's offense?

With a host of players who had never participated in the postseason, the Red Sox looked like an inexperienced club for much of the first two games. Ultimately, that was one of the unrecognized costs during the transition and makeover of the club. While players like Wakefield, Derek Lowe, Jason Varitek, and Pedro Martinez had participated in the postseason, newcomers like Millar and Walker had not. Ortiz had a limited and unspectacular postseason history, as did Mueller. All of that raised serious questions about the Red Sox' ability to compete, particularly with a bullpen that came with yellow warning labels.

The Red Sox lost Game 1 in 12 excruciating innings, 5–4, the final run of the game scoring when Oakland catcher Ramon Hernandez bunted for a hit against Lowe, who was being used as a reliever in the wake of an earlier meltdown by the radioactive Red Sox relief corps. The Red Sox had taken a 4–3 lead into the bottom of the ninth before Kim reverted to his 2001 form with the Diamondbacks, walking one batter and hitting another to put the tying run in scoring position. Having lost faith in the right-hander by that point in the season, Sox manager Grady Little called upon left-hander Embree to face Oakland designated hitter Erubiel Durazo, who promptly tied the game with a two-out single to center. In the innings that ensued, thanks largely to closer Keith Foulke, the A's silenced the Red Sox until Hernandez's dramatic bunt hit.

Faced with little time to dwell on the defeat, the Red Sox went out and dropped Game 2 by a 5–1 score, looking lifeless against A's left-hander Barry Zito, the man who had edged out Martinez and Lowe for the Cy Young Award a year earlier. As the teams left Oakland and headed for Boston, there seemed little doubt that the A's were the better and far more seasoned team, blessed with a big advantage in the area that mattered most, especially during the playoffs: pitching.

"Nothing is over yet," said center fielder Johnny Damon as players packed their belongings for the return flight to Boston. "We were hoping we could advance [to the next round] with a win at our place, but we know we have to come back here. And if we win Game 3, we're definitely coming back here."

Said reserve infielder Lou Merloni, recalling that the Red Sox were in a similar 0–2 series predicament to the Cleveland Indians in 1999 before rallying to win three straight games: "It was a lot worse [in 1999]. First of all, Pedro came out of Game 1 and we thought he was done for the series. Then we went home and our number three or number four hitter went down [in Garciaparra], so I thought that was a lot worse. They still have to come and beat us at our best, which is at our place. I just hope the fans are ready."

Of course, they were.

With the Red Sox facing elimination, Little handed the ball for Game 3 to Derek Lowe, who had followed up his Cy Young–caliber season of 2002 with a 17-7 performance in 2003, albeit with a significantly higher ERA (4.47). Matched against left-hander Ted Lilly, Lowe pitched brilliantly, holding the A's to just one unearned run over seven innings. The game was tied at 1 in the bottom of the 11th inning when Trot Nixon pounded a two-run home run against reliever Rich Harden into the center-field seats, giving the Red Sox their first victory of the series, 3–1, and injecting life into both the Red Sox and their fans.

They were alive.

While the Boston offense had managed just three runs in Game 3— all things considered, the Oakland pitchers were still beating the Boston hitters—a funny thing was happening: the Red Sox pitching staff, particularly the bullpen, was starting to jell. Excluding Lowe's performance as a reliever in Game 1—he was, after all, a starter—Red Sox relievers had allowed just one run while striking out 11 during their first nine innings of the series. In the wake of Kim's meltdown in Game 1 of the series—the pitcher responded to boos during introductions at Fenway Park by flipping his middle finger at the Boston crowd—Little had settled into a bullpen rotation of Embree, Timlin, and Williamson, the last of whom was now closing. In Game 3, Timlin and Williamson had combined for four scoreless innings, allowing Nixon the opportunity to homer against Harden.

Suddenly, Billy Beane's theories were being validated. *There was no way to predict postseason performance.*

Still, as much as the Red Sox were thrilled at the developments in their bullpen, their offense—specifically David Ortiz—was a growing concern. After finishing the regular season with a career-best 31 home runs and 101 RBIs (Jeremy Giambi, we hardly knew ye), Ortiz had opened his first career playoff series with the Red Sox by going 0-for-13 with five strikeouts. By the time Ortiz came to bat in the eighth inning of Game 4 against A's closer Foulke, Ortiz's slump had expanded to 0-for-16 with six strikeouts, the kind of performance that had led many to wonder whether Ortiz was the kind of player who could succeed only during the regular season, who could hit against bad and mediocre pitchers but not good ones. As quickly as the Red Sox bullpen had unexpectedly blossomed, Ortiz seemed to be wilting.

Faced with the most critical at-bat of the series to that point, Ortiz stepped in against Foulke with two outs, two runners on base, and the Red Sox facing a 4–3 deficit. A mere four outs remained in the Boston season. An extremely durable reliever whose best pitch was a changeup that darted down and away from left-handed batter, Foulke nonetheless elected to throw Ortiz a *fastball* on the sixth pitch of the at-bat, a mistake that resulted in a laserlike two-run double that gave the Sox the lead.

Closer Williamson then came in and continued the illogical renaissance of the Boston bullpen, striking out two batters in a one-two-three ninth to give the Red Sox a pulsating 5–4 victory that forced a fifth and final game of the series.

In Oakland.

"My heart is racing, man. It's unbelievable," said the usually even-keeled Red Sox pitcher and 38-year-old veteran John Burkett, the Sox' starting pitcher in the game. "It's off the charts. We've been fighting and scratching all season long. It's just unbelievable. Things are just flying through my mind right now. It's going to be the best flight I've ever taken."

At least one that took place on an airplane.

As expected, Game 5 was a struggle. The Red Sox put together one rally against Zito, who had shut them down in Game 2, but the club managed four runs. Martinez handed a 4–3 lead to Timlin and Embree, who combined for a scoreless eighth. Little opened the ninth by giving the ball to Williamson, who had been brilliant to that point in the post-season.

And then, without warning, it was as if the Red Sox regressed to the days of midseason, when their bullpen could not get anyone out.

With the series—and season—hanging in the balance, Williamson walked the first two Oakland batters of the ninth inning, Scott Hatteberg and Jose Guillen, the latter of whom was playing with a wrist injury and was known for swinging at anything close to the strike zone. As a result, the A's quickly had runners at first and second with nobody out, leaving Little with no choice but to go to a member of his starting staff, Lowe, in yet another closing situation. Though the A's rarely bunted to sacrifice runners—yet another tenet of the "Moneyball" philosophy was to avoid giving away outs whenever possible—Ramon Hernandez (he of the bunt single in Game 1) gave himself up to move runners to second and third. The A's then sent up Adam Melhuse to pinch-hit for the struggling Jermaine Dye, lining up three consecutive left-handed hitters against sinkerballer Lowe.

Two days after starting Game 3 at Fenway Park, Lowe stood on the mound of the Network Associates Coliseum on Oakland with one out, runners at second and third, the Boston season once again on the line. Only two years earlier, during the breakdown that was his final season as

Red Sox closer, Lowe's difficulties were largely the result of two things: shakeable confidence and an inability to retire left-handed batters, who hit a whopping .371 against him. But largely as a result of those struggles, the Lowe of 2003 was an entirely different pitcher, particularly in the wake of Game 3. He was pitching well, so his confidence was high. And his difficulty against left-handers in 2001 had forced him to refine his skills; he could now throw his best pitch, a darting sinker, to both sides of the plate.

Under impossible pressure, Derek Lowe peered in to catcher Jason Varitek, the man with whom he had been traded to Boston in 1997.

Derek Lowe struck out Melhuse for the second out.

Then he walked Chris Singleton to load the bases.

Then he struck out Terrence Long to end the game, the final pitch a banana-curved sinker that started at Long's right hip before swerving back to catch the inside corner of home plate. Strike three.

Game, set, and match.

"If you had any doubts about his heart, there are absolutely no doubts now," Red Sox general manager Epstein said of Lowe amid the Boston clubhouse celebration. "That was as clutch as you can possibly be. I don't know how many pitchers in the game have the guts to make those pitches."

Said Varitek of his friend and batterymate: "That strike-three pitch was the best pitch he's ever made."

The matchup most everyone wanted to see was set. In the next round of the playoffs, the Red Sox would face the New York Yankees for the right to go to the World Series.

AS DISAPPOINTINGLY as things turned our for the Red Sox in the 2003 American League Championship Series, a critical metamorphosis took place. Boston grew into a legitimate, indisputable threat to the mighty New York Yankees, the team that Sox president Larry Lucchino had dubbed "the Evil Empire."

In the process, during a series that was nationally televised, most of the United States of America saw the Red Sox as an appealing, striking contrast to the corporate, cleaned-and-pressed Yankees, the embodiment of American big business. By then, the Red Sox had long since adopted a rodeo slogan coined by Millar—"Cowboy up"—and turned it into their rallying cry. The Red Sox, in some ways, were seen as a collection of hard-livin', beer-bellied softball players who possessed, more than anything else, *grit*, which endeared them to most anyone who had ever had to endure a struggle of any kind. The Yankees were seen as cold and efficient. But the Red Sox won in spite of their flaws and because of their determination, all while celebrating an individuality that seemed to fly in the face of everything the Yankees stood for. "Nothing comes easy for us," Millar said proudly before the series began. "And we don't want it to be easy for us."

Continuing the pattern that was set early in the postseason, almost nothing went according to script. While they had long since mastered Sox ace Pedro Martinez, the Yankees lost to knuckleballer Tim Wakefield in Game 1 before beating a weary Lowe in Game 2. The series then went back to Boston, where Game 3 pitted Martinez against Roger Clemens in a rematch of their one-sided bout from 1999. The difference this time was that Martinez was inexplicably flat, making him nothing more than chum for the sharks of the New York lineup. Martinez allowed runs to New York in the second, third, and fourth, when he desperately fired a pitch behind Yankees outfielder Karim Garcia, hitting Garcia between the shoulder blades and bringing decades of Red Sox–Yankees hatred to new heights. Later in the game, when Sox slugger Manny Ramirez reacted angrily to a Clemens pitch that Ramirez deemed too close for comfort, the benches emptied and a scrum ensued, leading to the unforgettable scene of Martinez grabbing elder Yankees bench coach Don Zimmer by the head and pushing him to the ground.

Martinez acted like a bullfighter.

The Yankees thought it was bull. "You know the kind of respect I have for Pedro's ability to pitch, but I didn't care for that," dignified

Yankees manager Joe Torre said of Martinez's pitch to Garcia, speaking on behalf of his team.

Said Martinez of the Zimmer incident: "I would never raise my hand against Zimmer or Torre or anyone that age. I was just trying to push him away or dodge away, and his body fell. I hope he's fine."

As it was, Martinez's antics worked, at least to a degree. While the pitcher effectively got the Yankees off their game and sufficiently settled down to hold New York scoreless over the balance of his outing, the Yankees nonetheless emerged with a 4–3 victory. Wakefield continued his mastery over New York in Game 4 with a superb 3–2 victory, but the Yankees again defeated Lowe, this time in Game 5, to take a 3–2 series lead. The series then shifted back to New York for Games 6 and 7, leaving the Red Sox with a seemingly impossible task. They had to beat the Yankees twice if they wanted to advance to the World Series, and they had to do it at Yankee Stadium, where New York had pulled off more than its share of miracle victories during the Yankees' storied history.

Facing a 6–4 deficit entering the seventh inning of Game 6, the Red Sox rallied for three runs against a pair of Yankee relievers, beginning with Jose Contreras, the Cuban pitcher over whom the clubs had battled during the off-season. Contreras had been an enormous disappointment during his first season, particularly against the Red Sox, who had pounded him for 12 runs in 4⅓ innings, an embarrassing ERA of 24.92. Contreras pitched so poorly at times that the New York media already considered him a colossal bust, further driving home the point that the game on the field could be completely unpredictable, during the regular season or the playoffs. The Red Sox had *wanted* Contreras, after all. Yet there he was, dragging down the Yankees.

The score remained 7–6 in favor of the Red Sox entering the ninth inning, when the relentless Nixon contributed his second major blow of the postseason, belting a two-run home run off left-hander Gabe White to give the Sox a spongy 9–6 lead. The extra runs were invaluable against the Yankees, particularly in a playoff game at Yankee Stadium, and Williamson continued a generally stellar postseason—he finished with a 1.12 ERA, 14 strikeouts, and three walks in just eight innings—by closing out the Yankees in the bottom of the ninth.

Between Boston and New York, there would be a seventh game, a final contest of winner-take-all.

And the starting pitchers would be none other than Martinez and Clemens.

"You guys have the dream matchup of the playoffs right now. You've got Roger against Pedro," Sox reliever Embree said after the Boston victory in Game 6. "There are some kids who have had that dream. They've played in the backyard using those names. And that's what you're going to have."

As it was, the pitching matchup never really developed. In a complete reversal of Game 3, Clemens came out flat and failed to survive the fourth inning, leaving with nobody out, two men on base, and a 4–0 deficit. The Red Sox appeared on the verge of blowing the Yankees out when Mike Mussina (normally a starter) entered the game in relief and quashed the Boston threat, keeping New York within a reasonable distance. Still, Martinez seemed to be cruising along without much difficulty, taking a 4–1 lead into the seventh inning.

In having more success against Martinez than any other team during the pitcher's tenure in Boston, the Yankees had used a consistent and reliable formula. Even if Martinez retired them, Yankees batters made the pitcher work for his outs, driving up the right-hander's pitch count and wearing him down. By the time the sixth or seventh inning rolled around, Martinez had typically reached his projected pitch limit for the day, forcing the Red Sox to dip into their bullpen. It was then that New York fully exploited the advantage they possessed with the impenetrable closer Rivera, scoring against the overmatched Boston bullpen while the New York bullpen shut down the Boston lineup. It was a plan that seemed to work almost every time.

Yet, in Game 7 of the 2003 American League Championship Series, Martinez was both effective and efficient, mowing the Yankees down through six innings. The score was still 4–1 in favor of Boston when the Yankees rallied for a run in the seventh on a home run by the good Giambi—Jason—and the Yankees had two other men on base when Martinez struck out second baseman Alfonso Soriano to end the threat. Martinez pointed to the heavens and returned to the Boston dugout, where both he and teammates seemed to assume that his work was done for the night.

It wasn't.

After Boston took a 5–2 lead in the top of the eighth on a home run by the awakened Ortiz, Martinez made a surprising return to the mound in the bottom of the ninth inning. He retired Nick Johnson before the Yankees strung together four hits—three of them doubles—giving New York seven hits against Martinez (four for extra bases) during the Yankees' last nine at-bats against him. By the time manager Grady Little came out of the Boston dugout to lift Martinez from the game, New York had tied the score at 5 and put the go-ahead run on second base.

Slightly more than two weeks after dreading the presence of any Boston reliever, most Red Sox fans had long since been screaming for Little to summon Embree, Timlin, or Williamson, each of whom had pitched exceptionally well in the postseason. Embree and Timlin got the Red Sox through the rest of the eighth and the ninth, but with the score now tied at 5, Little was reluctant to use Williamson, whom he needed to close the game if the Red Sox took the lead. When Mike Timlin walked off the mound to end the ninth inning, he, Alan Embree, and Scott Williamson had combined to allow one run—*one*—in 24.1 postseason innings during which they had amassed 26 strikeouts.

Nobody had seen it coming.

Now faced with the unenviable task of matching up with bulletproof closer Rivera in the extra innings of a tie game in the deciding contest of the American League Championship Series, Little turned to Wakefield, whose two starts in the series had produced a 2-0 record and 2.08 ERA. Wakefield breezed through the 10th, retiring the Yankees in order, but Torre sent Rivera back out to the mound for an unprecedented third inning, during which the Yankees closer retired the Red Sox on 11 pitches. The good news for the Sox was that Rivera was now absolutely, positively finished for the night, meaning that Wakefield and the Red Sox had only to make it through the bottom of the 11th to have another chance to score.

On Wakefield's first pitch of the 11th inning—the final pitch of a 2003 Red Sox season that had effectively begun with the appointment of a new general manager—New York Yankees third baseman Aaron Boone launched a historic solo home run into the left-field seats at Yankee Stadium that gave New York an electrifying 6–5 victory. The Yankees and their fans celebrated wildly as the stunned Red Sox looked on in disbelief. A soul most undeserving of this agony, Wakefield hung his head as he walked off the field; later he broke down in the Boston clubhouse. He told teammates that he feared becoming the next Bill Buckner, the first baseman who had allowed Mookie Wilson's seemingly harmless ground ball to go through his legs in the Red Sox' catastrophic loss to the New York Mets in Game 6 of the 1986 World Series, a moment that lived in infamy.

"Derek [Jeter] told me the ghosts would show up eventually," a beaming Boone, who joined the Yankees in a midseason trade, said after the glorious Yankees comeback. "When I joined the Yankees, this is the kind of thing I thought I could be a part of. It's the perfect ending."

As for the Red Sox, the defeat concluded a postseason that had been, as much as anything else, *im*perfect. The Red Sox lost their offense against Oakland, but they found their bullpen. And in the end, they lost the final game of their season the way they had won so many others, the victorious team showing inspiring character despite facing a seemingly impossible deficit.

In the end, the Red Sox and Yankees played 26 games in 2003, New York winning 14 and the Red Sox claiming 12. Had the Red Sox pulled out Game 7, the teams would have finished a perfectly even 13–13. Prior to Boone's homer, Boston and New York had scored precisely 29 runs each in a series that ultimately was decided by the unpredictable flight of a knuckleball.

"If we played 100 times," said Red Sox pitcher Derek Lowe in a somber Boston clubhouse after the game, "I think we'd win 50 and they'd win 50."

Lowe was right, but Tim Wakefield proved to be wrong.

He did not become the next Bill Buckner.

That was a burden to be saddled on someone else.

THIS IS THE YEAR

THE RED SOX APPEARED ON THE VERGE OF BREAKING UP ANY-way, so maybe it was no surprise that John Henry, Larry Lucchino, and Theo Epstein considered ripping it all apart.

Even though John Henry's former team, the Florida Marlins, was playing the New York Yankees in the World Series—the Marlins would defeat the exhausted New Yorkers in six games—Henry had little interest in watching. As much as anyone in New England, Henry had been captivated by the renegade 2003 Red Sox, had believed in them, if for no other reason than he had *felt* they were going to win. Logical and analytical by nature, Henry had made his fortune devising formulas to forecast the commodities market, and he knew that, on paper, the 2003 Red Sox had flaws. What he also knew was that the Red Sox had a defiance as potent as their lineup, and he, like many, had seen the Red Sox overcome deficits to win time and time again.

To most everyone, the 2003 Red Sox had proved an old adage: Where there's a will, there's a way.

When Aaron Boone's final blow landed in the left-field seats at Yankee Stadium, the reality seemed impossible. *Was it really over?* The Red Sox had overcome so many odds, so frequently defied probability, that no one had bothered to consider the possibility of defeat. There was always the chance of losing, to be sure, but few had stopped to think of what it would feel like, how it would happen, largely because the 2003 Red Sox inspired such confidence. Years later, Red Sox manager Terry

Francona, a coach on the Oakland A's team that had similarly lost to the Red Sox on the final pitch of a decisive series game, articulated the peculiar phenomenon. "Everyone says the season winds downs and it doesn't. It comes to a crashing halt," Francona said. "You show up to play every day and then all of a sudden, it's over."

In Boston, never was that truer than in October 2003.

Hounded by reporters for his thoughts on the season and, more specifically, the fate of manager Grady Little, Henry finally addressed the media on October 19, the date of World Series Game 2, with a group e-mail sent to reporters of the *Boston Herald*, *Boston Globe*, and *Providence Journal*, among others. That was how Henry preferred to do things. The new owner of the Red Sox was a deeply sensitive man who liked to think before he acted or spoke, and so e-mail frequently served as the best way for him to express his thoughts and emotions. Henry simply found it easier that way. The new owners and operators of the Red Sox were a well-constructed management team, and each brought something to the table—Henry's money and mind, Lucchino's instincts and combativeness, television producer Tom Werner's insight into the Sox-owned New England Sports Network—and Henry frequently left the press briefings to someone else. More often than not, that someone was Lucchino, who generally oversaw the day-to-day operation of the Red Sox on all levels.

But even as John Henry typed away on October 19, it was as if he were speaking from the heart. Wrote the owner:

As much as I love some of the Marlins players and root for them to win, I have no interest in watching this series. The only interest I currently have in baseball is to prepare for next season. The supportive communications I have received from fans has been shocking and has stirred me greatly—emotionally.

Initially, I thought New Englanders would just finally throw up their hands. But their level of commitment and resolve is astonishing and deserves our full attention to moving this franchise forward without a break. It shows you how little I know about the toughness of this region. And it shows me how tough I need to be in making sure that we accomplish our goals.

So I'm riding their "wave," so to speak. They've given me the energy to move forward without having to get away from it all. I thought I would have to get away from it all to recharge and start again. But they have refocused me. And I can tell you that Theo and Larry did not take a one-day or even a half-day break this week. I don't think they needed an external force to recharge themselves. This franchise is in very good shape with these two leading it.

How amazing is it, that even the angriest/saddest/most broken-hearted fans offer thanks and remain determined to see this team prevail? It's astonishing. I'm not listening to the radio, so maybe things are different there. I just know what comes directly to me.

There isn't anything I wouldn't do for these [fans]. You know, there isn't anything these people wouldn't do for the Red Sox. We owe them.

Eight days later, the Red Sox began one of the most fascinating, pivotal, and tumultuous off-seasons in their history by firing Little, who was coming under tremendous scrutiny following his decision to stick with Martinez in the eighth inning of Game 7.

In retrospect, Grady Little never had a chance. Truth be told, Henry had expressed a desire to change managers back in June while the Red Sox were playing the St. Louis Cardinals, a series during which the Red Sox lost two of three to extend a poor stretch during which they dropped 10 of 15 overall. The Red Sox subsequently swept the Houston Astros in a three-game series to right the ship; and there were also those who felt that changing managers during the middle of the season was not necessarily the best thing. Back in 1996, in fact, Dan Duquette had cited that as the reason he elected to stick with Kevin Kennedy, who was fired at the end of the year and replaced with Jimy Williams. But *during* that season, Williams was busy serving as the third-base coach of the Atlanta Braves, and there was no way that Duquette could conduct the kind of thorough search he wanted. If he changed managers during the middle of the year, there was a good chance he would do so again after the season, which would only create more instability. So Duquette chose to ride it out.

Still, by the time the 2003 Red Sox lost to the Yankees, Little's rope was already short. Like Henry, Lucchino and Epstein declined to address questions about their manager in the wake of the eighth-inning breakdown, and that was an indisputably bad sign. If Little's job were safe, after all, upper management would have come right out and said so, putting an end to all speculation and doubt. Instead, the Sox waited and deliberated. By the time they emerged from their bunker as if announcing the election of a new pope, the verdict was in. Little was out.

To their credit, Sox officials treated Little quite well upon his departure, giving him what amounted to a $310,000 severance package that included only about $60,000 in bonuses accrued by the manager. The remaining $250,000 was an offering of the club's gratitude. Later, some Sox officials acknowledged that part of the reason Little's job hung in the balance for so long was because the organization was split on the manager's fate. Young general manager Epstein was believed to be truly in Little's corner. Lucchino was believed to have some sentiment for keeping Little—it was Lucchino, after all, who had hired him. But the Red Sox president also recognized that owner Henry would likely cast the deciding vote. Just before arriving in Boston, Lucchino's relationship with his former boss, Padres owner John Moores, had deteriorated considerably, and Lucchino wasn't about to jeopardize a relationship with another owner if it really came down to it.

Grady Little was hardly surprised when the ax fell. "I'm prepared for the likelihood [of being fired]. . . . I'm not sure I want to manage that team," Little, by phone from his North Carolina home, told the *Globe*'s Gordon Edes in the days leading up to his dismissal. "If they don't want me, fine, they don't want me. If they want me back, then we'll talk and see if I want to come back up there. That's the way I feel about it.

"All I know is, when I left there, there was some hesitation. That's all I need to know," Little continued. "If Grady Little is not there, he'll be somewhere. Right now I'm disappointed that evidently some people are judging me on the results of one decision I made—not the decision, but the results of the decision. Less than 24 hours before, those same people were hugging and kissing me. If that's the way they operate, I'm not sure I want to be part of it."

Concluded the manager: "Just add one more ghost to the list if I'm not there, because there are ghosts. That's certainly evident when you're a player in that uniform."

So, from Aaron Boone and Derek Jeter to Grady Little, that is what the compelling 2003 Red Sox season—like so many others in club history—had dissolved into: talk of *ghosts*.

In fact, as much as the public and media focused on Little's decision in Game 7, Red Sox officials insisted they had far bigger reasons for dismissing their manager. (Epstein, for one, went so far as to say that Little would likely have been fired even if the Sox had won the World Series, which seems preposterous.) Over time, Sox officials privately revealed that they thought Little frequently was unprepared, that he was dismissive of some of the new-school theories of modern baseball, that he had a closed mind. As a result, Little's game-management skills suffered. Sox officials argued that the decision to stick with Martinez was not a cause for Little's dismissal as much as it was a symptom of his shortcomings, and further examination suggested that upper management of the club had a strong case.

When Little sent Martinez back out to the mound for the eighth inning, he made the decision primarily with his heart. By that point in Martinez's career, there was considerable documentation to prove that Martinez was a seven-inning pitcher, that 100 pitches was his limit, and the pitcher had reached both thresholds when Little sent him back out to pitch. It was as if Little were managing the Martinez of the late 1990s, when Jimy Williams was the Boston manager and Little was his bench coach, and the Red Sox entrusted most every critical situation to their then-peerless ace. During those years, no matter how many pitches Martinez had thrown or innings he had pitched, the bottom line was that Williams trusted Martinez more than he did any other pitcher on his staff, and so he left the ball in the hands of his best option. And usually it worked.

So, who could blame Little? He had seen Martinez succeed in similar situations time and time again, no matter how great the pressure or consequences. Yes, Red Sox relievers had been pitching well of late, but Boston's bullpen had been nothing short of a demolition site for the better part of two years. If Grady Little had scant faith in the Boston bullpen and supreme confidence in Pedro Martinez, it was entirely understandable, given the track of Little's career path, recent Red Sox history, and Martinez's place as one of the great pitchers and competitors of all time.

In the end, Little got in the way.

Annoyed, the men who now ran the Red Sox wanted to do their best to ensure that something like that never happened again.

WITH OR without Grady Little, Theo Epstein knew the Red Sox had to address their greatest need: pitching. Even with Pedro Martinez and Derek Lowe coming off 20-win seasons during the fall of 2002, Epstein felt the club was a starter short entering the 2003 campaign. The young general manager subsequently engaged in trade discussions with a number of clubs, including the Montreal Expos, who had a young and talented right-handed pitcher named Javier Vazquez. Though Vazquez went just 10-13 with a 3.91 ERA during the 2002 season, he was still just 25 years old. He was improving. Most evaluators believed that Vazquez's won-lost record was a poor indication of his ability, mostly because the Expos had been a bad team during the bulk of his career.

For all of the statistics that new-school executives now had at their disposal, in fact, wins and losses remained one of the few areas where all baseball evaluators generally agreed. As much as someone might describe a pitcher like Martinez or Lowe as "a 20-game winner," wins were often the worst way to evaluate a pitcher's impact on a team. Wins were a *team* statistic, after all, even if pitchers were credited with them individually. A pitcher could work nine innings, allow one run, and lose just as easily as he could go five innings, allow five runs, and win. The end result ultimately depended on how many runs his team scored for him. And while there was a feeling in baseball that statistics were generally accurate when measured over time—this is what people like Billy Beane relied on—there were cases where the final numbers did not accurately reflect a player's performance.

During his first off-season as general manager, in fact, Epstein believed he had found such a pitcher in right-hander Ryan Rupe, who had gone 5-10 for a wretched Tampa Bay Devil Rays outfit. Rupe also had a high ERA (5.60), but many of his other pitching statistics were in line with those of a far more effective pitcher. Rupe allowed fewer hits (83) than he had innings pitched (90), for instance, and his walk total (25) was relatively low. The Red Sox interpreted this as a sign that Rupe had had some unusually bad luck, and they claimed him on waivers because they deemed him a worthwhile gamble.

As it turned out, Rupe got off to a poor start with Boston, then suffered an arm injury that ended his season (and, effectively, his career) after just four games in a Boston uniform.

While Epstein was not able to acquire Vazquez following the 2002 season, he renewed talks with the Expos after the Red Sox' near miss in 2003. By that point, the Red Sox had determined that their best chance at acquiring an impact starting pitcher was through trade, and they had identified free agent Keith Foulke as their closer of choice. Foulke was the same pitcher who had made the curious decision to throw David Ortiz a fastball (instead of his best pitch, a changeup) at the most critical moment of Game 4 of the AL Division Series between the Red Sox and Oakland A's, but he was coming off a sensational year in which he went 9-1 with a 2.08 ERA and 43 saves. In 72 outings, Foulke had pitched 86⅔ innings—a high number for a closer—and the A's had used him in tie games as well as in save situations, the latter being close games in which Oakland had a lead.

The Red Sox did not see Foulke as a closer as much as they saw him as a good relief pitcher who happened to close, and the latter appealed to them far more given their feelings on closers in general. Still, Epstein had long since dismissed the notion of entering another season trying the closer-by-committee experiment, though he continued to believe that the system could work with the right people and the right manager. Regardless, Foulke was a perfect fit for what the Red Sox believed in— versatility—and Epstein made it a point to inform Foulke's agents, the Beverly Hills Sports Council, that Foulke was a priority for them. At the time, Foulke's performance put him in a position to earn an annual salary in the range of $6 million to $7 million, a figure that would likely be excessive for a team like the A's, depending on the length of the con- tract. Still, because Foulke had some desire to stay with the A's, who had acquired him only a year earlier in what turned out to be a one- sided deal for right-hander Billy Koch, Epstein knew that the negotia- tions for the reliever could take some time.

In baseball, the free-agent season consisted of countless moving pieces, all built around a calendar of various deadlines. In the case of Foulke, the calendar required that Oakland offer him salary arbitration at the end of the first week in December, which had various implica- tions. If, by that time, Foulke had not drawn significant interest from other clubs—extremely unlikely given his performance—he might have agreed to go back to Oakland on a one-year contract for a salary greater than $6 million. The A's might ask Foulke to be patient while they explored other possibilities, something the A's were required to do given their payroll. In any case, all teams were simultaneously looking to fill several openings, which required all involved parties to be patient.

So, even during a the courting process during which teams and free agents were forbidden to discuss financial terms of a deal, someone like

Epstein could call Foulke's agents and tell them that yes, the Red Sox had interest; yes, their interest was considerable; yes, Foulke was a priority. Foulke's agents could then assess other clubs' interest before beginning talks, all while knowing the Red Sox were there, ready to move at the proper time.

With all of that understood, Epstein continued his pursuit of a top starter, a search that could have taken him in any number of directions. While a deal with the Expos for Vazquez seemed unlikely—in earlier talks, the Red Sox had offered a package that included left-hander Casey Fossum and third baseman Shea Hillenbrand, who had since been dealt for Byung-Hyun Kim—Epstein also explored the possibility of signing free-agent right-hander Kelvim Escobar. Epstein also knew that right-hander Curt Schilling was available from an Arizona Diamondbacks team that, like Montreal, was downsizing its payroll. Despite winning the World Series in 2001—Schilling was named co–Most Valuable Player of the World Series along with left-hander Randy Johnson—the Diamondbacks had to cut payroll considerably. The glitch in talks was that Schilling possessed a no-trade clause and had told Arizona officials he would not go to Boston, which seemed to leave the Sox on the outside looking in.

Still, while many believed that Arizona was working toward a deal with the New York Yankees, the Red Sox persisted. Frustrated by their inability to reach terms with New York—the Yankees also were in on Vazquez—Arizona officials agreed to get more serious in talks with Boston to see if the teams could at least agree on personnel. Diamodbacks general manager Joe Garagiola Jr. gave the Red Sox a list of players divided into two groups—A and B—and listed four players in each group. The Arizona GM then assured the Red Sox they could pick two players from each group and they would have the foundation of a deal for Schilling.

Among a group of eight, it was up to the Red Sox to decide which four. Said one Sox official later of the deal: "It was like ordering off a Chinese menu."

When the Red Sox reviewed the list of players in whom the Diamondbacks had interest, their spirits perked up. Among those listed in Group A was pitcher Jon Lester, a promising left-hander the Sox had selected with their first pick in the 2002 amateur draft, when Mike Port was the interim general manager. While Epstein had no intention of giving up a prospect like Lester, he deemed two of the other players in Group A expendable: Fossum and young left-hander Jorge de la Rosa, both of whom had been drafted under Duquette. The remaining two players (from Group B) turned out to be pitcher-outfielder Michael Goss (another Duquette product) and pitcher Brandon Lyon, the latter of whom Epstein had claimed off waivers.

When all was said and done, Epstein deemed the potential deal so good he couldn't turn it down. In exchange for Schilling, who was a potential ace, all the Red Sox had to surrender was three young players of debatable talent whom the new Sox operators had not drafted and another whom they had plucked from another organization.

All the Red Sox had to do now was convince Schilling that Boston was a place he should seriously consider.

When news of the discussions between Boston and Arizona leaked, most Red Sox fans thought the news too good to be true. Schilling had veto power on the deal, many stressed, and he had already made it clear that he would not come to Boston. Nonetheless, the veteran right-hander was willing to meet with Epstein, assistant Jed Hoyer, and team president Larry Lucchino, all of whom arrived at Schilling's home in Arizona just before Thanksgiving. While Schilling would later admit that he was turned off by Lucchino, he and his wife, Shonda, took a liking to Epstein and Hoyer, who shared Thanksgiving dinner with the Schilling family. During the stay of the young Sox executives, Schilling expressed a concern about pitching at Fenway Park—a fly-ball pitcher, Schilling had a tendency to give up home runs. Hoyer flipped open his laptop and showed Schilling reassuring data.

Impressed by the knowledge and persistence of both Epstein and Hoyer, Schilling almost instantly became more receptive to pitching for

Boston, a fact that spoke to his competitiveness and open-mindedness. Most veteran players would have selected the Yankees when given a choice between Boston and New York. As talented a team as the Red Sox possessed, the Yankees were seen as the surer thing, the place to go to win another title. That was what Roger Clemens had done. That was what Mike Mussina had done. And though the latter had yet to win a title in New York, he had played a significant part in defeating the Red Sox in Game 7, shutting down the Red Sox in relief after Clemens crumbled.

But for Schilling, the Red Sox suddenly represented a challenge, the opportunity to do something that few others had. Now he could *beat* New York. Now he could be the man who brought a championship to Boston. Once the Red Sox convinced Schilling that his concerns about the ballpark were baseless—in Arizona, in fact, Schilling had demanded that the retractable roof at Bank One Ballpark be closed when he pitched to cut down on opposing homers—Schilling quickly agreed to a two-year, $25.5 million contract extension (through 2006) that included an option for a third season (2007). Schilling negotiated the deal on his own, without an agent—this was something he was quite proud of—and it included some unique provisions that Major League Baseball banned from all future contracts. If the Red Sox were to win the World Series at any point during Schilling's career with the team, his salary in the next season would increase by $2 million. Additionally, Schilling's option for 2007 (valued at $13 million) would instantly become guaranteed, meaning that Schilling could gain as much as $21 million if he could bring a championship to Boston.

On November 28, 2003—the day after Thanksgiving—the Red Sox announced that they had acquired Curt Schilling from the Arizona Diamondbacks for Fossum, de la Rosa, Lyon, and Goss—and that Schilling had agreed to a two-year contract extension, with the possibility for another season.

"When they left that first night, Shonda and I looked at each other and realized this was a group of guys determined to put us in a Red Sox uniform—not at all costs, but at the right cost," Schilling said of the Red Sox contingent led by Epstein. Added Schilling while pointing at a replica of the World Series trophy in the sitting room of his Arizona home: "They didn't bring me [to Boston] to pitch well. They brought me here to put one of those on their mantel. If that doesn't happen, to me, this contract would be a failure."

Clearly, Curt Schilling was willing to invest in his ability.

Nonetheless, Schilling's nature being what it was, some Sox fans wondered: How would someone like Schilling affect a Boston clubhouse where, in 2003, chemistry had been one of the team's greatest strengths? Indisputably, Schilling was a peerless competitor, though the mention of his name prompted many in baseball to roll their eyes. Schilling was not seen as a clubhouse detriment as much as he was, at times, a clubhouse nuisance, the kind of player who frequently had an answer for *everything*. Once asked to describe Schilling, former Philadelphia Phillies general manager Ed Wade had referred to the big right-hander as "a horse" every fifth day (when Schilling pitched) and "a horse's ass" on the remaining four, and that assessment had all but become the epitaph on Schilling's career. But the Red Sox had strong clubhouse leadership—catcher Jason Varitek, first baseman Kevin Millar, and center fielder Johnny Damon all had value in that regard—and Schilling was simply too good to pass up.

Still, even before he arrived in Boston, there were flashes of Schilling's self-importance, which made it critical that the Red Sox have a clubhouse who could handle such a strong personality. Of course, the Red Sox did.

"When the paper comes out, there's a W or an L next to my name. I've never read a box score where the catcher or the pitching coach got a win or a loss," Schilling said. "That's *my* game. That's what they pay me for." Added the pitcher: "I don't get mad at errors. Errors present a challenge to me. But the one thing I will not tolerate is someone not being [mentally] into the game."

If those remarks reflected any feeling that Schilling was bigger than the team—it wasn't *his* game, after all, it was *theirs*—they also contained more than a measure of honesty. Where many pitchers saw a teammate's error as a get-out-of-jail-free card—in many cases, subsequent runs were then not the responsibility of the pitcher, who became exempt from blame—Schilling took the opposite approach. He pitched *better*. During his career with the Sox, Schilling would go on to make a major-league-record 69 consecutive starts without an unearned run, an accomplishment that might be considered a fluke were it not for one thing: Schilling also owned the *second*-longest such streak in baseball at 53 starts. Schilling fit in well with a Red Sox club that stared down the New York Yankees and repeatedly won in spite of its flaws.

Curt Schilling didn't make excuses.

And he was there when his team needed him most.

AFTER THE playoff loss to the Yankees, Grady Little was not the only man whom the Red Sox wanted to dispose of.

They didn't care much for Manny Ramirez, either.

Three seasons into his eight-year, $160 million contract with the Red Sox, Ramirez had produced 111 home runs, 336 RBIs, and enough maddening behavior to make the Red Sox wonder whether it was all worth it. In the wake of a new collective-bargaining agreement signed by baseball owners and players late in the 2002 season, baseball was in the midst of what Henry, Lucchino, and Epstein liked to call a "market correction," which was to say that salaries were coming down. Ramirez's average annual salary of $20 million was second in all of baseball to that of Texas Rangers shortstop Alex Rodriguez, who had signed a historic 10-year, $252 million after leaving his first organization, the Seattle Mariners, for a mediocre Texas club. Red Sox owners seemingly had a philosophical opposition to paying *anyone* $20 million a year— committing such a high percentage of resources to one player was bad business, they felt—particularly one who frequently acted like, well, a 13-year-old.

During his first three seasons in Boston, Ramirez had had *issues*. On one occasion in 2001, for example, he asked to go on the disabled list during a series in August, when the Red Sox were fighting for their playoff lives; on another, while on a rehabilitation assignment, Ramirez actually expressed a desire to stay in the minor leagues altogether. Part of the reason the Red Sox had hired Little was because they felt he could tap into Ramirez's talent—in fact, Ramirez played in a career-high 154 games for Little in 2003—but even Little had his issues with the player, benching him for an early-September 2003 game against the Chicago White Sox after Ramirez had refused to pinch-hit a day earlier, in Philadelphia.

The Red Sox won both games in spite of the player, whose antics were so familiar to teammates that they learned to shrug them off. "What can I say?" one Sox player asked later during Ramirez's career in Boston, following a game at Tampa Bay in which Ramirez asked for a day off when the Sox were badly undermanned. "He's not like the rest of us."

Sox officials had a slightly less diplomatic view. "Manny's a turd," one club rep said at the end of the 2003 season.

Consequently, just two days after firing Little, the Red Sox took the unprecedented action of placing Ramirez on waivers on October 29, which was akin to the owner of a luxury car placing the vehicle in front of his home with the sign "Please Take." Even with the keys in the ignition, the one catch was that the owner had to take on the remaining loan payments, in this case the approximately $100 million remaining on the player's contract.

Incredibly, though the Red Sox were all but giving away perhaps the best run producer in baseball since Ted Williams retired in 1960—statistically, based on RBIs per at-bat, this was true—not a single team took the bait.

The only question was whether the Red Sox had expected them to.

"Probably not," Epstein admitted in a private conversation as events were unfolding.

Still, while many believed the Red Sox were conveying their

dissatisfaction with the player, the reality was that Ramirez wanted out too. In fact, Sox officials had discussed the maneuver with Ramirez's agent, Jeff Moorad, before placing the player on waivers. Even if no one claimed Ramirez, the sides agreed that the Sox might be able to determine which teams, if any, had a genuine interest in the player, and such a discovery could help facilitate a trade that would get Ramirez out of Boston and free the Red Sox from a contract and the irresponsible behavior that they had no desire to keep.

At roughly the same time all of this was taking place, Rodriguez was trying to leverage his way out of Texas, where the Rangers had only regressed since the player arrived. Unsurprisingly, most everyone in the world with any interest in baseball came to the same conclusion: if both Ramirez and Rodriguez were unhappy and wanted out of their deals, why weren't the players simply traded for one another?

It made all the sense in the world.

Yet, while the Red Sox were eager to shake things up in the wake of their loss to the Yankees, the matter was more complex than it seemed. For starters, Ramirez played left field and Rodriguez played shortstop, which was a problem in and of itself. Current Red Sox shortstop Nomar Garciaparra was one of the centerpieces of the team, after all, though Henry, Lucchino, and Epstein had long since grown tired of him, too. Prior to the 2003 season, the Sox had offered Garciaparra a four-year, $60 million contract that the player rejected, largely because he wanted a salary that would put him more in line with Rodriguez ($25.2 million a year) and New York Yankees shortstop Derek Jeter ($18.9 million). The problem was that the market had changed considerably since Rodriguez and Jeter signed their deals—Jeter, like Ramirez and Rodriguez, agreed prior to the 2001 season—and that Garciaparra (advised by agent Arn Tellem) rejected the proposal, in part because he deemed it nothing more than an opening offer.

As it turned out, Red Sox officials weren't playing negotiating games. Their $60 million offer, which proved to be a good one, was the best they would make to their shortstop, to whom they later offered a four-year, $48 million deal. Factoring in future contracts, Garciaparra's decision to reject the $60 million package would ultimately cost him between $27 million and $28 million in earnings from 2005 to 2008.

Still, if the Red Sox were to trade Ramirez for Rodriguez—and they were not sure they could—they needed to trade Garciaparra, too. Thus, dealing away Ramirez would require not a renovation but a *reconstruction* of the entire Boston batting order, which was no small task for any team to undertake. Showing the kind of fearlessness they would display throughout their ownership, Henry, Werner, Lucchino, and Epstein pursued the deal anyway.

Given the magnitude of the trade—the complexities of the deal, the personalities involved, the potential to alienate Garciaparra—the Red Sox did their best to operate discreetly, though their attempts at secrecy would go for naught. (Lucchino, for his part, liked to say that there were "no secrets in baseball.") But after initiating discussions with the Texas Rangers, who were receptive to a deal, the Red Sox wanted to speak with Rodriguez directly. Because such a meeting would violate baseball's tampering rules, the clubs were required to get permission for the meeting from baseball commissioner Bud Selig, who signed off on the clubs' request. Henry and Rodriguez later had lunch together to discuss the prospect of Rodriguez playing for the Red Sox, a move the player would have to approve because his contract with Texas possessed a no-trade clause.

When word of the meeting between Henry and Rodriguez leaked in the *Herald*, Red Sox officials and Selig denied such a meeting. That was hardly a surprise. The Sox wanted neither to call attention to the talks nor to rankle Garciaparra, who was still under contract with Boston for another year. Selig had a responsibility to the teams first, and acknowledging such a meeting would complicate the process. Baseball salaries had grown so preposterous prior to the recent "market correction" that economics were playing a part in virtually every trade—let alone one as big as this—so the commissioner had to consider the economic realities facing all clubs when any trade possibility arose, no matter how complex.

In fact, just two years after Rodriguez, Ramirez, and pitcher Mike Hampton signed megadeals—Hampton's contract with the Colorado Rockies was worth $121 million over eight years, an average of more than $15 million a season—the three clubs that signed those players were already showing regret. Hamptons had already been traded to the Atlanta Braves, with his contract being split three ways, portions going to Colorado and the Florida Marlins. And now Ramirez and Rodriguez were being looked upon as solutions for one another.

Unsurprisingly, then, economics came to play a huge role in negotiations between the Red Sox and Texas Rangers, both of whom wanted to save some money on the deal. Deeming Rodriguez a superior player, the Rangers wanted the Red Sox to pay a portion of the approximately $100 million due Ramirez over the remaining five years of his contract, asking Boston for a reported $5 million annually (or about $25 million overall). The problem was that Rodriguez had roughly $186 million remaining on his contract, and Boston officials had no intention of taking on *more* long-term money *and* paying part of Ramirez's salary, too, no matter how much Ramirez appeared to be overpaid at the time.

Consequently, the sides haggled.

"The only way it makes sense for the Rangers is if there were financial considerations that gave us the ability to significantly improve our team in '04 and beyond. If that doesn't happen, there will be no trade," Rangers owner Tom Hicks told reporter T. R. Sullivan of the *Fort Worth Star Telegram*. Added Hicks: "My belief is [Rodriguez] will end up being our shortstop. . . . We haven't gotten a compelling offer to make us want to do it."

Paying close interest to all of this was Garciaparra, who was on his honeymoon in Hawaii with new wife and women's soccer star Mia Hamm when news of the meeting between Henry and Lucchino broke in the *Herald*. Agent Tellem called the *Globe* and suggested that the Red Sox' actions "were a slap in the face" to his client; Garciaparra called the *Herald* and expressed a feeling of hurt, playing on the emotions of Red

Sox fans who had seen him excel for the team since he broke into the big leagues with his historic rookie season of 1997. Though Garciaparra's performance had begun to slip by the end of 2003—he was now a very good player, but no longer a great one—fans had not forgotten Garciaparra's greatness from 1997 to 2000.

"Basically, what I'd like to say is that I know there's always been this speculation that I'm unhappy there [in Boston]. I've heard it and read it—that I want to go home [to California] and I'm unhappy—and I don't know where that comes from," Garciaparra said. "No words have ever come out of my mouth—publicly or privately—that I don't want to be there. I also believe that my actions have shown I don't want out of there. I go out there and play hard and give it my all, day in and day out, not just on the field, but off. I have a [charitable] foundation there. I'm coming back in January to do my 10th hitting camp, I think. Before we got married, my wife and I purchased a new home [in the Boston area]. If you look at all that, I wouldn't do all that stuff if I wanted to leave." Added the onetime wonder boy of the Red Sox, when asked to explain how news of the Rodriguez meeting made him feel: "I think I'm kind of like the fans are. If you were a fan looking at this, you might think, 'Are they really considering this option?' I've always respected the uniform that I've worn. It's been the only uniform I know and it's the only uniform I want to know for my entire career. That's basically how I feel."

Though Red Sox officials remained mum at the time, the club found Garciaparra and Tellem to be terribly disingenuous. Later, after continued criticism from Tellem, Henry revealed that Garciaparra and his agent had been kept abreast of all options concerning the player's future, including the possibility of a trade. While the matter dissolved into a classic case of he said, she said (or, more accurately, he said, he said), the most likely scenario was that the sides had agreed that the Red Sox would explore trade talks after contract negotiations had reached an impasse. Concern from the Garciaparra camp grew only after news of the Rodriguez meeting had been leaked, and Tellem and Garciaparra thought that the club had leaked the information to prepare for a public campaign against Garciaparra. *Nomar won't re-sign here and Manny's unhappy*, was the message they anticipated from Red Sox management, *so they've left us with no choice.*

As all of this was unfolding—and refusing to give up hope that a deal for Rodriguez could be struck—Henry and Lucchino sent Epstein to baseball's annual winter meetings in Dallas and instructed him to line up the best possible deal for Garciaparra, assuring him that the club would be able to move quickly if and when the Red Sox were able to complete the Ramirez-Rodriguez deal. As if he were trying to prequalify for a new homeowner's loan, Epstein met with Chicago White Sox general manager Kenny Williams, who had a problem similar to Epstein's. Like Garciaparra, All-Star White Sox outfielder Magglio Ordoñez was eligible for free agency at the end of the season, and Chicago officials seemed resigned to the fact that they would not be able to keep the player. Ordoñez and Garciaparra had reasonably comparable contracts—Ordoñez had one year and $14 million remaining, Garciaparra one year and $11.5 million—so the sides quickly came to an understanding. If Boston could come to terms on a deal for Rodriguez that would send Ramirez to Texas, the Red Sox would ship Garciaparra to the White Sox for Ordoñez.

Faced with that scenario, Red Sox officials were downright giddy. In Rodriguez, the Red Sox saw a better all-around talent around whom the club could better market its product—neither Garciaparra nor Ramirez was especially receptive to the media—and the inclusion of the talented Ordoñez in the deal would allow the Red Sox to swap a shortstop and an outfielder for an outfielder and a shortstop. All that remained was for the Bosox to sort out the financial aspect of the Rodriguez deal, which was no small feat given the size of the contracts.

By that point, too, the Red Sox had consummated the deal with closer Foulke, meaning that Boston had added Schilling and Foulke to a pitching staff that had needed help at both the front end and the back end. Many regarded those tow pitchers as the best available starter and reliever, respectively, on the trade or free-agent markets over the winter, which led to an obvious question: Given that the Red Sox already had the best offense in baseball, why weren't they prepared to just go to spring training with their current collection of talent?

"I hear what you're saying," Epstein told a *Herald* reporter in a moment of candor. "But it's more complicated than that."

As much as Garciaparra and Ramirez offered to the Red Sox lineup in 2003, after all, Epstein had information that most people did not: namely, that Ordoñez—and not a collection of prospects or minor leaguers, as many had speculated—was the prize he could acquire for Garciaparra. Furthermore, while Ordoñez also could leave the club via free agency after 2004, the Red Sox would have a far easier time finding an outfielder to replace Ordoñez's contributions than they would finding a shortstop who could replace Garciaparra's output, all of which made the potential of the Rodriguez acquisition all the more appealing. By making both trades, Epstein believed, the Red Sox could remain championship contenders in 2004 *and* be better positioned for the long term.

Given those realties, the Red Sox' motivations for making the deal were great. Sox officials subsequently resumed talks with the Rangers in hopes of coming to some agreement on terms, at least with regard to the annual $5 million subsidy that the Rangers were seeking so that they could augment their pitching staff. One such solution involved the inclusion of a young pitcher in the deal—again, the name Jon Lester came up—an option that made far more sense to the Sox than paying roughly $30 million a year ($25 million for Rodriguez, $5 million to Texas for Ramirez) in salaries. A year earlier, in fact, the Red Sox and Rangers had discussed a trade for veteran left-hander Kenny Rogers that would have required the Sox to give up a package built around Lester. In that deal, the Sox would also have received a young, then-unproven left-handed hitter named Travis Hafner. There was a time when Sox officials actually believed the deal was done. Instead, at the last moment, the Rangers pulled out and instead traded Hafner in a package to the Cleveland Indians for catcher Einar Diaz and right-handed pitcher Ryan Drese.

Still, even if the Sox could find a way around the $5 million subsidy, there was the issue of Rodriguez's contract, which Sox officials deemed the far bigger hurdle. The team subsequently sent representatives to meet with Rodriguez and his agent, Scott Boras, with a proposed restructuring of the player's contract, a matter that would require the approval of the Major League Baseball Players Association. The Red Sox were optimistic that the deal could be done—and that they could make the trade for Rodriguez—when union deputy Gene Orza dealt what proved to be the fatal blow to a soap opera that had gone on far too long and toyed with the emotions of far too many people. "The association had to turn down the renegotiation of Alex's contract that the Red Sox proposed because it was clear it crossed the line separating restructuring and reductions—and by a huge margin," Orza said in an issued statement. "We did suggest an offer the club could make to Alex that would not do that, but as was its right, the club chose not to make it."

Lucchino was furious, issuing his own statement saying it was "a sad day" when the union stood in the way of its constituency, in this case Rodriguez. Lucchino was a longtime union adversary, and his anger continued to boil in subsequent days when Texas owner Hicks imposed a Christmas deadline on any deal involving Rodriguez, and Lucchino emphatically declared any chance of Rodriguez coming to Boston was "dead" as the New Year approached. Hicks similarly assured reporters that Rodriguez would be on the Texas roster on Opening Day 2004, and in late January 2004 the Rangers conducted a gratuitous press conference during which they named Rodriguez their team captain. Said Rodriguez during the charade: "I definitely think I'm going to be here for a long time."

So, while the Red Sox appeared to have an extemely talented team as 2003 turned to 2004, team officials nonetheless felt a little frustrated. Their ultimate Red Sox makeover would not come to fruition. Nomar

Garciaparra and Manny Ramirez were staying in Boston, and Alex Rodriguez was staying in Texas.

Or so everyone thought.

ULTIMATELY, IT all came back to Aaron Boone, who had already done enough damage to the Red Sox to last an eternity.

But in mid-January 2004, while New York Yankees general manager Brian Cashman was vacationing with his family in Anguilla, Aaron Boone struck again.

To most baseball executives, January was the rare time of year when they were afforded a brief respite from their work, when most of the off-season work had been accomplished and only housekeeping matters remained. Spring training was roughly a month away, and there were still things to deal with—most notably, teams had potential arbitration hearings with players who qualified—but such negotiations, like most, got productive only at the 11th hour. Furthermore, arbitration cases required both the team and the player to submit proposed salaries, which meant that the sides already were within range of a deal. If the team proposed a $1 million salary and the player responded with a request of $1.5 million, it served all parties to split the difference and settle at $1.25 million for the coming year. Ultimately, neither side wanted to endure an arbitration process that former Red Sox general manager Dan Duquette frequently described as "distasteful," and so rarely did the cases reach a hearing.

By that point in the off-season, too, Cashman felt he had sufficiently fortified the Yankees' roster in the wake of Boston's acquisition of Schilling and Foulke, making the deal the Red Sox had tried to make a year earlier: he traded for Javier Vazquez. New York's loss to the Florida Marlins in the World Series had left the Yankees feeling as if they needed a good young pitcher to augment their staff, and there were those in baseball who preferred Vazquez to Schilling, particularly over the long term. Schilling might be the better pitcher *now*, many reasoned—and even that was debatable—but Vazquez certainly would be the better pitcher *later*, primarily because he was 12 years younger. The Yankees, too, had a dynamic offense, and Cashman felt there was little left to do to improve his club.

So he went on vacation.

And that's when he found out that Aaron Boone had hurt his knee while playing *basketball*, an injury that would likely result in Boone's missing the entire season.

Given the time of year—and fearing that New York's state of desperation would badly hurt the club's leverage—Cashman began a swift fact-finding mission that led him to a most clever conclusion: Rodriguez. Though Rodriguez had already established his place as one of the greatest shortstops of all time, Cashman knew that the Rangers were eager to move the player's contract—in fact, Cashman had spoken with the Rangers about Rodriguez as far back as October—and he also knew that Rodriguez badly wanted out of Texas, preferably to a far more competitive team. When the Yankees and Rangers had first discussed Rodriguez, Cashman and other Yankees officials dismissed the possibility out of hand, primarily because the Yankees had the multitalented Jeter at shortstop. So, throughout the entire saga that was the Ramirez-Rodriguez trade discussions between the Red Sox and Texas Rangers, nobody deemed the Yankees a factor.

Including the Yankees and Red Sox themselves.

But when Boone went down, that all changed. From the time the thought first crossed Cashman's mind—why not Rodriguez at third base!—to the time New York executed one of the greatest trades in baseball history, roughly two weeks passed. Texas owner Hicks subsequently took jabs at the Red Sox by noting how discussions with the Yankees were so easy and professional, and the news of Rodriguez going to New York stuck both the Red Sox and their followers like a cruel dagger. *Trumped again.*

Stunned by developments they had not seen coming, Red Sox officials fell all over themselves trying to make a last-gasp run at the Rangers and Rodriguez, but to no avail. Sox officials called upon one former Sox player and former Rodriguez teammate Bill Haselman to see if Rodriguez would consider changing his mind, but Haselman's involvement was leaked to the media, revealing the Red Sox' desperation. Roughly four months after Boone's home run had landed in the left-field seats at Yankee Stadium, New York had now replaced him with the otherworldly Alex Rodriguez, whose acquisition came shortly after the Yankees had acquired Javier Vazquez, too. Few Red Sox followers paid much attention to the fact that the Yankees traded highly productive second baseman Alfonso Soriano to Texas in the deal—how much had the Yankees really gained in the end?—but after the Red Sox had publicly failed in their pursuit of the player, it was agonizing to think that Boston had failed so miserably where the Yankees had succeeded so effortlessly. "It will suffice to say that we have a spending limit and the Yankees don't," Red Sox owner Henry wrote to reporters in an e-mail all but stained with tears and spilled milk.

Baseball doesn't have an answer for the Yankees. Revenue sharing can only accomplish so much. At some point it becomes confiscation. It has not and will not solve what is a very obvious problem. More often than not, $50 million on average will not allow an MLB franchise to field a highly competitive team. Every year there will be an exception, but that is really the baseline number. So what has meaning are the dollars spent above $50 million. Most clubs can perhaps afford to spend $10 million to $25 million above that figure trying to compete. A few can spend as much as $30 million to $60 million above that. But one team can and is spending $150 million incremental dollars, and at some point 29 owners and their players say to themselves, "We can't have one team that can spend 10 dollars above the baseline for every incremental dollar spent by an average team." One thing is certain the status quo will not be preserved."

Replied megalomaniacal Yankees owner George Steinbrenner in a statement that all but chuckled at the Red Sox' whining: "We understand that John Henry must be frustrated, embarrassed and disappointed by his failure in this transaction. Unlike the Yankees, he chose not to go the extra distance for his fans in Boston. It is understandable, but wrong that he would try to deflect the accountability for his mistake onto others and to a system for which he voted in favor. It is time to get on with life and forget the sour grapes."

To their credit, Red Sox players engaged in no such self-pity. During the 2003 season, after all, the Red Sox believed they were every bit as good their New York rivals, no matter how Game 7 of the American League Championship Series turned out. Boston played New York to the bitter end. For all of the potential changes that could have taken place between the 2003 and 2004 seasons, there were those players who expressed delight at the fact that the core of the Red Sox remained intact, that they had added Schilling and Foulke without affecting their nucleus, that they could make another run at the Yankees with the same group that had tasted the bitterness of defeat. "Nobody said it would be easy and George [Steinbrenner] is going to do whatever it takes to stop us," said left-handed reliever Alan Embree. "I think [the A-Rod trade] is kind of exciting . . . [because] they're worried about us. They know we have a very good ballclub."

Said backup catcher Doug Mirabelli: "I think there's definitely respect for the Red Sox there, but I don't know if they'd admit that. They know they've got a fight on their hands every time they play us, regardless of who they've got on their team. . . . Look, A-Rod would help any team, but, still, on paper, the Red Sox are right where they need to be."

Back and forth, the volleys bounced between Boston and New York. In some ways, it seemed as if the 2003 season never ended.

IN THEIR search for Grady Little's replacement, the Red Sox wanted two things. First, the Red Sox wanted someone who possessed Little's interpersonal skills, who could handle the considerable egos and strong personalities that came along with a high player payroll. Additionally, the club wanted someone more skilled in game management, who fully appreciated that good game decisions frequently resulted from preparation, from playing out potential scenarios before they actually occurred.

Once the Red Sox settled on Terry Francona, the new manager's skills were immediately put to the test.

The son of a former major-league player, Terry Jon Francona was known to most people in baseball as Tito, which just so happened to be the name of his father. Terry Francona was selected in the first round (22nd overall) by the Montreal Expos in the 1980 amateur draft, and he made his major-league debut the following season, batting a respectable .274 in 94 at-bats. Francona subsequently had a nomadic, injury-plagued 10-year major-league career during which he played for five organizations, serving largely as a pinch hitter and part-time player. By the time he played his last major-league game at the age of 31, Francona had 1,731 career at-bats—the equivalent of roughly three full major-league seasons—and a career .274 batting average that matched the precise number from his rookie season. Joked the affable Francona much later during his career as a coach and manager: "Basically, I was a horse-shit player."

He was being far too hard on himself. What he had been, in reality, was a mediocre one.

But what Terry Francona may have lacked in productivity on the field, he generally made up for with smarts and affability, the latter of which served him well. Francona frequently endeared himself to people with self-deprecating humor, and he had spent countless hours in major-league clubhouses and stadiums during the career of his father. During all of those years, Francona learned most everything about the life of a ballplayer, from the travel to the dedication to the ruthlessness with which the game could operate. More than anything else, what Francona learned was about the *people* who played the game and worked in it, be it as a member of the grounds crew or the pitching staff or the front office.

And he learned to appreciate all of them.

By the time he became manager of the Red Sox at the age of 44,

Francona had served as a minor-league manager and major-league coach, completing the proverbial circle that was his playing career. His only stint as a major-league manager came with a dreadful Philadelphia Phillies organization from 1997 to 2000, a four-year period during which the Phils were an abysmal 78 games under .500. Most recently, Francona had served as the bench coach for the Oakland A's team that blew a 2–0 series lead against the Red Sox in the 2003 American League Division Series, a defeat that stung all of the A's given their consistent success during the regular season under general manager Billy Beane.

Roughly a month later, when the Red Sox came looking for a manager, Francona blew away the rest of the field, which included, among others, former Sox shortstop Glenn Hoffman, then a coach with the San Diego Padres. Said Red Sox general manager Theo Epstein on the eve of Francona's hiring: "He's a pretty impressive guy."

Still, even the most seasoned manager would have had his hands full with the 2004 Red Sox, who were a potential time bomb despite an abundance of talent. First, the Red Sox had pressure to win, particularly with new acquisitions Schilling and Foulke having joined a club that had come within five outs of advancing to the World Series. Second, the Sox had a number of players in the final year of their contracts, from Pedro Martinez to Jason Varitek to Nomar Garciaparra to Derek Lowe, and such realties could be a distraction. Third, the Alex Rodriguez soap opera had blown up despite the wishes of Ramirez (who wanted to leave) and Garciaparra (who wanted to stay, at least publicly), the latter indicating he was hurt by the entire series of events.

For the new manager of the Red Sox, there was a great deal of fence-mending to be done. "I wanted to establish relationships as quickly as possible," Francona said when asked about the earliest days in his first spring training with the team. "I guess I was at a little bit of a disadvantage at the beginning because we were coming off a winter where we put Manny on waivers and a trade with Nomar fell through. If I tried to just jump in . . . loyalty takes time." Added the new skipper: "Part of the reason you try to build relationships is because there comes a time when you're going to have to tell someone something they don't want to hear."

While Francona made his relationships inside the Boston clubhouse an obvious priority, he generally adhered to that belief regardless of whom he was dealing with. Francona similarly cultivated relationships with reporters and team executives beyond Epstein, with whom he would have to work in concert daily. Epstein, after all, was a new-age executive who was far more involved in the day-to-day operation of the club than Lou Gorman, who preceded Duquette, and the game on the whole had changed considerably in that regard during the last several years. One of the side effects of Beane's "Moneyball" philosophy in Oakland was that general managers became more involved in the day-to-day operation of the club, and that required an entirely new breed of manager who was secure enough to have the GM in his office nightly, who recognized that the GM would have more of a say in game decisions, who viewed himself as just part of the process. In former days, baseball insiders generally operated with the assumption that it was the general manager's job to procure talent and it was the manager's job to use it. But that had changed.

Beyond that, particularly during the early years of his tenure, Epstein was omnipresent, making it a point to sit in every day on his manager's pregame meetings with the media, largely because he thought it was the proper thing to do. (Epstein saw it as a sign of both solidarity and accessibility.) In fact, the move was terribly unusual in most baseball clubhouses, and looked to the media as if the young GM didn't trust his manager or, worse, wanted to control him. Only after some time did Epstein begin leaving Francona alone to deal with reporters—Epstein had similarly been present for Little's gatherings—though the practice was understandable considering that Epstein was entering just his second full season as a GM.

Now, given the change in managers, too, many had concerns. Even if the Red Sox had the players to compete with the Yankees, Francona and

Epstein were in their first year together, with a combined year of experience in Boston between them.

If Francona was feeling any pressure, he certainly did a good job of hiding it. While the manager was using much of the spring to familiarize himself with his players, the Red Sox quietly went about the business of preparing for the season. It was one of the beauties of a veteran team. Though the Red Sox had a number of contract issues—it was extremely unlikely that Martinez, Varitek, Lowe, and Garciaparra would be signed before the start of the season—the spring generally went off without a hitch. Privately, Martinez felt threatened by the presence of Schilling and grumbled about his presence—"If they want him, why don't they just say that?" said the temperamental ace—but much of the grousing was a result of the players' having too much time on their hands. Spring training was far too long, most players agreed, though it had long since become a moneymaker for clubs. Veteran players, in particular, frequently found the spring routine to be monotonous, and it took only until the middle of March for players to begin getting restless. *Can we start the season now?*

Like Martinez, Garciaparra was sulking some, though most everyone knew that such issues would disappear as soon as the season started, so long as the Red Sox won. The most notable flare-up of the spring came when Sox president Larry Lucchino approached pitcher Lowe before the start of a spring game and berated him over the actions of Lowe's agent, Scott Boras, during frustrating contract discussions. Lucchino and Boras were historic adversaries—like Superman and Lex Luthor—and each seemed to bristle at the mere mention of the other's name. So, when the Red Sox got nowhere in discussions with Boras, Lucchino took it out on the player.

Said one Red Sox employee when asked of the incident: "Part of the reason [Lucchino and Boras] hate each other is because they're so much alike."

After all, what did people expect from two good lawyers?

Otherwise, the spring went off without incident, which was just as well. The 2004 Red Sox had a great deal at stake, and everyone knew it. The Red Sox were loaded with talent—with or without long-term contracts—and they had indisputable character, at least based on the results of 2003. Nobody knew about Francona or Schilling or Foulke, but the pursuit of Rodriguez made it clear that the nucleus of Martinez, Varitek, Garciaparra, and Lowe was likely gearing up for what Kevin Millar might have referred to as a final rodeo. A new year needed a new motto, of course, but the Sox knew it was time to cowboy up. "They've made it pretty apparent this is probably the last time the four of us will be together," admitted Varitek, who typically did not call attention to such matters. "We've got to hold on to that and win. . . . I'm just getting ready to play the season. I'm going to go out there and keep this [team] together. We'll try to win a championship."

Anything less would be considered a failure.

HAD THINGS started poorly, there is no telling what might have happened to the 2004 Red Sox. Boston players might have begun grumbling about their contracts, about the changes the team tried to make over the winter, about how management played with their heads. The excuses were all at the ready. Players generally resist change, but this ownership had long since made it clear that change was preferred. Instead, only enhanced by the additions of Schilling and Foulke, the Red Sox opened 2004 like a team on a mission.

After opening the season with a 7–2 loss to the inferior Baltimore Orioles, the Red Sox won 15 of their next 20 games to finish April with a sterling record of 15-6. The Red Sox had not really begun to hit— they batted just .260 for the first month and averaged a shade over five runs game, a significant drop from 2004—but that only fueled the notion that these Red Sox were different, better. The Red Sox could pitch. Francona opened the season with a starting rotation of Schilling, Martinez, Lowe, Tim Wakefield, and the enigmatic Korean Kim, who had been changed back to his preferred role of starter after the Foulke acquisition. The fortified starting rotation also seemed to make the relief pitchers better by lessening the workload on Embree and Timlin, in particular. By expanding their pitching staff, it seemed, the Red Sox had succeeded in distributing the workload so that everyone could focus a little bit more, be a little more effective.

Still, as much as the 15–6 start had people beaming, the nature of Boston's 15 victories was far more important than the total. Before the end of April, the Red Sox played the Yankees *seven* times, taking three of four during a series at Fenway Park and sweeping all three games of a series in New York. In that series, the Red Sox won all three games by the combined score of 16–4, winning the finale 2–0 behind the brilliance of Martinez. Going back to the final two games of the 2003 American League Championship Series, the Red Sox had won four of their final five games in New York, the sole loss being the Game 7 defeat in which the Sox held a 5–2 lead entering the bottom of the eighth inning. Clearly, the Red Sox were not afraid to go into the lion's den.

"We all remember Game 7, but this is a new year," said quotable first baseman Millar. "We went out and played a good series and that tells you about the character of this team. We haven't clicked all the way through offensively, but we will. For now, we're just getting Ws, and that's what it's all about."

Even the Yankees seemed to know that the Red Sox were more formidable, that the club appeared more driven. During spring training, before the clubs had even played a meaningful game, Yankees shortstop and captain Derek Jeter praised the Red Sox for making "some good additions," most notably Schilling. Jeter had been a part of the Yankees team that had lost to Schilling, Randy Johnson, and the Arizona Diamondbacks in the 2001 World Series, and he was particularly keen when it came to evaluating a player's competitiveness and drive. Jeter correctly saw such qualities in Schilling, and it was as if the respected Yankees captain knew, on some level, that Boston had gained the upper hand.

Of course, Jeter being Jeter, he also knew that the Red Sox still had to beat the Yankees on the field. "They've added some quality

TOP LEFT: Often criticized for being cold and robotic, former Red Sox GM Dan Duquette showed rare emotion when he addressed reporters after being fired by the new Red Sox owners on February 28, 2002. Nonetheless, in acquiring such players as Pedro Martinez, Jason Varitek, Derek Lowe, Manny Ramirez, and Johnny Damon, Duquette played a major role in the construction of the Boston's dynasty. (Jim Mahoney, *Boston Herald*)

TOP RIGHT: After much of Boston grumbled during the political process that was the sale of the Red Sox, new owner John Henry and team president Larry Lucchino took time for a celebratory toast upon taking formal ownership of the club on February 27, 2002. A day later, they began putting their mark on the club by firing Duquette. (Jim Mahoney, *Boston Herald*)

BOTTOM: While the search for Duquette's replacement was centered on Oakland A's GM Billy Beane, it was Lucchino protégé Theo Epstein who ultimately moved into the hot seat just before Thanksgiving 2002. With Lucchino looking over his shoulder, Epstein began his reign as GM by saying he hoped to turn the Red Sox into "a scouting and player development machine." (Mike Seamans, *Boston Herald*)

TOP LEFT: During his first winter as GM, Epstein built a dynamic Boston offense by acquiring, among others, Todd Walker, Bill Mueller, Kevin Millar and, of course, David Ortiz. The 2003 Red Sox subsequently set a major league record for slugging percentage en route to victories like this one, a 25–8 victory over the Florida Marlins on June 23 in which the Red Sox scored 14 runs in the first inning. Note the scoreboard in the background. (The Marlins, anchored by Josh Beckett, went on to win the World Series.) (John Wilcox, *Boston Herald*)

TOP RIGHT: While countless New Englanders screamed at their television sets demanding that manager Grady Little remove ace Pedro Martinez from Game 7 of the 2003 American League Championship Series in New York, Little controversially opted to stay with his ace. The New York Yankees promptly tied the game and went on to defeat the Red Sox in extra innings to advance to the World Series against Florida. (Mike Seamans, *Boston Herald*)

BOTTOM: Joining Bucky (Fucking) Dent in the long line of Red Sox killers, Aaron (Fucking) Boone struck the decisive blow against the Red Sox with this solo home run against Tim Wakefield in the bottom of the 11th inning in Game 7. Had the Red Sox won the series, Wakefield would have been elected Most Valuable Player of the ALCS. (Matt West, *Boston Herald*)

TOP LEFT: More resolute than ever in the wake of their Game 7 loss to the Yankees, the Red Sox fortified their pitching staff during the offseason by acquiring ace Curt Schilling and closer Keith Foulke. Said Yankees shortstop Derek Jeter of the changes by the Red Sox: "They've made some good additions. They've added some quality guys and the big one is Schilling. Obviously, you win with pitching and defense and they've added a quality guy." (Renee DeKona, *Boston Herald*)

TOP RIGHT: During the same winter that they added Schilling and Foulke, the Red Sox also replaced Little with Terry Francona, whose only previous managerial experience came during a wretched four-year stint with the Philadelphia Phillies. Few envisioned Francona as the man who eventually would post the highest postseason winning percentage by any manager in history. (John Wilcox, *Boston Herald*)

BOTTOM: Manny Ramirez endured more than his share of ups and downs during his time in Boston, sometimes missing games for vague or unspecified reasons. On May 11, 2004, Ramirez returned from an excused absence during which he passed the United States citizenship exam, greeting his fans in left field at Fenway Park with a miniature version of the American flag. Said Ramirez of the citizenship exam: "It was fifteen questions. They give you the book. It's not hard. You just have to study the questions." (Dave Goldman, *Boston Herald*)

TOP LEFT: After qualifying for the playoffs for a second straight season, the Red Sox returned to the American League Championship Series against New York. The Sox faced a 3-0 series deficit when David Ortiz hit a game-winning home run against Yankees reliever Paul Quantrill, which triggered this celebration at home plate. In subsequent years, the scene would become strikingly familiar. (Dave Goldman, *Boston Herald*)

TOP RIGHT: One night after dealing the decisive blow against Quantrill, Ortiz sent the ALCS back to New York with a game-winning single against right-hander Esteban Loaiza in the bottom of the 14th inning to give the Sox a 5–4 win. The postseason win for the Red Sox was their third straight to end with a hit by Ortiz, whose performance that October turned Big Papi into a baseball demigod. (Mike Seamans, *Boston Herald*)

BOTTOM: Fueled by the heroics of Ortiz and Schilling, the Red Sox completed the greatest comeback in the history of team sports by going to New York for Games 6 and 7 of the 2004 ALCS, the latter by a lopsided 10–3 score. The comeback made the Red Sox into America's darlings and sparked an incredible celebration on the hallowed ground at Yankee Stadium. (Dave Goldman, *Boston Herald*)

TOP LEFT: Playing in the World Series for the second time in his career, Manny Ramirez was a force in a four-game sweep by the Red Sox over the St. Louis Cardinals. Less than a year after the Red Sox first put Ramirez on waivers and then had a deal in place to trade him, Ramirez went 7-for-17 with a home run and 4 RBIs to be named the World Series Most Valuable Player. (Matt Stone, *Boston Herald*)

TOP RIGHT: Regarded as a sound offensive and defensive player before coming to Boston, Renteria nonetheless led the major leagues with 30 errors in 2005. Thus was born a talk-radio scapegoat—"Error Renteria," they called him—whose stay in Boston proved remarkably brief. (Stuart Cahill, *Boston Herald*)

BOTTOM: By the time the Red Sox recorded the final out, the 2004 World Series was a forgone conclusion. As reliever Keith Foulke looks towards home plate to celebrate, Doug Mientkiewicz secured the baseball that resulted in a legal dispute between the player and franchise. The St. Louis player who made the last out? That's Edgar Renteria, who signed a four-year, $40 million contract with the Red Sox during the offseason. (Matt Stone, *Boston Herald*)

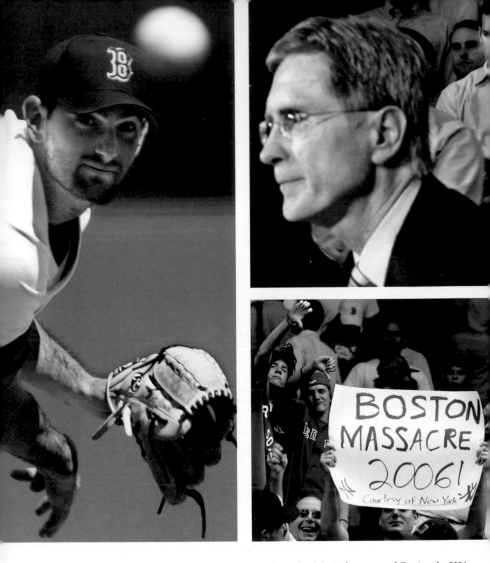

LEFT: While allowing Pedro Martinez and Derek Lowe to leave the club via free agency following the 2004 championship season, GM Theo Epstein signed pitcher Matt Clement to a three-year, $25.5 million contract. Clement got off to a terrific start in Boston before proving to be a major bust, making the offseason of 2004–05 one of the more costly in recent Red Sox history. (Matt Stone, *Boston Herald*)

TOP RIGHT: Following the frustrating 2005 season, the seemingly unthinkable happened when Epstein, citing irreconcilable difference with Sox president and mentor Larry Lucchino, abruptly resigned from the club. Owner John Henry was stunned by the decision, going so far as to say: "I have to ask myself if maybe I'm not fit to be principal owner of the Boston Red Sox." (Mark Garfinkel, *Boston Herald*)

BOTTOM RIGHT: After a winter of discontent dominated by Epstein's resignation and eventual return, the 2006 Red Sox got off to a fabulous start before crumbling in the last two months. While Epstein stood pat at the trading deadline, the New York Yankees added Bobby Abreu, who was among the many players to hurt the Red Sox during a five-game Yankees sweep at Fenway Park in August. Naturally, comparisons were drawn to the "Boston Massacre" of 1978, when the Yankees similarly wiped out the Sox during a late-season four-game series. (Matt West, *Boston Herald*)

TOP LEFT: Once again motivated by their failures, the new operators of the Red Sox acted aggressively following the 2006 season, spending a total of $103.11 million to sign Japanese pitcher and phenom Daisuke Matsuzaka. Shown here during the postseason, Matsuzaka won 15 games during the regular season and struck out 201 batters. (Nancy Lane, Boston *Boston Herald*)

RIGHT: For all of the attention heaped on Matsuzaka, left-handed reliever Hideki Okajima played just as big a role—or bigger—in the success of the 2007 Red Sox. As the primary set-up man to closer Jonathan Papelbon, Okajima posted a sterling combined ERA of 2.25 during regular and postseason play. (Lisa Hornak, *Boston Herald*)

BOTTOM LEFT: While Theo Epstein would not have made the deal for Josh Beckett, veteran evaluator Bill Lajoie did. Empowered by Lucchino to run the Red Sox following Epstein's resignation, Lajoie acquired third baseman Mike Lowell and Beckett, who subsequently won 20 games during the 2007 championship season and turned in one of the all-time great postseason performances. (Nancy Lane, *Boston Herald*)

LEFT: Upon striking out Colorado Rockies pinch hitter Seth Smith for the final out of the 2007 World Series, Red Sox closer Jonathan Papelbon leaped for joy. Regarded as Boston's long-term answer to New York Yankees great Mariano Rivera, Papelbon did not allow a run in his first 14 ⅔ career postseason innings. (Nancy Lane, *Boston Herald*)

RIGHT: Seen as a necessary cost in the Josh Beckett deal, Mike Lowell came to the Red Sox following a miserable 2005 campaign with the Florida Marlins, during which he was one of the worst everyday players in baseball in which he batted a mere .236 with eight home runs. Two years later, Lowell's two seasons in Boston had produced an aggregate batting average of .305 with 41 home runs, 200 RBIs, and a World Series Most Valuable Player Award. (Matt Stone, *Boston Herald*)

guys and the big one is Schilling," Jeter concluded during the spring. "Obviously, you win with pitching and defense, and they've added a quality guy."

While Schilling faced the Yankees only once during the first seven games—he defeated them in Boston, 5–2—the Red Sox had other reasons to be optimistic. During a 3–2 extra-inning win at New York on April 24, Foulke made his first profound impact, pitching two scoreless innings—the 10th and the 11th. In that way the game was a striking replica of Game 7, when the Sox had no one to match up against the great Mariano Rivera, allowing Boone to open the bottom of the 11th with his game-winning home run against Tim Wakefield. But in 2004, at least in April, the Red Sox had an antidote. After Foulke matched Rivera's two scoreless frames with his own two, the Red Sox rallied for a 3–2 win against right-hander Paul Quantrill.

Suddenly, it seemed, the Red Sox were using New York's own strategy against the Yankees. "Last year, we didn't have a guy that could go out there and throw a scoreless [10th] and a scoreless [11th]," noted veteran reliever Timlin. "As strong as [Foulke] is, he probably could have thrown another inning. The extra dimension we have—we have a three-inning closer, basically."

And the Yankees had a lost a critical advantage.

Almost predictably, the Red Sox subsequently went into a minislump, at one point losing five straight after the emotional games in New York. The team then went through a mediocre May and continued to slumber into June, winning enough games to stay in the thick of playoff contention, losing enough to avoid pulling away from the pack. Boston's defense during the time became a particular concern of Epstein—Jeter stressed pitching *and* defense, remember—and while the Red Sox were not playing poorly, there was a feeling through the organization that the club should be playing better.

The good news? To that point, the Red Sox had played the entire season without Garciaparra, who had suffered a peculiar injury to an Achilles tendon during spring training. While the "official" story was that Garciaparra bruised the area while being hit with a ground ball during spring training, Red Sox officials later suggested privately that Garciaparra suffered the injury while playing soccer during the off-season. (By that point, the relationship between team and player was dead.) Regardless, Garciaparra was hurt yet *again*, and there were those in the Boston organization who felt Garciaparra was being especially deliberate in rehabilitating the injury, partly because he was headed for free agency, partly because he wanted to tweak Sox officials who he felt had jerked him around during the winter.

Whatever the reason, Garciaparra postponed his return to the club by an extra day as the Sox neared the middle of June, a move that irked Sox officials to no end. For all of the talk about Garciaparra being the poster boy of the Red Sox, team officials found him to be chronically unhappy and impossible to communicate with, which made for a bad combination. Garciaparra was so structured and rigid at times that even fans watching the game on television found it disconcerting—before each pitch of every at-bat, Garciaparra would step out of the batter's box and nervously tug at his batting gloves several times—and some even called the New England Sports Network to request that Garciaparra not be shown on their television screens during those moments.

For sure, Nomar Garciaparra was a worrywart.

And that was true *before* he entered the pressure-packed and final year of his contract.

When Garciaparra finally did return to the Red Sox, Epstein's concerns about the defense only became greater. Garciaparra now lacked the mobility and agility he had possessed before the injury, and his range in the field had diminished considerably, at least according to data that Sox officials used to evaluate defense. Sox officials believed that Garciaparra had become one of the worst—if not *the* worst—defensive shortstops in baseball, and Epstein, in particular, felt that poor defense at that position (and at first base) was potentially a fatal flaw for a team that desired nothing less than a championship.

Given Garciaparra's status as an organizational icon, however, the

Red Sox felt it was nearly impossible to trade him without at least some justification.

Late in June, they got the little leverage they needed.

Having slipped a sizable five and a half games behind the suddenly surging Yankees, the Red Sox went back into New York on June 28 for a series of considerable importance. As it was that season, games between New York and Boston had taken on ridiculous importance in the wake of the 2003 ALCS, and now the Yankees could deal the Red Sox a devastating blow. If New York could win two out of three games—or, perhaps, sweep—Boston's chances of winning a division championship would almost be extinguished, even with half the season still to play.

Consequently, after New York won the first two games of the series to increase the lead to seven and a half games, the Red Sox faced what qualified as a virtual must-win situation. Francona posted a lineup that did not include Garciaparra, who was being given the night off as part of a prescribed program to manage his injured Achilles. Still, in the testosterone-filled world of professional sports, many felt that Garciaparra should have barged into Francona's office and demanded to play in a game of obvious importance, something Garciaparra saw no need to do.

As it turned out, the Red Sox and Yankees played 13 innings that night in a game many would later regard as one of the greatest regular-season games of all time, a 5–4 Yankees victory that included the spectacular, unforgettable sight of Jeter diving headfirst into the stands to catch a foul pop-up. When Jeter emerged from the box seats looking battered—Yankees GM Brian Cashman all but sprinted through the media work room to check on his captain—the image only magnified Jeter's reputation as one of the truly great combatants in sports history.

Meanwhile, through it all, Garciaparra sat on the bench. Francona sometimes hoped that Garciaparra would demand to play.

Alas, he did not.

Said Schilling of Jeter after the game, pointing to his fingers: "That's why he's got four of those big fucking rings right here."

The implication was obvious: *And that's why Garciaparra does not.*

Roughly one month later, prior to a July 31 games at Minnesota and with the Red Sox nursing a 57-45 record—the revamped Sox had gone a mediocre 42-39 over a half season since their fast start—young general manager Theo Epstein grabbed his overpaid team by the collar and gave it a hard, angry shake. After tossing and turning all night, after insisting that he would not trade arguably the greatest shortstop in Red Sox history despite persistent trade speculation, Epstein traded Garciaparra and minor-league outfielder Matt Murton in a three-way deal that brought the Red Sox a super defensive shortstop, Orlando Cabrera, and a skilled defensive first baseman, Doug Mientkiewicz. Epstein also executed another trade in which he acquired outfielder Dave Roberts from the Los Angeles Dodgers for an unknown minor leaguer named Henri Stanley, but it was the Garciaparra trade that drew far more attention for obvious reasons. It was a bona fide blockbuster.

"The safe thing would have been to play it out. The safe thing to do would have been not to touch it," Epstein said. "But in my mind, we were not going to win the World Series as is."

While Garciaparra expressed shock at the deal—"My initial reaction was, 'Wow,' " he claimed—the Red Sox, in fact, were believed to have engaged in some discussion with agent Arn Tellem about the possibility of a trade. Still, Epstein had learned in 2003 that it made no sense to make a deadline trade purely for the sake of making a deadline trade—he especially regretted the 2003 acquisition of starter Jeff Suppan—and so he was convinced, as recently as one day before dealing Garciaparra, that he would not be trading away his shortstop. But somewhere in the final 24 hours, perhaps buoyed by a youth that inspired him to be daring, Epstein pulled the trigger on one of the most aggressive trades in Red Sox history, a deal he felt would have significant impact.

If Epstein was right, he would become a hero.

If he was wrong, he might be remembered by some in the same manner as former Sox owner Harry Frazee, the man who sold Babe Ruth.

"If we're going to beat Anaheim," Epstein said privately, acknowledging that the Red Sox had all but shifted their focus to the wild-card race, "then we needed to improve our defense."

Two months still remained in the 2004 regular season.

But the Red Sox were running out of time.

UNLIKE NOMAR Garciaparra, Orlando Cabrera was a socially energetic sort who bounced around the clubhouse like a firefly. His teammates took a liking to him almost immediately. And while Cabrera was a lesser offensive player than Garciaparra, he possessed relatively good offensive skills while rating far better defensively, which made Red Sox officials feel as if they had improved their team.

What Cabrera gave the Red Sox, too, was an indisputable *edge*, something that some Sox players felt was an important element in their future success. In many baseball clubhouses, Hispanic players bonded to one another, forming cliques that were no different from inner-city ethnic neighborhoods. Yet even the American-born members of the Red Sox noted that Cabrera was unafraid to challenge even an accomplished player like Manny Ramirez, whose nonchalant nature often led many to wonder whether Ramirez truly cared. "He was the only guy who would chew out Manny's ass," one American Sox player said of Cabrera years later. "Even David [Ortiz]—it's not really his nature to get in someone's face. But Cabrera didn't give a shit."

Indeed, as much as most every player in the Boston clubhouse respected Garciaparra's ability, most were happy he was gone. Garciaparra's poor relationship with management had dramatically affected the player's mood, and many teammates found Garciaparra to be increasingly negative. Too often, in the final days of his career with the Red Sox, it seemed as if Garciaparra could not get past the bullshit, could not allow himself to do the only thing everyone (including himself) wanted him to do: enjoy playing baseball.

The acquisition of Cabrera was one catalyst for the Red Sox turnaround, but not the only one. Just before the Garciaparra deal, the Red Sox had played another emotional series against the Yankees—this one in Boston—during which the clubs engaged in a bench-clearing brawl when Sox catcher Varitek wrestled Alex Rodriguez to the ground. Rodriguez had been hit by a pitch thrown by Sox starter Bronson Arroyo and immediately began shouting profanity at the pitcher—"Fuck you," Rodriguez snarled—and Varitek immediately put himself between Rodriguez and his pitcher in hopes of preventing an altercation. When Rodriguez would not relent, Varitek snapped. "Basically, I told him to get the fuck down to first base," Varitek would say later. When Rodriguez declined, a donnybrook ensued.

The Red Sox then rallied for a ninth-inning win that ended with gritty third baseman Bill Mueller hitting a game-winning home run against Mariano Rivera, a victory many would later credit as the alarm that awakened the slumbering Red Sox. It was not. Though Boston also won the series finale with the Yankees, the Red Sox subsequently went 4-5 in their next games to immediately relapse into a coma. It was during the same span that Epstein executed the trade for Cabrera, whose arrival similarly had little effect on the Sox for a two-week period.

In fact, after losing to the Chicago White Sox on August 15, despite all that had happened along the way, the Red Sox had gone a perfectly mediocre 17-17 over a span of 34 games, leaving them with an overall record of 64-52 with 46 games to play.

And then, as if recognizing that it was time to start playing to their capabilities, the 2004 Red Sox took off on one of the great runs in the history of any franchise, let alone theirs. Over the final seven weeks of the regular season, the Red Sox went 34-12 to nearly erase what had seemed like an insurmountable 10½-game lead over the New York Yankees in the American League East. In fact, Boston actually closed to within one and a half games of New York following a series-opening win at New York on September 17, another game in which the Red Sox rallied against the inimitable Rivera. By then, the Yankees looked like the Red Sox of June—frustrated and unraveling—and even the typically cool Rivera at one point threw his hands in the air when Yankees center fielder Kenny Lofton inexplicably allowed a Red Sox hit to fall at his feet. "Without question, this is a blow to their ego," Sox pitcher Arroyo said after the win. "You start getting a little closer [in the standings] and people start doubting themselves a little bit."

Though the Yankees pulled together to salvage the final two games of the series and all but secure the division title, that victory was relatively inconsequential. Though the Red Sox publicly said that winning the division was a goal, the presence of the wild-card berth gave the Sox a fallback into the postseason. Epstein and manager Francona subsequently agreed that the best thing to do was for the Red Sox to get their house in order, to get their players rested, to get Boston prepared to play the emotionally demanding games of October. Yes, the Red Sox wanted to win the division, they all said, but not at the cost of damaging their chances at a world title. So, having pulled away from all other contenders for the wild card, the Red Sox concluded the 2004 regular season with 64 losses and 98 victories, their highest total since winning 99 games during the heartbreaking season of 1978. That was the year of Bucky Dent and Boston's unforgettable loss to the Yankees in a one-game playoff, a tiebreaker that would not have been necessary had the wild card then existed.

"This is the beginning," Francona declared after the Red Sox clinched a playoff spot with a victory at Tampa Bay on September 27. "I think the players feel that way too."

Said pitcher Pedro Martinez, making his fourth trip to the playoffs during his seven years in Boston: "I'm expecting to go further and further. I don't want any more of [just] clinching the wild card. I want to go further and I'm pretty sure the whole team feels the same way."

Indeed, had the Red Sox held a vote, the outcome would have been unanimous.

WITH THE New York Yankees so far ahead of the Red Sox in July, general manager Theo Epstein's focus at the trading deadline was on finding a way for the Red Sox to beat out the Anaheim Angels in the American League wild-card race. As it turned out, by virtue of Anaheim's victory over Oakland in the AL West Division, both the Angels and Red Sox qualified for the postseason. And even then, Epstein didn't have to worry about the Angels.

In 2004, more than any other year in recent memory, the American League was a two-team race.

Sufficiently rested after having clinched the AL wild-card berth with a week to play—in fact, the Red Sox clinched a playoff spot as the wild-card team before the Angels did so as a division champ—the Red Sox entered the 2004 postseason with their team in order. Francona had settled on a playoff rotation of Curt Schilling, Pedro Martinez, Bronson Arroyo, and Tim Wakefield—in that order—which meant primarily two things.

First, Schilling—and not Martinez—was the ace of the staff.

Second, Derek Lowe was the odd man out.

Of course, neither Martinez nor Lowe was particularly happy about those decisions, but nobody seemed to worry. Contract issues had been simmering with the club since spring training, after all, but the Red Sox were able to put aside all issues and focus once the season began. The 2004 Red Sox had played their best baseball of the season when they absolutely, positively had to, and Francona was confident that his players would rise to the challenge of playing in October.

With Schilling leading the way in Game 1, the Red Sox manhandled the Angels in the first two games of the series, both played on Anaheim's home field. The combined score of the victories was 17–6, and only once did Anaheim seem to have control of either game, possessing a 3–1 lead entering the sixth inning of Game 2. Then Sox catcher Jason Varitek hit a two-run home run against Angels starter and ace Bartolo Colon—because the Angels had to play meaningful games on the final weekend of the regular season, Colon was not available until Game 2—and the Red Sox followed by teeing off for five more runs in the final three innings against the allegedly invulnerable Anaheim bullpen, leaving little doubt as to the identity of the superior team.

Even Martinez, who had pitched poorly in September and seemed to spend much of the year sulking in Schilling's shadow, regained his swagger. "I was a number one [starter] today. That's all that matters to me," Martinez said following Game 2—after insisting previously that he was not hurt by Francona's decision to go with Schilling in Game 1. "I don't care what all the experts out there have to say. I just do my job. I let go of my ego. I swallowed it because, to me, anytime they give me the ball I'll pitch. I'm special. I'm a number one. I don't care how many games I have to wait." If Martinez's pride was hurt—and it was—he was not about to let it show.

Still, that a pitcher as great as Martinez could be shaken revealed just how emotionally brittle baseball players could be, no matter how accomplished. Going back to the time he was traded to the Red Sox, Martinez had always sought attention, craved it, *needed* it. Nobody wanted to be loved as much as Pedro. Even when the Red Sox assured Martinez's return to the club in 2004 by prematurely picking up an incredible $17.5 million option, the club's decision was driven largely by the desire to keep Pedro happy, and most Sox officials believed that a happy Pedro was a productive Pedro. At his core, Martinez was extremely good-hearted and deeply sensitive, but his speech in the wake of Game 2 was nonetheless capable of drawing a soft chuckle. In a scene reminiscent of Michael Jordan's visit to *Saturday Night Live*, Martinez sat before a crowded room and explored his self-esteem as if he were sitting with Stuart Smalley. *I'm good enough, I'm smart enough, and people like me.*

With two wins in their pocket and just one win shy of a return trip to the American League Championship Series, the Red Sox returned home for Game 3, their first postseason home games since losing to the Yankees in Game 5 a year earlier. The Sox raced to a 6–1 lead before a relatively impotent Anaheim lineup rallied for five runs in the seventh inning—the final four came on a grand slam home run by eventual American League Most Valuable Player Vladimir Guerrero that tied the game at 6—but even then, Anaheim seemed destined for elimination. The game remained deadlocked until the bottom of the 10th inning—as he had done against New York earlier in the the season, Foulke shut down the opposition in the late innings—when Johnny Damon led off with a single. The Angels then negotiated their way through the next two Red Sox hitters—second baseman Mark Bellhorn (who had replaced Todd Walker during the off-season) and Ramirez, bringing David Ortiz to the plate with the series-clinching run on base.

One year after opening the postseason with an 0-for-16 performance against the Oakland A's, Ortiz stepped into the batter's box against Anaheim pitcher Jarrod Washburn having collected five hits in his first 10 at-bats of the series. Ortiz also was coming off a regular season during which he batted a career-best .301 with 41 home runs and a whopping 139 RBIs, numbers that had validated his place as one of the elite sluggers in all of baseball. Only a year earlier, of course, the Red Sox had had Ortiz sitting on their bench behind the immortal Jeremy Giambi, yet here was Ortiz now, having turned into the kind of prolific slugger that made Theo Epstein look like a genius.

On Washburn's first pitch, a belt-high fastball that caught too much of the plate, Ortiz pounded a drive to deep left-center field that disappeared over Fenway's most distinguishing characteristic—the left-field wall—for a two-run home run that gave the Red Sox an 8–6 victory and a sweep over the completely overmatched Angels. The victory made Boston an incredible 37–12 in 49 games since the middle of August, sent the Sox back to the AL Championship Series, and continued to make a growing legend of Ortiz, whose late-inning production was starting to become routine.

"We went through a lot of this last year but it never gets old," general manager Theo Epstein said of the late-inning dramatics in the old ballpark. "[Ortiz] never ceases to amaze me. In a spot like that, he's the guy you want at the plate."

Said Angels manager Mike Scioscia, similarly acknowledging Ortiz's ascension to star status in Boston: "He found a home here and he's been incredible to say the least."

With their return trip to the ALCS clinched, the Red Sox awaited their opponent. The New York Yankees held a 2–1 series lead over the

Minnesota Twins in the American League's other semifinal, and Game 4 of the series was not scheduled until October 9, the day after the Red Sox wiped out the Angels. Sox players publicly took the politically correct approach and indicated that they had no preference regarding their opponent, but privately they admitted that they wanted a date with the Yankees, with whom they had unfinished business, particularly after a regular season during which tensions between the teams escalated to heights that had not been reached in more than a quarter century. "If we're ever going to win this thing," said reliever Alan Embree, "it's probably fitting that we do it going through [New York]."

On October 9, 2004, despite facing a 5–1 deficit entering the eighth inning, the Yankees rallied for a 6–5 victory that eliminated the Twins from the American League playoffs.

One year after Aaron Boone's homer, the rematch was set.

And while the Red Sox beamed at the opportunity to exact revenge, all of New England soon was reminded of an old and familiar adage: *Be careful what you wish for.*

THE 2004 American League Championship Series will forever be regarded as one of the most fascinating competitions in the history of team sports. New York will remember it as a tragedy. Boston will remember it as a fairy tale.

The entire story is best told in two parts.

As a result of their division title, the Yankees earned home-field advantage in the series, meaning New York would host Games 1, 2, 6, and 7. Despite that, somewhat incredibly, the Red Sox actually were favored by Las Vegas oddsmakers. Most attributed that peculiarity to the presence of Schilling, who had long since developed a reputation for being a big-game pitcher. The Yankees did not appear to have the pitching to match up with either Schilling or Pedro Martinez, and many prognosticators went so far as to suggest that the Red Sox would win the series in fewer than the maximum seven games.

All it took was one game for people to begin changing their minds.

Unbeknownst to many, Schilling had suffered an ankle injury late in the season, a problem he aggravated in the Game 1 victory over Anaheim. Most people didn't give the problem a second thought, because Schilling cavalierly brushed it off, but it did not take long to see that he was badly affected. The Yankees scored two runs in the first inning and four more in the third before taking an 8–0 lead into the seventh inning, by which point Schilling had long since left the game and introduced an entirely new element into the competition.

Without Schilling, the Red Sox of 2004 were not much better than the Red Sox of 2003, if at all. And everyone already knew how that chapter turned out.

"If I can't go back out there with something better than I had in Game 1, I'm not going back out there," a matter-of-fact Schilling said when asked about his future availability in the series following the 10–7 loss. "This isn't about me. It's about winning a world championship. If I can't do better than I did, I won't take the ball again."

And if he didn't take the ball again, the Red Sox probably didn't stand a chance.

Nonetheless, the Red Sox had little choice but to move on to Game 2, a contest that produced another defeat. Taunted by a New York crowd throughout the night—in September, after another frustrating loss to New York, Martinez had all but preordered the razzing by referring to the Yankees as his "daddy"—Martinez allowed three runs in six innings, which would have been enough to win on most nights. The problem was that sinkerballer Jon Lieber had completely shut down the prolific Red Sox attack, inducing one quick out after the next while allowing just three hits. The result was a 3–1 Boston loss that left the Red Sox faced with a 2–0 series deficit, a fact that did not begin to measure the extent of the damage.

In the first two games, the Yankees had defeated both Schilling and Martinez, Boston's two best pitchers. And there was the real possibility that Schilling was not coming back.

While Red Sox fans began to fret, Sox players went about the business of preparing for Game 3, to be played in Boston. Rain forced the postponement of play for one day, and those believing in omens did not have to look far to see a suggestion that the Red Sox were already doomed. "It's unfortunate if they feel that way," Red Sox outfielder Johnny Damon said when asked if it was understandable for some fans to feel pessimistic. "They've seen [failure] in the past, but this team is different. We know we can do it—it's just a matter of doing it."

Roughly 24 hours later, in the most important game of the 2004 Boston baseball season to that point, the Red Sox did nothing less than throw up on themselves. Scoring multiple runs in the first, third, fourth, fifth, seventh, and ninth innings, the Yankees pounded out 22 hits and battered the Red Sox 19–8. Things got so bad that Terry Francona was forced to use his scheduled Game 4 starter, Tim Wakefield, in relief. The desperation move meant that Francona would hand the ball to the previously demoted Derek Lowe for Game 4, the first of at least four consecutive games the Red Sox would play (if they were lucky) with no margin for error.

For all of the hype and talk about the highly anticipated rematch between Boston and New York, the series was rapidly becoming a dud. The Red Sox were hurt—on a number of levels—and the Yankees were using them to wipe up the blood.

"It's definitely embarrassing," Arroyo said after the game. "You try to forget about it during the regular season, but when it's crunch time, to get destroyed like that and have a football score up there, it's definitely embarrassing."

Said Francona months later: "If I was on a radio talk show, I would have said the Yankees were going to win [the series]. You had to."

In baseball history, after all, no team had ever overcome a 3–0 series deficit to come back and win a best-of-seven affair.

NO MATTER what David Americo Ortiz achieves in his professional career, nothing will match his accomplishments of October 2004. During his career with the Red Sox, Ortiz would go on to have better seasons than the one he had in 2004, when he finished fifth in the American

League Most Valuable Player Award balloting. But in October, when a team needed it most, no player has ever done what Ortiz did for the Red Sox against the New York Yankees.

With the Red Sox facing elimination, Ortiz delivered game-winning hits in the 12th and 14th innings of Games 4 and 5, Red Sox victories by the respective scores of 6–4 and 5–4. In both cases, the Yankees led the game entering the eighth or ninth inning. Calling upon their experience of having defeated the great Mariano Rivera during the regular season, the Red Sox pinned blown saves on Rivera not once, but *twice* in the next two games, each of which ended with a mighty swing of Ortiz's bat. In the first game, after hero-in-the-making Dave Roberts stole second against Rivera and scored the tying run on a Bill Mueller single in the ninth inning, Ortiz hit a two-homer homer against Paul Quantrill to win the game in the 12th. On the next night, Ortiz battled through a 10-pitch at-bat against Esteban Loaiza before delivering a single to center field that sent the series back to New York.

"I hope people appreciate what he's doing right now," Red Sox outfielder Gabe Kapler said in the wake of Ortiz's heroics. It's not that easy."

Said Ortiz after Game 4: "Things can change. You never know what can happen from now on. We played a really good game [in Game 4]. It was a totally different game than the one we played [in Game 3]."

And if anyone knew about change, it was Ortiz.

Labeled lazy and uncooperative during his career with Minnesota by former Twins manager Tom Kelly, Ortiz was now becoming a star in Boston. No Red Sox player since Carl Yastrzemski in 1967 had delivered the kind of drama Ortiz began producing during the 2004 playoffs, when Ortiz almost single-handedly refused to let the Red Sox lose. And as the series progressed, the greatness of Ortiz's performance only grew. Because the Red Sox were able to extend the series, because team doctor Bill Morgan found an innovative way to treat Schilling's injury by essentially sewing a dislocated ankle tendon back into place, Schilling was going to try to take the mound for Game 6 in New York. And if Schilling could pitch reasonably well, if the Red Sox could win

Game 6, the Yankees would be forced to play a seventh game with the knowledge that they were on the verge of the greatest collapse in baseball history.

And it was all because of Ortiz.

Said the slugger in his memoirs, *Big Papi*: "On two straight nights, against the Yankees in the American League Championship Series, I had two walk-off hits. My phone was ringing off the hook. The chances of anybody getting two walk-off hits like that, in about 24 hours, are probably about the same as a team coming back to win four straight after losing the first three games of a seven-game series. But we were halfway there, bro. The series was now three games to two. And we were going back to New York."

Never in their history had the Red Sox been happier to go back to New York. The club's confidence had been restored. The Yankees were now the ones feeling the heat, and New York began showing signs of cracking in the eighth inning of Game 6, after a courageous outing by Schilling in what forever came to be known as "the Bloody Sock Game." His problematic right ankle sutured in place, Schilling pitched seven stellar innings as blood from the procedure seeped through to the surface of his sock, an image that television producers were all too eager to play up. He was on the bench when Yankees third baseman Alex Rodriguez, after grounding to pitcher Arroyo, swiped at the pitcher's glove in attempt to knock the ball free. Umpires quickly conferred and deemed that Rodriguez had committed interference, effectively stifling a New York rally in what would prove to be a 4–2 Red Sox win.

After the game, Red Sox players pulled aside reporters and asked them to "call out" Rodriguez in print for what they perceived as a tactless maneuver, something Rodriguez would never live down.

As for Schilling, his legacy as a member of the Red Sox was forever cemented. "Our team doctor is a fucking genius," the pitcher said in a private moment while getting dressed in front of his locker.

Unsurprisingly, given the manner in which the Yankees were unraveling, Game 7 was never really a contest.

One night after Schilling's heroics, Lucchino aide Charles Steinberg was standing in one of the cavernous hallways in the depths of Yankee Stadium just before the start of the seventh game. Steinberg expressed the hope that the Red Sox would score quickly and jump to a big early lead, thereby taking the New York crowd out of the game. No one with the Red Sox wanted anything ever remotely resembling the events of October 2003. The Red Sox then went out and took a 6–0 lead through the first two innings—the big blow was a grand slam by Johnny Damon against Javier Vazquez, the same pitcher Epstein had more than once tried to acquire—and the Red Sox never really looked back. The Yankees got as close as 8–3 before finally succumbing 10–3; Boston had clubbed New York over the head.

On the field at Yankees Stadium and in the Boston clubhouse after the game, the celebration lasted for quite some time. Derek Lowe, who had started Game 7 on just two days of rest after opening the playoffs in the bullpen, looked as wide-eyed as a child on Christmas morning despite the effects of a long, emotional season. Martinez, too, looked as happy as ever. Sox executives John Henry, Tom Werner, Larry Lucchino, and Theo Epstein all joined the Boston players frolicking about in the champagne drizzle while, roughly 200 miles away, an entire city watched on live television with awe and disbelief.

The Red Sox just came back from three games down to beat the Yankees.

Meanwhile, in a relatively tame corner of the Boston clubhouse, Red Sox pitcher Tim Wakefield was speaking with reporters when a clubhouse attendant called him away, informing Wakefield that Yankees manager Joe Torre was waiting on the phone. It was only a year earlier that Aaron Boone had hit Wakefield's trademark knuckleball into the left-field seats at Yankee Stadium, only a year since Wakefield feared he had become the next Bill Buckner. Now Torre was calling to offer Wakefield his congratulations, to remind him that the bad times exist to make the good times that much better.

"When we got that final out, I wanted to stand on that mound as long as I could and relish the fact that I got to walk off the field a winner this time," Wakefield said. "For us to win four in a row from these guys really shows the determination and the guts we have in this clubhouse." Continued Wakefield, who had been with the club longer than any other player: "This is as big as the World Series. To be down 3–0, losing Game 3 the way we lost it, with the way we won Game 4 and the way we won Game 5, then coming back and winning Game 6 and Game 7 here, it's tremendous, not only for this organization, but for the city and the fans that stuck around through thick and thin for us."

As it turned out, Tim Wakefield was 100 percent correct.

It *was* bigger than the World Series.

THE ST. LOUIS Cardinals never had a chance. Boston steamrolled St. Louis in four straight games by a combined score of 24–12 to win its first World Series since 1918, officially declaring an end to Boston's stained past. During the Series, the Red Sox never trailed. And during a postseason in which one Red Sox player after the next seemed to redeem himself, Manny Ramirez was named the Series Most Valuable Player.

Only a year earlier, the Red Sox had placed Ramirez on waivers for the purpose of releasing him, a maneuver that led to the Alex Rodriguez saga. Since that time, there had been many crossroads at which the Red Sox might have gone in a different direction. In the end, the Red Sox won eight straight games after entering the ninth inning of Game 4 of the American League Championship Series trailing the New York Yankees 4–3. It was then that their final race to immortality began with a stolen base by Dave Roberts, who had slid under the tag of shortstop Derek Jeter by a fraction of a second.

What if Roberts had been out?

What if Ramirez had been traded?

What if Ortiz had never been given a chance?

Where would the Red Sox be now?

"If we had lost that fourth game to the Yankees, we'd be saying 'How do we fix it?'" acknowledged manager Terry Francona, whose career similarly was resurrected. "Now we're asking, 'How do we keep this thing together?'"

In the end, they didn't.

WHAT A HANGOVER

THE PARTY ALWAYS ENDS, OF COURSE, THOUGH THE CELEBRATION following Boston's first World Series title in 86 years sometimes seemed to last forever. The Red Sox savored the moment as long as they could, and the words they spoke on the night of October 27, 2004, echoed through the New England winter.

"We'll never hear the '1918' chants again," said Tim Wakefield, the Sox' senior statesman. "It's huge for the franchise. Ever since Mr. [John] Henry and Mr. [Tom] Werner and Larry [Lucchino] took over they've pointed us in the right direction. People that have lived there longer than I have had too many sad days. Now they can rejoice in the city of Boston."

Said catcher Jason Varitek, who joined the Red Sox in 1997: "I can't explain the great feeling we have for the whole New England area. They can finally rest. They can finally take a nap. Some people that have suffered a long time can finally go to sleep."

Added pitcher Derek Lowe, who was credited with the win in all three postseason series clinchers, against the Anaheim Angels, New York Yankees, and St. Louis Cardinals: "We're finally winners. We're not the happy guys that came in second, the so-close-but-so-far kind of thing. There are so many people who deserve credit for this. I was happy to see [longtime Red Sox player and coach] Johnny Pesky here and I saw a tear in his eye. I hope the Red Sox bring everybody back [from the past to celebrate]. This isn't just the 2004 Red Sox. This is 86 years here."

Of course, the Red Sox being the Red Sox, the event was not completely devoid of tension. Just prior to the celebratory "rolling rally" orchestrated by the office of Boston mayor Tom Menino, Sox president Larry Lucchino chastised manager Terry Francona upon learning that Red Sox players had declined to wear their game jerseys for the parade. But even then, the blowup was brief and insignificant. All of New England was in such good spirits that nothing could take away from the Red Sox' fabulous achievement, which still seemed too good to be true.

They were down 3–0 to the Yankees.

It was over.

And then they won eight in a row.

Despite poor weather in Boston, the parade commemorating the Red Sox' historic championship drew an estimated 3.2 million spectators, according to the *Boston Herald*. Red Sox players piled onto Boston's celebrated duck boats, then cruised around the city and into the Charles River, which brought more than a touch of anxiety to at least one Red Sox player. "When we drove off the road and pulled into the Charles River, I looked at everybody and I was like: 'How is this thing going to float, dude?'" Red Sox designated hitter David Ortiz wrote in *Big Papi*. "Everybody laughed. But it was really cold outside and I don't really like the water, so I put on a life vest. Everybody cracked up."

Amid the laughter, Ortiz's words proved both ironic and terribly appropriate. For much of October, after all, he had served as Boston's life vest. And now, with the Red Sox' season but a memory, many wondered: *How are the Red Sox going to keep this thing afloat?*

While much of New England continued to celebrate in the immediate aftermath of Boston's 2004 World Series victory—over the winter, the Red Sox took the championship trophy on a tour of New England cities and towns—Theo Epstein had no choice but to get right back to work. Like every organization, the Red Sox constantly had to balance the short term against the long, and Epstein had long since concluded that the Red Sox needed to be infused with youth. Epstein's roots were in the minor leagues and player development, and he knew that for the Red Sox to make consistent runs at the world title, the club had to rotate its stock to avoid getting stale. New blood always needed to be brought in, just as the Atlanta Braves had done annually while dominating the National League East for more than a decade.

It was out with the old, in with the new.

Of course, planning and executing those changes was far more complex and difficult than many would have assumed. In his capacity as general manager, on what might as well have been a mental spreadsheet, Epstein had to know the Red Sox' long-term salary commitments projected out over a number of years along with information concerning potential eligible free agents following a given season. He had to know which Red Sox prospects were most likely to develop, their estimated date of arrival in the major leagues, how they might be able to contribute. Constantly, he needed to weigh all of those things against one another to determine what was the best course of action for now *and* for later, and those two things did not always align.

Sometimes, Epstein found, he had to sacrifice some of the present for more of the future.

The off-season of 2004–5 was one of those times.

For obvious reasons, much of the discussion concerning the future of the 2004 Red Sox centered on the three longtime cornerstones now eligible for free agency: Pedro Martinez, Derek Lowe, and Jason Varitek. Garciaparra would have been the fourth member of that group, but Epstein had traded him in July. Garciaparra's replacement, Orlando Cabrera, also was eligible for free agency, leaving Epstein with a considerable task entering the off-season. If all of those players filed for free agency, the Red Sox faced the prospect of being without two of their more reliable starting pitchers, their catcher, and their shortstop. The nucleus of the team might be all but gutted, though New England was in such a state of bliss that no one seemed to recognize the magnitude of the problem.

And there were other troubles. *Boston Globe* columnist Dan Shaughnessy was the first to report that the Red Sox and first baseman Doug Mientkiewicz were involved in a dispute over the baseball used to record the final out of the World Series. As the Boston first baseman in the ninth inning, Mientkiewicz had caught closer Keith Foulke's underhanded toss to retire Edgar Renteria (remember the name) for the final out. Anticipating such a moment—talk about premeditation—Mientkiewicz had the ball authenticated by representatives from Major League Baseball immediately after the contest, then later joked to Shaughnessy that the value of the ball would help pay the college tuition for one of his children.

Lucchino, naturally, was furious, believing the baseball was the property of the club and should be shared with fans as if it were a museum artifact or, perhaps, the *Mona Lisa*.

Months passed before the sides finally reached an agreement, with Mientkiewicz donating the ball to the National Baseball Hall of Fame in Cooperstown, New York.

By the time that happened, the Red Sox had a very different look.

HAVING SURVIVED the departures of Roger Clemens and Mo Vaughn, many Bostonians had long since assumed that Pedro Martinez would be a casualty. In 2004, frequently pitching as if he were merely trying to avoid injury in a free-agent year, Martinez finished 16-9 with a 3.90 ERA, the latter the highest number in his career to that point. Martinez's nine losses also were more than he'd had in the 2002 and 2003 seasons *combined*, and many in baseball had concluded that Martinez was a shoulder injury waiting to happen. No one was willing to suggest that Tommy Lasorda was right—Martinez had 182 career wins by then—but the writing was on the wall: Pedro Martinez's best days were well behind him.

Of course, Martinez didn't see it that way, and he entered the free-agent season seeking a four-year contract that would pay him $13 million to $14 million per year, placing the total value of such a package

in the range of $52 million to $56 million. The Red Sox had no intention of going that far. Red Sox officials began discussions with
Martinez by offering a guaranteed two-year contract with an option
for a third season, then stood by as the player fielded offers from other
clubs. Boston kept the door open enough so that Martinez could always go back to them, so that it *appeared* as if the club had a genuine
interest in keeping the player, but the Red Sox privately hoped that
Martinez would get such a good offer elsewhere that he would choose
to leave the team.

In that way, it was Roger Clemens all over again. Observed Dan
Duquette from afar when the Red Sox' initial offer to Martinez was
made public: "It means they don't want him." Eight years earlier, after all, it was Duquette who had taken a similar approach with
Clemens.

Beyond the obvious drop in Martinez's skills, the player's attitude
had soured, too, during his final years with the Red Sox. After arriving in Boston seeking the recognition he had forever lacked, Martinez
had grown tired of the constant attention. While once he had seemed
to enjoy the banter with reporters and to embrace his role as a baseball spokesman, he now withdrew. The media seemed to wear him
down. He resented Red Sox management for bringing in Curt
Schilling—he resented Schilling, too—and he referred to new, young,
and analytical Red Sox executives as "computer geeks," sometimes to
their very faces.

The way Martinez looked at it, the Red Sox now seemed ungrateful
for all that he had done for the franchise, for whom he went 117-37 with
a 2.52 ERA and averaged a stunning 10.95 strikeouts per nine innings
pitched during the seven seasons from 1998 to 2004. He had won two Cy
Young Awards and helped the Red Sox to a World Series title.

Of course, though Martinez neglected to recognize it, he had also
been paid in excess of $90 million.

And in the end, the truth was that he needed a change of scenery as
much as they wanted to give him one.

"Why am I here? Because I felt a lack of interest from the Red Sox," Martinez told the *Herald*'s Michael Silverman in an exclusive interview on December 16, 2004, after signing a four-year, $53 million contract with the New York Mets. "I think a player that has achieved what I have achieved should not be subject to anybody's time, or thoughts on time. I have been waiting for three years to get things done with the Boston Red Sox.

"I meant it in an honest way. I'm very straightforward, as you well know, and I'm a proud man. I represent a lot—not only as a man but as a player. And for my country, it's important that somebody make a statement and understand how to deal with this situation and lead by example. If I let somebody mistreat a player like I am, what's the hope going to be for the rest of the people that are coming after me? I'm not saying that the Boston Red Sox mistreated me, but what I'm saying is they should have shown a little more interest than they showed, even though they were negotiating and were probably being cautious. But I was always honest about what I wanted, how I wanted it, and I made a lot of sacrifices to give Boston the opportunity to keep me."

Publicly, at least, Red Sox officials feigned disappointment at Martinez's departure—"We lost a Hall of Famer today," Epstein said like a bad actor on the day Martinez agreed with the Mets—but club officials privately were thrilled. In their minds, Martinez was a time bomb. His shoulder would fail him. Though the Sox ultimately increased their offer to the pitcher to three years at $40 million with an option for a fourth season—Martinez wanted to be paid more than the $13 million the Sox were due to give Schilling—they did so knowing that Martinez had a better offer elsewhere. They seemed to purposely drag their feet in negotiations so that Martinez would get annoyed, frustrated, *emotional*.

Still, even as the Martinez saga played out the way the Red Sox expected it to, the greater question was obvious: what were the Sox going to do to replace him? The trade and free-agent markets were relatively strong with regard to pitching after the 2004 season, and the Red Sox believed they could make their staff better and younger. Epstein had now participated in three drafts since joining the Red Sox—two as general manager—and the front office believed that those drafts would soon begin to bear fruit. At the same time, the Sox had to replace Martinez and Derek Lowe, the latter of whom they had similarly cast aside for an assortment of reasons.

Said Lowe when asked what he and his representatives had heard from the Red Sox with regard to a new contract: "Nothing."

As was the case with Martinez, Sox officials had long since grown tired of Lowe, albeit for entirely different reasons. A sinkerballer who relied on the movement of his pitches more than sheer arm strength, Lowe possessed a remarkably resilient arm and was an exceptional athlete. In the 2003 Division Series against Oakland, he had appeared in three games—two as a reliever, one as a starter—and closed Game 5 after starting Game 3 only two days earlier. In 2004, he pitched Game 7 of the AL Championship Series against the New York Yankees on a mere *two days of rest*, giving the Red Sox six superb innings while allowing just one run in Boston's runaway victory. At just 31, Lowe was still young and he was *durable*, though his performance had deteriorated steadily since his 20-win season of 2002.

Over his last three seasons in Boston, Lowe went from 21 wins to 17 to 14 while his ERA went from 2.58 to 4.47 to 5.42. Prior to the playoffs, remember, Lowe had been pitching so poorly that the Red Sox had left him out of their postseason rotation altogether, and it was only during the crisis that was the first three games of the AL Championship Series against New York that Lowe was forced into a much bigger role.

When it came, Lowe's performance was nothing short of spectacular. In five appearances (three starts) during the 2004 postseason, Lowe went 3-0 with a 1.86 ERA.

But Red Sox officials viewed Lowe's effort in October 2004 as the exception rather than the rule. And there were other factors that may (or may not) have affected their decision. By the time Lowe had thrown his last pitch for the Red Sox, the pitcher had been making frequent appearances in the *Herald's* widely read gossip column—the Inside Track—most as the result of a deteriorating relationship with his wife, Trinka, and Lowe's frequent appearances in the city bars. The latter, in particular, led Sox officials to suggest privately that Lowe's off-field behavior was a force behind their decision to let him go.

But the team's actions belied its words. Partly to replace Lowe, the Red Sox signed veteran left-hander David Wells, who was both older than Lowe—Wells was 41—and reputed to be a drinker. In fact, in his autobiography (*Perfect, I'm Not*), Wells caused quite a stir by suggesting that he had pitched a perfect game for the New York Yankees while drunk. But because the Red Sox were able to acquire Wells at the extremely affordable price of a guaranteed $8 million over two years, they were willing to make sacrifices they did not care to make for the far more expensive Lowe.

As it was, Lowe never received even a gratuitous offer like the one presented to Martinez. "They made it perfectly clear right after the World Series that nothing was going to happen," Lowe told reporters in Los Angeles after signing a four-year, $36 million deal with the Dodgers in January. "They definitely have a plan and there's nothing wrong with having a plan."

While Wells helped solve part of the Red Sox' pitching dilemma—at least in the short term—the club exhausted several options before finding a younger starter who would serve a bigger role in their rotation. (In short, the Sox were looking for someone with more of Lowe's durability and more of Martinez's talent.) The club began the off-season by pursuing free-agent right-hander Brad Radke, a steady, efficient, and cerebral pitcher who had spent his entire career to that point with the Minnesota Twins. Like the older, left-handed Wells, Radke was a marksman who rarely walked batters, which made all the sense in the world for a Red Sox team that had embraced at least part of the offensive "Moneyball" philosophy by emphasizing on-base percentage. If the Red Sox were going to stress on-base percentage to their hitters, they needed their pitchers to be equally efficient in keeping opposing hitters *off* base. One of the ways to do that was to find pitchers who rarely issued walks, and Wells and Radke were regarded as two of the best control pitchers in baseball.

Much to the Red Sox' chagrin, Radke turned down a three-year, $27 million offer and took less money (two years, $18 million) to remain in Minnesota, where he finished his career. Radke's decision made him that rarest of professional athletes—someone who actually took *less* to remain in a better personal situation—and served as a fitting contrast to Martinez.

Pedro Martinez took more to jilt the Red Sox. Brad Radke took less to do the same.

For Epstein, the contrast provided fitting bookends on what would be a terribly frustrating off-season.

"It was a better offer [from Boston], but I wanted a certain number," Radke said during spring training 2005 in Fort Myers, Florida, where, ironically, both the Red Sox and Twins trained. "And if the Twins landed on that number, I was going to sign. For the Red Sox organization to have an interest in me, that's an honor. . . . I was just looking for a fair deal. I didn't want to lead [the Red Sox] on or anything. Signing with your current team is your first priority. I wasn't looking for [the most] money. I was looking to be treated fairly and to be happy."

While Radke went by the boards, the Red Sox had a number of other options that seemed palatable, beginning with right-hander Tim Hudson, then of the Oakland A's. Hudson was a fierce competitor who had become a team leader with the young, upstart A's, but Oakland general manager Billy Beane had been growing concerned that Hudson was losing some effectiveness while suffering from a succession of nagging injuries. Like Martinez, Hudson was not especially big, and his delivery generated such torque that many wondered about his long-term durability. Hudson also was entering that stage of his career when his salary would begin to escalate rapidly, and Beane had deemed the winter following the 2004 season the time when he might be able to get the greatest value in trading away his staff ace.

Despite the praise being heaped upon Beane, the secret to Oakland's recent success was simple: pitching. In Hudson, left-hander Mark Mulder, and left-hander Barry Zito, the A's had a group of three starters that was better than any in baseball. All three of the pitchers were young, which meant that their salaries were relatively low, though part of the reason Oakland had to adopt a creative offensive philosophy built around on-base percentage was because Beane chose to commit a significant percentage of his finances toward pitching. Still, the general manager pulled it off by building decent offensive teams despite a ridiculously low payroll, and Oakland's combination of excellent pitching and serviceable offense allowed the A's to qualify for the playoff every year from 2000 to 2003.

But when the A's lost the American League West Division to the Anaheim Angels and missed the playoffs in 2004, Beane started to wonder: *Maybe it's time to shake this up.*

Like Epstein, Beane had long since begun to prepare for the day that the A's couldn't retain any combination from the group of Hudson, Mulder, and Zito, drafting pitchers and developing them in the Oakland minor-league system. One of those pitchers was Rich Harden, a hard-throwing right-hander who had already reached the major leagues and whom many regarded as the heir apparent to Hudson. Another was right-hander Joe Blanton, who had similarly soared through the organization. Beane made it clear to teams that Hudson was available by trade during the offseason of 2004–5, and a number of teams lined up to sit with Beane concerning his bulldog ace.

Of course, the Red Sox were among them.

While most everyone in baseball thought highly of the 29-year-old Hudson—to that point in his career, he was 92-39 with a 3.30 ERA in a six-year career—Red Sox manager Terry Francona was a huge fan. Francona was a bench coach for manager Ken Macha on the 2003 Oakland team that had lost to the Sox in the playoffs, and he knew that Hudson's personality and character—what baseball people frequently referred to as "makeup"—were in line with the pitcher's considerable ability. The transition from a small market like Oakland to a big market like Boston could overwhelm some players—many had feared that Johnny Damon, for instance, would have difficulty with the switch—but Francona knew that Hudson could handle it, that he would thrive in Boston, that he was precisely the kind of personality the Red Sox needed in a high-intensity market. Said Francona in a private moment as the Red Sox went through their winter checklist like a quarterback reading through his progressions: "The guy I'd love to see us get is Hudson."

Billy Beane knew that too. Which is precisely why Beane ended up trading Hudson to the Atlanta Braves in the National League.

To the surprise of many, Beane also traded away 27-year-old left-hander Mulder, similarly sending him to the National League (in this case, the St. Louis Cardinals). Both players had immediate physical problems in the National League—it was as if Beane were psychic—though Hudson would rebound to go 16-10 for the Braves during the 2007 season.

Despite thinking they had made a good play for Hudson, Red Sox officials felt as if they were spinning their wheels in talks with Beane. The existence of the wild-card berth had changed the baseball playoff structure considerably since its introduction, most notably in that it meant teams from different divisions were competing against one another for the same playoff spot. As much as Beane's A's were competing against teams like the Angels and Seattle Mariners in the American League West, they were also competing against teams like the Red Sox. Dealing someone like Hudson to a power like Boston could deal a huge blow to Oakland's playoff chances somewhere down the line. So Beane seemed to indulge Sox officials by sitting down to talk trade with them, but he had no intention of sending them his best pitcher.

Moreover, there were palpable, indisputable rivalries among some of the game's new and bright young general managers: from Epstein,

New York Yankees general manager Brian Cashman, Beane, and Cleveland Indians general manager Mark Shapiro. While many of them claimed to be friends—and Beane and Toronto Blue Jays general manager J. P. Ricciardi did share a very close personal relationship—there was always a wall between most of them. Each wanted to beat the others, and the obligation to the job always outweighed any personal allegiances, at least when it came to baseball. Said a frustrated Epstein while standing with assistant Jed Hoyer outside the Anaheim Marriott, the host hotel of the 2004 winter meetings: "We feel like we've made [Beane] an offer that is probably better than anyone else's, but the bottom line is that Billy won't trade him to us."

While being thwarted in their attempts to acquire Radke or Hudson—as well as in their "efforts" to retain Martinez—the Red Sox were discussing a long-term contract with free-agent right-hander Carl Pavano (yes, him again). Now seven years removed from the Dan Duquette deal that sent him to the Montreal Expos for Pedro Martinez, the soon-to-be-29-year-old Pavano had finally blossomed into a frontline starting pitcher, albeit a little later than many thought. Pitching for the Florida Marlins in 2004—Pavano had been dealt to Florida, oddly enough, in the deal that had sent Cliff Floyd to Montreal on what proved to be Floyd's stopover to Boston—Pavano had gone 18-8 with a 3.00 ERA in 222⅔ innings, totals that made him arguably the most desirable free-agent pitcher of the off-season. Pavano was younger than Martinez and, at 6-foot-5 and 230 pounds, built to last—or so everyone thought—and he drew interest from the Red Sox as well as from the New York Yankees, who were also trying to inject their pitching staff with additional youth in the wake of their epic collapse to the Red Sox.

Epstein understood as well as anyone the irony of pursuing Pavano. To replace Pedro Martinez, the Red Sox were trying to bring back the very pitcher whom they had traded for Martinez in the first place.

As was the case with Radke and Hudson, the Red Sox failed in their chase for Pavano, who ultimately agreed to a four-year, $40 million deal with the New York Yankees. At the time, it was difficult to tell where the

Sox had placed Pavano in their pecking order, though ultimately it did not matter. Assuming the departure of Martinez, the Red Sox had Radke, Hudson, and Pavano as the top three options on their replacement list—and the club failed to acquire any of them. Epstein believed in spending responsibly—"By definition, any time you sign a free agent, you overpay," he was always eager to point out—but the problem was that the Red Sox still needed another pitcher, and the club was now sliding well down its depth chart.

By the time the Red Sox got to Matt Clement, though club officials would never admit it, the team was desperate. Several teams had been eyeing Clement, and the Red Sox had touched base with the pitcher's representative, Barry Axelrod, early during the free-agent recruiting process. But privately, the Red Sox hoped it would never come to that, because any sincere attempt on their part to sign Clement would indicate that the Sox had missed out on choices A, B, C, and, perhaps, D.

Nonetheless, having just turned 30, Clement was an intriguing talent. Having spent the majority of his career with bad teams, Clement entered the off-season of 2004–5 with a mediocre career record of 60–62 to go along with a 4.34 ERA. From 1999 to 2004, Clement had pitched an average of slightly more than 190 innings per season, suggesting that he was at least durable. Epstein and many other Sox baseball officials believed Clement was a better pitcher than his record suggested—in that way, he was a little like Ryan Rupe—and they believed that pitching in Boston, with the Red Sox offense supporting him, Clement would be far more effective. The Red Sox also believed that Clement would benefit greatly from working with catcher Jason Varitek, whom the club was optimistic about re-signing.

So, on December 18, 2004, having exhausted all other options, the Red Sox signed Matt Clement to a three-year, $25.5 million contract with the hope that he could at least replace Derek Lowe.

"The Red Sox probably did the least recruiting, or if not the least, then they didn't put on the full-court press," agent Barry Axelrod told the *Herald*'s Michael Silverman, explaining why Clement chose the Red

Sox over other suitors. "The Red Sox' game plan was very calculated. Theo, whom I admire greatly, very early on told us he was very interested and wanted to be on the list, but on the list of teams with conditional interest. Names like [Brad] Radke, [Carl] Pavano, and Pedro [Martinez] had to be eliminated first. He told us, 'If Pedro doesn't work out for us, we're going to be very hot and heavy for Matt,' and he kept in touch with us. Some teams were hot and heavy from the get-go and were always, 'Let's go now,' but Theo was not like that."

There was a reason. Theo Epstein wanted to do better.

In the midst of finalizing the Clement negotiations, with his pitching staff in order—at least somewhat—Epstein also focused his attention on shortstop, where he had taken a tack like the one he took with Axelrod. From the start, Epstein had called the agent for shortstop Edgar Renteria to express interest in the player, but on a condition: Epstein first had to see how things shook out with his pitching staff. Epstein believed the price for all talent had become grossly inflated during the 2004–5 off-season, and he was cautious about overspending on anyone. The Red Sox had all but written off shortstop Orlando Cabrera despite how well Cabrera fit in with the club—as was the case with Lowe, Sox brass privately cited "off-field issues"—but they also believed they had other options. The Red Sox had a supremely talented shortstop in their minor-league system—a Dominican-born player named Hanley Ramirez, who had been signed under Dan Duquette—and Epstein regarded Ramirez as a can't-miss prospect. The problem was that Ramirez was still more than a year away from playing in the major leagues, and the Red Sox needed a stopgap solution.

Though Epstein told Renteria's agent, Barry Meister, that the Red Sox needed to see how their pitching played out before making a serious offer on the player, that was only partly true. The Red Sox also believed that the Anaheim Angels might trade their shortstop, David Eckstein, a chronic overachiever who had actually begun his career in the Boston organization before being released by Duquette. (It was one of the underplayed blunders of the Duquette era.) But when the Red Sox and

Angels could not come to terms on a deal—and when the Sox couldn't acquire free-agent shortstop Craig Counsell—the club turned its attention to Renteria, particularly when it became clear that Wells and Clement would cost the Sox considerably less than they had thought they might invest in their pitching staff.

A native of Colombia, the 29-year-old Renteria was regarded as that most complimentary of all things by baseball evaluators: a winner. Renteria was a sound defensive player (he had won two Gold Glove Awards already), and he already had five career trips to the postseason, most recently with the 2004 St. Louis Cardinals team swept by the Red Sox in the World Series. Of course, Renteria was the same man whom Sox closer Keith Foulke had retired for the final out of the World Series, though he had previously been 5-for-14 in the Series, a .357 batting average. Entering the Series, Red Sox officials had been so concerned about Renteria that they had stressed to their pitchers that he and the St. Louis first baseman, the sensational Albert Pujols, were to be pitched to with the utmost caution and respect. That was how much they thought of him.

On December 18, 2004—the same day they reached contractual terms with Clement—the Red Sox introduced their new shortstop, Edgar Renteria, to the Boston media and fans during a press conference at Fenway Park. Even with the talented Hanley Ramirez on the horizon, Epstein felt that Renteria was a good signing, a safe investment. Renteria was the kind of player who would have value on the trade market, Epstein believed, and the Sox also had the option of moving Renteria to another position, perhaps third base, because Bill Mueller's contract was to be up at the end of the 2005 season. In the long term, there was the chance that the Red Sox could have *both* Edgar Renteria and Hanley Ramirez, the latter of whom was athletic enough to play another position, perhaps center field.

No matter what happened in the future, Epstein saw Renteria as a good player, and no team could have too many of those. "Edgar's one of the most complete and dynamic players in the game. He does everything well," Epstein said on the day Renteria was signed. "That's hard to find, especially at the shortstop position. Offensively, he's a very solid hitter, a tough out. He's not an easy guy to pitch to. . . . And he's not a prolific power hitter, but he has a lot of pop. And defensively we have him as one of the top guys in all of baseball. He's very sure-handed, consistent, with good range, and he's fun to watch play shortstop."

Not long after Renteria signed with Boston, Cardinals manager Tony La Russa second-guessed the move, saying Renteria's quiet and sensitive nature was a poor fit for Boston. Most assumed that La Russa, frustrated that St. Louis could not keep one of its better players, was just whining that a bigger, wealthier club had lured away one of his stars. The Cardinals then replaced Renteria with Eckstein, who was released by the Angels. (If only the Red Sox had known.) The Angels subsequently signed Red Sox reject Orlando Cabrera to a four-year, $32 million deal—an $8 million annual average that was $2 million a year less than Renteria's $10 million—completing a game of musical chairs at one of the most important positions in baseball.

When the music stopped, Theo Epstein had his shortstop. He had lost Pedro Martinez and Derek Lowe, replacing them with David Wells and Matt Clement. He had just one more vacancy to fill. He had to sign a catcher.

DURING THE purge that was the 2004–5 off-season of the world champion Boston Red Sox, Jason Varitek was the one exception. Long regarded as the backbone of the Red Sox—many thought him as vital to Boston's success as Derek Jeter was to New York's—Varitek ultimately agreed to a four-year, $40 million contract that was to keep him in Boston through the 2008 season. There was a shortage of catching throughout the major leagues—historically, it had been an extremely difficult position to fill—and the Red Sox' decision to give Varitek such a big contract further magnified the importance of Dan Duquette's trading-deadline deal with the Seattle Mariners in July 1997.

Even Epstein, who rarely let emotion cloud his judgment, recognized Varitek's importance as a leader and a clubhouse presence, as the team's *soul*. Upon arriving in Boston prior to the 2002 season, Epstein came with the preconception that Varitek was terribly overrated, that Boston could find a far more affordable catcher who could give the club the same productivity or more at a lesser price. For a time, the Red Sox actually tried to trade him. Later, during the height of "Moneyball," it was suggested that Billy Beane would have made trading Varitek one of his first moves had he become general manager of the Red Sox, replacing Varitek with someone like Mark Johnson, whom Beane actually acquired for the Oakland A's in December 2002, after Beane had backed out of the deal to become general manager of the Red Sox.

But after being around Varitek every day and seeing firsthand what the Red Sox catcher brought to the team, Theo Epstein did a complete 180-degree turn, admitting as much during a discussion with a *Herald* reporter during the 2004 season.

"Is there any one player here who has changed your initial opinion of him the most?" the reporter asked.

"Yeah," Epstein replied. "Varitek."

Indeed, Jason Varitek was that rare player whom everyone respected, from reporters to teammates to team executives to fans. He was a professional in every sense of the word. Though some reporters found Varitek to be terse, even uncooperative, in interviews, much of that impression was forged during Varitek's early years with the club, when the player was still trying to establish himself. By the time the Red Sox won the 2004 World Series, Varitek's importance to the team was indisputable. Managers and coaches raved about his work ethic, commitment to detail, thorough preparation. In 2001, when the Red Sox ultimately unraveled in a season that led to the firing of manager Jimy Williams, a season-ending injury to Varitek was seen by many as more damning than injuries to either Nomar Garciaparra or Pedro Martinez. Without the latter two, the Red Sox continued to have some success. But once Varitek was lost to a broken elbow—an injury he suffered while diving into the on-deck circle to catch a foul pop-up in a game the Red Sox were winning by a landslide—it was as if the team's spinal cord had been ripped out. (Any suggestion that the events were unrelated was destroyed in 2006, when Varitek was lost to a knee injury and the team similarly came unglued.)

Varitek's injury was symbolic, a fact that was duly noted. Though he could just as easily have let the ball drop at no cost to the Red Sox, he made the play. Jason Varitek had one speed.

After protracted negotiations with agent Scott Boras, the Red Sox and the player came to terms, just before Christmas, on a four-year, $40 million contract. Though the Red Sox privately had been feeding the media information about how the productivity of catchers plummeted after their 35th birthday—Varitek would turn 33 in early April 2005—the club uncharacteristically caved in and gave Varitek four years. Boras, who had been seeking a five-year contract and was known to shoot for the moon, showed similar deference to his client and budged some, making it seem as if everyone knew that Jason Varitek wanted to remain in Boston, that the Red Sox wanted to keep him in Boston, and that both sides would make some sacrifices as a result.

While many media members questioned whether the Red Sox bid against themselves in the negotiations, they badly missed the point. Jason Varitek was vital to the on-field and off-field success of the Red Sox. The Red Sox *had* to keep him.

"We could not be happier. It's not every day that you're lucky enough to find a player who embodies everything you want your franchise to be," Epstein said at the Varitek signing. "When you're lucky enough to have that player, you don't let him get away. You lock him up for as long as you can and you make him the rock of your franchise."

The Red Sox gave their catcher something else besides the four-year, $40 million contract; they officially named him team captain. In the process, the Red Sox took the highly unusual step of stitching a C on the player's jersey, a custom typically practiced in hockey, but never before done in baseball. Varitek balked some at the gesture, in part because some regarded the letter as pretentious, but he eventually agreed, ultimately because he was proud of it. As much as any other athlete, Varitek was the kind of player who liked to show up and do his job, who liked to lead by example, who discouraged the making of excuses, and who believed that success went to those who worked hardest for it. He was hardly a self-promoter. But if someone who mattered took notice of his approach and wanted to recognize him for it, then Varitek felt he should accept the praise graciously. The C on his jersey, he believed, was proof that his way worked.

"Being a Red Sock, the city, it pulls a lot out of me because I think a lot of my values, a lot of the fans' values, a lot of the guys who played here have the same values," Varitek said. "They like to get dirty, fans like us to get dirty. We want to play hard and leave what we have on the field, and that's what they demand out of you here. It was for the longest time to win a championship here, to win one. Now we've won one. Now it's giving these people the same opportunity and the same chance to win another championship."

In December 2004, with all that had already happened to the Red Sox, it was if the Red Sox were letting their fans know: *We're moving on now. But we're taking Jason Varitek with us.*

IN A place like Boston, after an 86-year drought, winning one World Series is hard enough. Winning two in a row is damn near impossible.

If the Red Sox didn't know that already entering spring training 2005, they were about to find out. As good as the Red Sox were in 2004—and they were arguably the greatest team in franchise history, going 45-15 over their final 60 regular- and postseason games—the Sox had their share of luck, too. During the four ALCS wins over the Yankees and the World Series win over the Cardinals, every bounce seemed to go Boston's way. In Game 7 of the ALCS and Game 1 of the World Series, for instance, Sox second baseman Mark Bellhorn *twice* homered off the right-field foul pole. Those two blasts accounted for two of Bellhorn's three career postseason home runs, all of which were hit for the Red Sox in 2004. Of the 72 home runs Bellhorn had hit overall in regular-

and postseason play, 27 came in slightly more than a year with the Red Sox—an astonishing 37.5 percent of his career output.

Not long after Bellhorn's homers disappeared into the night, so did Bellhorn. Before the end of the 2005 season, the Red Sox released him.

Still, while most every championship team could cite a player like Bellhorn, the Red Sox had had other things in their favor too. During the entire 2004 season, the Red Sox did not have a single pitcher miss a start due to an injury, which was a truly astonishing development. Entering the season, Red Sox pitching coach Dave Wallace had said that his greatest fear concerning his team was injury, largely because Boston had little or no depth in the minor leagues. The trade for Curt Schilling had stripped away a few pitchers, albeit marginal ones, but even they'd had their place. During a 162-game season, a surplus of even mediocre arms was of great value given the attrition rate of pitching throughout the major leagues. Most teams had to plan on using at least seven or eight starting pitchers during the course of the year due to the inevitable injuries. The only thing teams could hope for was that the injuries were relatively minor and that they did not affect the best starters on the team.

In 2004, the Red Sox had no injuries to their starting pitchers. Schilling, Martinez, Lowe, Tim Wakefield, and Bronson Arroyo (the latter a nifty waiver-wire acquisition by Epstein in February 2003) made 157 of the team's 162 starts, with three of the remaining five going to the beleaguered Byung-Hyun Kim. (Kim started early in the year before being replaced by Arroyo due to continued ineffectiveness.) Of the remaining two Boston starts, one went to youngster Abe Alvarez when the club had a doubleheader early in the season, and the other went to Pedro Astacio in a meaningless September game after the Red Sox had clinched a playoff spot. That was the extent of any scrambling that Wallace and manager Terry Francona had to endure.

Though the Red Sox suggested that part of the reason for their pitchers' health was the manner in which they managed their staff, that was a self-serving explanation more than it was an accurate one. There wasn't a team in baseball that *tried* to injure its pitchers, and many teams handled their staff with the same philosophy as the Red Sox, giving their starters additional rest whenever possible. The bottom line was that the Red Sox, like the historic 2001 Seattle Mariners team that won 116 regular-season games and made it through the year with only five starters, were downright lucky. To get 157 starts from five pitchers was a wild aberration, something that historians like Bill James knew all too well.

What the Red Sox knew, too, is that such seasons could show up a little later than logic would suggest, like jet lag.

Before the Red Sox played even in a game in 2005, there were already signs that this year would be different. For starters, Schilling had undergone off-season ankle surgery in the wake of his October sacrifices, and it became increasingly clear during spring training that he would open the season on the disabled list; already, the 2005 Sox were trailing their blessed predecessors. By the end of the season, nine Boston pitchers would start games, most of them in place of Schilling, who, in the absence of Martinez, was now the undisputed ace of the staff.

The Red Sox wouldn't just lose more games to injury in 2005. They would lose *Schilling's* games.

Beyond Schilling's health, the most popular topic of spring training 2005 was obvious: 2004. For the first time in 86 years, the Red Sox were entering a season with the task of defending a world championship, and that served as a theme throughout the spring. No matter how much the Red Sox tried to escape it—and at times they did—the discussion always came back to October 2004. It was as if the season had never ended. Many Red Sox players had made appearances on national television broadcasts like *The Tonight Show* and *Late Show with David Letterman*, and that was just the beginning. Johnny Damon "wrote" a book, *Idiot*, a title that played off Damon's remarks during the postseason. ("We're just a bunch of idiots," Damon explained when asked how the Red Sox convinced themselves that they could overcome a seemingly insurmountable deficit.) Up and down the roster, players, coaches, and the manager were paid for speaking engagements and appearances. *Everybody* wanted a piece of the Red Sox, and the club often felt it had no choice but to oblige.

In Tampa, the spring home of the New York Yankees, the talk also centered on 2004. The Yankees had made significant changes during the off-season, bringing in Pavano for the long term and fortifying their starting rotation with left-hander Randy Johnson, the other half of Arizona's overpowering tandem that toppled the Yankees in the 2001 World Series. Given that Schilling was already in Boston and had been such a factor in the 2004 series between the teams, Johnson's presence in New York seemed only fitting. The entire baseball world was *still* talking about the Yankees and Red Sox, and not without reason.

During the 2003 and 2004 seasons, with each team winning an American League Championship Series, the Red Sox and Yankees had played 52 games in the regular season, with Boston holding a 27–25 edge. (In the postseason, it was 7–7.) During that time, the Red Sox outscored the Yankees by a mere 17 runs—a difference of one-third of a run per game. The 2004 season had been especially competitive. In the 26 games played between the teams during the most recent year, the Red Sox had scored 149 runs and the Yankees had scored 146. Derek Lowe's words in the wake of Boston's devastating Game 7 loss in 2003 were proving prophetic: "If we played 100 times, I think we'd win 50 and they'd win 50."

As eager as both the Red Sox and the Yankees were to put 2004 behind them, even the start of the regular season would not allow it. Thanks to a 2005 schedule that had been announced even before the team met in the '04 playoffs, the Red Sox and Yankees faced each other in the '05 season opener, at Yankee Stadium. The game featured the debuts of both Johnson and David Wells—the latter was filling in for Schilling against his former New York teammates—and the Yankees dominated, 9–2. The teams split the remaining two games of the series, the latter of which became overshadowed when Sox manager Terry Francona was driven away in an ambulance with chest pains before the game. Francona eventually was diagnosed with a viral infection that was one in a long list of maladies he suffered beginning in 2002, when he suffered a life-threatening pulmonary embolism. The Red Sox subsequently played the first week of the season without their manager, going 2-4 on a season-opening six-game road trip that also took them to Toronto.

Said Francona later that season when speaking to *Boston Globe* reporter Bob Hohler about the impact the setback had on him in 2005: "I never seemed to bounce back after that. It really took a toll."

Nonetheless, Francona was back in uniform and in the Boston dugout when the Red Sox played their home opener on April 11, 2005, against—who else?—the Yankees. Before Boston coasted to an 8–1 win behind starter Wakefield, the Sox handed out their championship rings in one of the truly unique days in the history of the organization, a celebration that even the Yankees seemed to enjoy. Led by manager Joe Torre and the elegant Derek Jeter, the Yankees applauded from their dugout as the Sox handed out their championship rings. And on a day when Dave Roberts and Derek Lowe returned to Boston despite being on the rosters of the San Diego Padres and Los Angeles Dodgers, respectively—the Sox had traded Roberts for outfielder Jay Payton, infielder Ramon Vazquez, and pitcher David Pauley—one of the biggest cheers of the day belonged to Yankees closer Mariano Rivera, whose contributions to the 2004 Red Sox (two blown saves) earned him a standing ovation.

While Rivera laughed and tipped his hat to the crowd, the former Red Sox took time to note what they were missing. "I was standing next to Jason [Varitek] and I said, 'You're lucky, you get to play here the next four years,'" Lowe said. "There's nothing like it."

After the game, Red Sox players seemed grateful to have been part of such a special event, though they felt something else, too: relief. The meetings with New York were especially draining during the season— for this reason, Francona despised the hype that came along with Yankees games—and the teams had already played six times before the

2005 season was two weeks old. As much as the Red Sox seemed content to celebrate 2004 one final time, they seemed more eager to begin 2005 so that their lives would once again possess some measure of normalcy. Going all the way back to the start of the dramatic 2003 season, the team had been on emotional overdrive for close to two years.

"I think today was a great day for closure," said first baseman Kevin Millar, effectively speaking for everyone in and around the organization. "It was a great day for everyone in the city to come out and celebrate together, but now we've got to turn the page and focus on this season and winning another championship."

Said a far more direct Francona in the privacy of his own office after most everyone had gone: "To be honest, I'm glad it's over."

The Red Sox looked exhausted.

And the season had just started.

WHEN THINGS got back to normal, it seemed as if the Red Sox regressed. The 2005 Red Sox went right back to being what they were in 2003 and 2002, a good offensive team with obvious flaws on the pitching staff. The absence of Schilling was not the only problem. Early in the year, it became terribly apparent that Keith Foulke was a shell of his former self. During the regular season and postseason combined, Foulke had pitched in 83 games covering 97 innings in 2004, and one could only wonder whether the workload had begun to catch up with him. Overall, from 2000 to 2004, Foulke had made 369 appearances in regular- and postseason play, an average of 74 per year. During the same period, no closer in baseball had pitched in as many games. In the end, the combination of workload and job stress—he was, after all, the closer—wore down a man who had been so durable that many baseball people had begun to regard him as indestructible.

But while Schilling was enjoying the continued praise that went along with his physical sacrifice during the playoffs, Foulke received no such latitude. Part of the reason was that Foulke had not undergone surgery, so most people assumed he was healthy. Part was that he was not nearly as endearing as Schilling, whom even members of Congress had suggested should be a "politician" when Schilling appeared in Washington during the congressional hearings on steroids. So Schilling got a free pass, while Foulke did not, even though the latter deserved one just as much as the former.

During his first season in Boston, Foulke had been nothing short of brilliant. In 72 regular-season appearances covering 83 innings, Foulke went 5-3 with a 2.17 ERA and 32 saves. In the postseason, he was even better. Foulke made 11 appearances in the playoffs—including all four World Series games—and posted a platinum 0.64 ERA, allowing just one run in 14 innings. He struck out 18 and was such an enormous factor in the club's success that many believed he, and not Manny Ramirez, should have been elected Most Valuable Player of the World Series.

But when Foulke struggled in 2005, he immediately became a target for media and fans, the latter of whom Foulke sparred with verbally. When the pitcher blew a game against the Cleveland Indians in late June, the fans at Fenway Park booed him mercilessly. Unlike Schilling, Foulke was not adept at public relations, at "playing the game" off the field as well as on it. "I'm not inviting them to my World Series celebration," a typically surly Foulke said when asked about the booing. "They can boo, they can cuss. . . . If they don't want me to do the job, tell them to go tell management. I've done a lot of good for this team. They pay their money. Let them boo. Does it look like it bothers me?" Added the pitcher, whose guts far outweighed his smarts: "[The fans] aren't going to make it any harder for me to look in the mirror, or more embarrassing for me to walk into this clubhouse and look into the faces of my teammates, than I [already] am to walk out and see Johnny from Burger King booing me."

Despite all that Foulke accomplished during his Red Sox career, it was the last remark that would serve as the legacy of his time in Boston. *Johnny from Burger King.* If it wasn't bad enough that Foulke was pitching poorly and was frustrated, now he was belittling the fans. Red Sox teammates and officials knew that Foulke was only making the entire matter harder, not easier, and that he had somehow managed to make himself a public enemy despite having been a conquering hero only months earlier.

Like Foulke, Schilling also failed to regain his 2004 form—in either 2005 or beyond. The 2005 season proved especially difficult because Schilling clearly lacked strength in his right ankle, and Sox officials privately wondered whether the pitcher's sacrifices had effectively cost him his career. But in Schilling's case, at least personally, the 2004 title had been worth precisely $15 million to him—thanks to his creative contract, he received a $2 million bump in pay in 2005 and was guaranteed a $13 million contract for 2007—though no amount of money could have equaled what he brought to the Red Sox and to Boston by delivering the team's first world title since World War I. Said Schilling when asked whether he had any regrets about pitching on an ankle that was sewn together during the playoffs: "If I never pitch another day in the big leagues, it will have been worth every day."

Through it all, the Red Sox remained in contention largely as the result of two things. First, the Yankees got off to a miserable start—they were a mere 11-19 after their first 30 games and were no better than .500 (39-39) roughly halfway through the season. Second, the Sox still possessed the same undying will to win that they had first displayed in 2003, thanks largely to the presence of players like Johnny Damon, David Ortiz, and Kevin Millar, the last of whom was struggling through a difficult year. Newcomer Matt Clement did more than his share to pick up the injured pitching staff—he went 10-2 in his first half season in Boston—and Schilling at least partially made up for Foulke's problems by briefly becoming the Boston closer.

The Red Sox were scrambling, to be sure, but their experiences during the previous years had made them adept during fire drills. But in the long term, the Sox knew, they would have difficulty if their pitchers didn't perform better, just like in 2003.

"It never fails," manager Francona said more than once as his team struggled through the regular season. "Whenever you think you have enough pitching or too much pitching, you're probably fooling yourself."

Deep down, the manager knew. The Red Sox didn't have enough.

WHEN THE Red Sox qualified for the postseason again in 2005, despite their considerable shortcomings, many regarded it as nothing short of a miracle.

The scientific explanation was that David Ortiz carried them there.

For all that Ortiz did for the Red Sox during October 2004, the 2005 season proved an extension of his heroics. The only difference was that the games didn't mean quite as much. In the wake of his October performance, Ortiz had garnered more fan votes to appear at the All-Star Game than any player in baseball, something never previously accomplished by a member of the Red Sox. Not one of the great players the Red Sox had boasted in their history—not Ted Williams, Carl Yastrzemski, Jim Rice, or Wade Boggs—had ever led in the fan balloting as Ortiz did in July 2005.

It was yet another reminder that the Sox were still feeling the effects of 2004. "I don't know. I guess people follow you and they really appreciate what we do on the field," Ortiz said when asked about his new popularity. "They appreciate the good things they hear about you, I guess. That has a lot to do with it."

Said pitcher Clement, who similarly represented the Sox at the All-Star Game: "Obviously, you had to be under a rock to not see what he did in the playoffs last year. It shows how much the Red Sox are in demand. It shows the kind of presence he's become in baseball."

And as impossible as it seemed, Ortiz was still growing in stature. In fact, thanks largely to the production of Ortiz and Manny Ramirez, the Red Sox were able to overcome most every shortcoming they possessed, from injuries to a relative shortage of offensive depth to the ineffectiveness of both their starters and relievers. In 2005, Ortiz and Ramirez were so damned good that it simply did not matter. Combined,

Ortiz and Ramirez would finish the 2005 season with 92 home runs and 292 RBIs—an average of 46 homers and 146 RBI *each*—and their final numbers were nearly a perfect split of their aggregate. Ortiz finished with 47 home runs and 148 RBIs, Ramirez with 45 homers and 144 RBIs.

Despite that parity, it was Ortiz whom many regarded as the team's obvious candidate for the American League Most Valuable Player Award, an honor for which only one other player seemed a true contender: Alex Rodriguez. While Ortiz was carrying the Red Sox, Rodriguez was similarly masking the deficiencies of the Yankees, following a disappointing New York debut in 2004 (a .286 average, 36 home runs, 106 RBIs) with the kind of monster season (a .321 average, 48 home runs, 130 RBIs) that many had envisioned when the Yankees acquired Rodriguez in the first place. The obvious difference was that Rodriguez played a position in the field (third base), while Ortiz did not, and no true designated hitter had ever been elected a MVP.

But if Rodriguez had a sizable advantage over Ortiz in the field, Ortiz had a similar advantage in one offensive statistic: clutch hitting. While numbers crunchers no less recognized than Bill James had argued that the concept of hitting under pressure was largely mythical—there was almost no way to effectively measure it—Ortiz was nonetheless convincing people based on what they *saw*. In situations defined as "close and late" by STATS Inc., Ortiz in 2005 led all major-league players in home runs (11) and RBIs (33) while batting a sterling .346. Rodriguez, by contrast, ranked a 29th and 66th in those same categories, suggesting that he and Ortiz did not belong in the same conversation on the topic.

From 2004 to 2006, Ortiz became so proficient at delivering game-winning hits that even mathematically minded Sox owner John Henry became convinced that the player possessed an indisputable intangible. And by the end of the 2007 season, Ortiz had an incredible 19 career *walk-off* hits, game winners that came on the final pitch of any contest. An incredible 16 of those hits came during his five-year career with the

Red Sox, with the large majority taking place from 2004 to 2006. Even more incredible was that of Ortiz's 16 walk-offs with Boston, 10 were home runs. Said manager Francona on repeated occasions during Ortiz's career in Boston: "I can't imagine anybody being more important to their team than he's been to ours."

In the final months of the 2005 season, Ortiz was a one-man wrecking crew. Beginning with a game-tying home run with two outs and the bases empty in the bottom of the ninth inning in a game at Detroit—such a hit was one of the many not reflected in the walk-off statistic—Ortiz single-handedly pulled the Red Sox back from the grave on several occasions. By then, the Yankees had long since righted their ship—going a sizzling 56-28 over their final 84 contests—and the Red Sox had grown so desperate in their bullpen that they were relying on rookies Jonathan Papelbon and Craig Hansen, the latter of whom had been drafted *in June* and was in the big leagues by September.

But thanks to Ortiz, the Red Sox stayed in the hunt. Two weeks after saving the Red Sox in Detroit, Ortiz hit a game-winning home run against the Anaheim Angels at Fenway Park. Shortly after that, he hit two homers in a game at Toronto, the second breaking a tie in the 11th inning. Not long after *that*, with the Yankees breathing down the Red Sox' necks and having pulled into a tie for first place in the American League East, Ortiz had another two-homer game to propel the Sox to a lopsided win at Tampa Bay.

Even Ortiz seemed to recognize that what he was doing far exceeded any reasonable expectations. "Looking back, I don't think I've ever played better than I did in the final two months of 2005, in August and September, for that long a period of time," Ortiz wrote in *Big Papi*. "Usually, when you get hot, it lasts a couple of weeks, maybe a month. Then you might cool off a little, even if for just a little while, and wait for the next hot streak. That's the way the game works sometimes, so you have to take every hit you get when you're feeling good at the plate. But in the final two months of 2005, it seemed like I felt good all the time. I don't know why. But every time I stepped up to the plate, no matter what the situation was, I felt like I was going to do some damage. My confidence was really high. And I think it showed."

That said, the Red Sox looked more vulnerable than ever. Despite Ortiz's two-homer game in Tampa, the Red Sox actually lost two of three during the series to the Rays, annually one of the worst teams in baseball. The Sox were banged up. They were tired and running on fumes. Their pitching staff was in shambles, without any apparent stability. Yet the Sox somehow remained in the race. Beyond the performance of Ortiz, Boston's place in the playoff race defied all logic. The Red Sox looked very much like a onetime champion boxer who made the poor choice to fight well beyond his prime, relying on grit and guile in the absence of speed and skill.

The Red Sox looked punch-drunk.

Yet they were still on their feet.

Ortiz seemed especially frustrated. For whatever reason, he seemed to have more energy than the rest of his teammates. Though hopelessly optimistic, even at the worst times, even Ortiz seemed to recognize that the 2005 Sox were on their last legs in Tampa. "This was the season for us to be 10 games up [on the Yankees]," Ortiz admitted to reporters after one of the Tampa defeats. "The Yankees can't play any worse than they did at the beginning of the season this year. They can't play any worse than that."

When the reporters cleared away from Ortiz's locker, the player continued packing his belongings for a flight to Baltimore, where the Red Sox would go on to sweep a three-game series that seemed more like a stay of execution. The Sox subsequently returned home for series against the Toronto Blue Jays and Yankees—yes, series with the Yankees were bookends to the 2005 Boston baseball season—and it was during the latter series, on the final weekend of the year, that the Red Sox lost the division to New York in a tiebreaker. Both clubs finished with 95 victories, leaving the Red Sox with yet another wild-card berth, but the second-place finish meant that the Sox would open the playoffs on the road against a Chicago White Sox club that had posted the best record in baseball.

Regardless, the trip to the playoffs was like a gift. The Red Sox didn't seem to belong there, and they knew it. During a private conversation with Francona, a reporter said to the manager that the Red Sox had no right making the playoffs, and the manager agreed: "Tell me about it," Francona replied. In its own way, that was a testament to the Red Sox' perseverance, to their drive, to their *instinct* to continue competing, like the punch-drunk fighter, because that was their nature.

Deep down, as the regular season was drawing to a close, even the players seemed to wonder how they were staying on their feet. "So what do you think?" Ortiz privately asked a *Herald* reporter after the crowd had cleared from his locker in Tampa. "Should we pack up or what?"

As it turned out, against all odds, the Red Sox ended up packing their bags for the playoffs to defend their world title.

But it was a very short trip.

THE SERIES against the White Sox really was no series at all. Because the Red Sox had to play to the wire to secure their place in the postseason—in the end, a breakdown by the Cleveland Indians got the Red Sox into the playoffs as much as Boston's never-say-die attitude— the Game 1 starter was Clement, who had deteriorated badly during the second half of the season. After going 10-2 with a 3.85 ERA during the first half of the year, Clement went 3-4 with a 5.72 ERA after the All-Star break. What happened to the Red Sox at the end of 2005 was what had happened to the Angels at the end of 2004. They had to expend so much energy during the final week of the season to get into the playoffs that they had nothing left when they got there.

Matched against White Sox ace Jose Contreras—traded by the Yankees to Chicago, Contreras had finally become the ace many had envisioned—Clement was slaughtered in Game 1. The Boston right-hander allowed five runs in the first inning and eight runs in 3⅓ innings overall, taking the loss in a 14–2 beating that put the Boston in an immediate hole. The Red Sox were much more competitive in Game 2 before a critical error by second baseman Tony Graffanino (acquired during the season to replace the ineffective Bellhorn) sparked a five-run Chicago rally, resulting in a 5–4 Red Sox loss and ruining what was otherwise a sensational performance by left-hander David Wells. The series moved back to Boston for Game 3, when the Red Sox were trailing 4–3 in the bottom of the sixth inning. Showing more life than they had at any other point during the series, the Red Sox loaded the bases with nobody out and appeared to be shifting the momentum when White Sox manager Ozzie Guillen went to his bullpen.

Facing the lower part of a Boston lineup that had led the major leagues in runs scored for a third straight season, White Sox right-hander Orlando Hernandez (a former Yankee) recorded the three biggest outs of the series, retiring Jason Varitek, Graffanino, and Johnny Damon without allowing the ball to leave the infield. As an elated Hernandez sprinted off the mound having stranded all three Boston runners, it was as if the customary sellout crowd at Fenway knew the Boston season was about to end.

Three innings later, when White Sox closer Bobby Jenks completed a perfect ninth inning by retiring Edgar Renteria on a groundout, the 2005 Red Sox season officially came to a close with a 5–3 defeat.

"We went so deep [into the playoffs] last year. We asked a lot physically of people that may have hurt us this year a little bit, but I don't think anybody would trade that," said Francona, whose club at one point played on 30 consecutive days during the month of September. "We won 95 games in a season that did not go right and I will not apologize for that. We busted our ass to do the best we could. . . . I was very proud of what we accomplished. The 95 wins—I think that could have slipped away from us a little bit because it was not easy for us to win games sometimes. I think we all found out that every time you think you have enough pitching, you don't. If you guys ask me about an excess of pitching in the future, I'll be thrilled."

The Red Sox found out other things, too, specifically about Clement. While the Red Sox had believed Clement could be a far more effective pitcher in Boston with a better team behind him, the 2005 season instead proved an old adage: You are what you are. Had Clement been the kind of frontline pitcher the Red Sox were hoping for, his previous teams (the Florida Marlins, San Diego Padres, and, most recently, Chicago Cubs) would have been elevated by his performance. Instead, the opposite happened. Clement's performance got dragged down by the teams for which he played, which meant that he was probably a mediocre pitcher, just as his career record and ERA suggested when he came to Boston in the first place.

But given the way Boston's previous off-season had gone, the Red Sox had had many targets on their off-season list before Clement. When the pitcher signed in Boston, Epstein knew he wasn't getting a staff ace. Publicly, Epstein acknowledged that the Red Sox needed more pitching, but privately, he had more in mind than just the 2006 season. The Red Sox were getting close to an influx of young talent from their minor-league system, Epstein believed, but the club would probably need another year to realize it. The club went into the off-season preaching caution—just as Sox officials had done a year earlier—and promptly began the organizational meetings that took place after every season, when clubs evaluated all of their players and made their plans for the winter. "This wasn't a perfect club—there probably wasn't a perfect club [in all of baseball] this year," Epstein said. "But the manager, the coaches, and the players were able to endure some things."

While the Red Sox got ready for winter, the White Sox breezed through the playoffs, finishing 11-1 to win their first World Series since 1917. (The Yankees, like the Red Sox, were eliminated in the first round, by the Anaheim Angels.) Chicago's season was a fitting development given that, a year earlier, the Red Sox had won their first world title since 1918, though most people in Boston didn't pay much notice when the White Sox swept the Houston Astros in four games. In New England, people were far more interested in how the Red Sox could fix things.

At the time, nobody envisioned the simmering controversy that would serve as the one truly dark period in the John Henry era.

ONE STEP BACK

FOR ANYONE INCLINED TO PAY ATTENTION, THERE HAD LONG been signs of an approaching conflict.

During the final two weeks of the regular season, after a trying 2005 campaign and all that had happened during the two years before it, both manager Terry Francona and general manager Theo Epstein showed signs of frustration. Francona snapped at WBZ-TV reporter Dan Roche for a relatively tame question during a pregame media session in Baltimore, an eruption for which Francona later apologized; Epstein was sitting in the visitors' dugout at Tampa Bay's Tropicana Field—where Ortiz had similarly expressed frustration—when the general manager showed rare emotion. "Let me tell you," Epstein said to a re-porter sitting nearby. "Being the general manager of your hometown team isn't everything it's cracked up to be."

Theo Epstein wasn't quite 32 when the 2005 baseball season ended, but he had far more on his mind than just the fatal flaws in his baseball team. For starters, Epstein could not understand why media and fans were incapable of seeing the bigger picture. Didn't they understand what he was trying to do? With the possible exception of the New York Yankees—or, perhaps, including them—expecting to win every year was unrealistic. Given Boston's resources, Epstein believed that the Red Sox should make the playoffs seven of every ten years, which was still a lofty goal. That kind of ratio should still deliver the Red Sox more than their share of world titles, though like Oakland A's general manager

Billy Beane, Epstein believed there were far more variables at play in the postseason than during the regular season. Regardless, he was willing to take his chances.

Beyond that, Epstein was growing increasingly frustrated with his contract negotiations, which were going nowhere. (Privately, Epstein allies said there were no negotiations at all.) Epstein's current contract was due to expire on October 31, 2005—as did those of many baseball executives, coaches, and managers—and he was annoyed that team president Larry Lucchino, who was representing the club in the matter, was taking things right down to the wire. In baseball, as in many professional sports, management contracts frequently were extended *before* the final year of any existing deal to avoid the appearance that an executive (or manager) was on the hot seat. If someone like, say, Terry Francona was allowed to go into the final year of a contract, it was undoubtedly an indication that Francona had to win to keep his job, and those were hardly the best terms under which anyone would want to perform.

As a result, people like Lucchino typically felt that they were being held hostage by the process, which often resulted in teams paying executives well after a member of management had been dismissed. Still, given the cutthroat nature of professional sports, most people regarded the extra year of security as being akin to a severance payment, which is why most contracts were extended a year early.

In Epstein's case, the matter was compounded by the fact that the Red Sox had entered the 2005 campaign *having just won the World Series,* which left little to debate concerning the job Epstein had done. During his first two years as general manager, Epstein had taken the Red Sox to Game 7 of the 2003 American League Championship Series (with one of the most prolific offenses in baseball history) and to their first championship in 86 years. There wasn't much of a gray area with regard to his impact. Yet Lucchino never addressed Epstein's contract during spring training and never engaged him on the matter during the regular season, which fostered understandable resentment in the young and talented general manager of the Red Sox.

By the time the Red Sox began their organizational meetings immediately after the loss to the White Sox, the tension between apprentice and mentor was palpable. According to author Seth Mnookin, who had been given an office at Fenway Park during the off-season to work on his book, *Feeding the Monster*—essentially, Mnookin was commissioned by owner Henry to write the Red Sox' answer to *Moneyball*—Epstein knew that things with the Red Sox might get worse before they got better. With regard to pitching, baseball's upcoming crop of free agents was particularly weak, and Epstein saw no sense in spending large sums of money for another mediocre pitcher like Matt Clement. He believed that patience was the far better course of action, that the Red Sox should be more open about acknowledging to their fans that they sometimes had to make long-term decisions that required short-term sacrifices.

At the very least, Epstein believed, the 2006 Red Sox would be a decent team. If things went right, they could make the playoffs again. But Epstein knew as early as the fall of 2005 that a world championship in 2006 was highly unlikely, and he believed that everyone should prepare for it. Said the young general in the organizational meeting, according to Mnookin: "We can be both a large-revenue club [that can afford to sign high-priced free agents] and have a strong farm system. But it's probably not going to be a seamless transition. This year we had a great year. We will probably be worse next year [in 2006]."

For Lucchino, who ran Boston's business operation, making such an admission to the fans was entirely out of the question. As it was, the Red Sox had the highest ticket prices in baseball and had sold out every home game for nearly two full seasons. (The streak began during May of the inspiring 2003 season.) Lucchino knew that any public admission of the club's intention to take the proverbial step back would significantly hurt the Red Sox' business operation on a number of levels. The Sox might not be able to command as much for their tickets, some of which would go unsold. Advertising revenue at the ballpark and the Sox-owned New England Sports Network would go down. The Red Sox would take a significant financial hit that would more than likely upset shareholders who had helped fund the sale of the Red Sox in the first place.

Both men made valid points.

But while the Red Sox internally tussled over these issues as they began preparing for 2006, the problems between Epstein and Lucchino clearly went beyond any difference in philosophy. In most major-league franchises the baseball operation and the business operation frequently clashed. What was good for the players wasn't always good for the organization, and the conflicts could range from the simple to the complex. Only a year earlier, Lucchino had wanted Red Sox players to wear their game jerseys in the cold and wet of their championship parade, prompting him to butt heads with his manager, Terry Francona, who had suggested that the weather made it difficult. Two years later, when the Sox were preparing to open their season in Japan against the Oakland A's as part of a Major League Baseball international promotional campaign, the Sox did so despite concerns over the obvious effect that such extensive travel could have on the players. Those were the kinds of internal disputes and negotiations that every team had to deal with.

In October 2005, there was clearly much more involved between Epstein and Lucchino. While the World Series victory of 2004 had made Epstein into a local celebrity, he had also matured considerably in the three years since he had been hired. Like nothing else, winning a world title could provide self-validation for a player, coach, manager, or executive in any sport, and even the older, more experienced Francona seemed far more sure of himself in 2005 than in 2004. Some of that was because Francona had already been around the block once, but some came from the respect people showed him after Boston's World Series title. Immediately after the World Series, for example, Francona was out dining with bench coach Brad Mills and their wives at Maggiano's, an Italian restaurant near Boston's famous Park Plaza hotel. When the couples got up to leave after a quiet meal during which not a single person bothered them for an autograph, the other patrons in the restaurant stood up and gave the manager and bench coach of the Red Sox a standing ovation. Said Francona years later: "It's still one of the cooler things that's ever happened to me."

In Epstein's case, the World Series win had a similar and predictable effect. Like the high school freshman athlete who was now a senior co-captain, Epstein seemed to feel empowered to speak, authorized to make decisions. He was more *secure*. Yet his relationship with Lucchino sometimes seemed as if it had not advanced at all—or if it had, it had advanced much slower—and that left Epstein frustrated, resentful, even downright angry.

By the time October 31 neared, Epstein was so blind with rage and the relationship between the two had deteriorated so badly that an explosion was inevitable. According to reports in the *Herald* and *Globe,* Lucchino's initial contract offer to Epstein put him in the financial class of someone like former Tampa Bay Devil Rays general manager Chuck Lamar, who had just been fired. (Epstein rightfully deemed that offer an insult.) Lucchino, meanwhile, seemed to think it preposterous that Epstein was seeking a salary that would put him in the same class as someone like accomplished and highly respected Atlanta Braves general manager John Schuerholz, who was believed to be earning somewhere in the neighborhood of $1.5 million.

And then there was this: Three years earlier, in their pursuit of Billy Beane, the Red Sox had agreed to pay Beane an average annual salary of $2.5 million before Beane backed out of the deal, leading the Sox to Epstein, whom they signed for a paltry $350,000 a year.

Now, Theo Epstein wanted his money and, more important, the respect that came with it.

And so back and forth the sides went.

Back and forth.

Back and forth.

On October 25, the night the Chicago White Sox defeated the Houston Astros in Game 3 of the World Series, *Boston Globe* reporter Gordon Edes uncovered the information that Epstein had a rejected a three-year proposal valued at $1.2 million per year, an eye-opening development for two reasons. First, despite getting within striking distance of Schuerholz's annual salary of $1.5 million, Epstein was digging in his heels. Second, some of Epstein's allies found it odd that such information would end up in the media, particularly when Epstein was not allowed to employ an agent in the talks. (This was one of Lucchino's conditions.) Ultimately, with the trust between Lucchino and Epstein having fully eroded, Epstein's camp concluded that Lucchino was now out to make the young general manager look like a greedy and ungrateful soul. "I can see the headlines now," one Epstein supporter privately cracked about what he perceived as a smear campaign. " 'Epstein Fails to Help Old Lady Across Street.' "

With the gloves now off, Lucchino and Epstein both went on the offensive, playing the *Globe* and *Herald* off against each other in what became an ugly, embarrassing, and very public dispute. Because the *Globe* had a 17 percent ownership stake in the Red Sox—and also because Lucchino and trusted aide Charles Steinberg had a long-standing relationship with *Globe* columnist Dan Shaughnessy that went back to when all worked in Baltimore—Boston soon became polarized like at no other time since New England Patriots coach Bill Parcells and owner Robert Kraft had a similar and very public power struggle during the Patriots' improbable run to the 1997 Super Bowl, where the team eventually lost to the Green Bay Packers. Parcells subsequently broke his contract with the Patriots to accept a job with the New York Jets, leading to a negotiation in which the Pats received compensatory draft picks.

Years later, by the time the Parcells-Kraft feud had fully played out, the Patriots had suffered through the disastrous reign of Pete Carroll, which in turn led them to hire longtime and trusted Parcells lieutenant Bill Belichick, now regarded as perhaps the greatest coach in NFL history.

What a long, strange trip it was.

In the case of Epstein versus Lucchino, the *Herald* and *Globe* engaged in a full-scale newspaper war, the former more frequently backing Epstein, the latter more frequently backing Lucchino. Despite it all,

Lucchino believed that the club and its general manager had reached an agreement on the night of Saturday, October 29, though Epstein still had his doubts. On the morning of Sunday, October 30, Epstein awoke to a *Globe* column (written by Shaughnessy) that unflatteringly painted Epstein as an ingrate who owed a great deal more to his mentor, a fact that made Epstein furious.

Shaughnessy's column came a few days after a *Herald* columnist had similarly skewered Lucchino, who was similarly enraged by the criticism. On the day the *Herald* column appeared, Lucchino was to make his weekly appearance on Boston's all-sports talk-radio station, WEEI. But he never went through with the appearance. "He can't come to the phone right now," Lucchino's wife, Stacey, reportedly told the station's producers. "He's busy shredding the *Herald*."

On Monday, October 31, 2005—Halloween—the *Globe* published a story indicating that Epstein and the club had agreed on a three-year contract that was to be announced that afternoon, the last day of Epstein's existing contract. The *Herald* took a far less optimistic approach, saying that Epstein's fate was still undecided, that the young general manager was infuriated by a weekend *Globe* report that characterized him in a poor light. By the end of the entire ordeal, dressed in a gorilla suit on Halloween night, Epstein left Fenway Park without being identified after having turned in his resignation, hitting the Red Sox and Lucchino with the kind of haymaker that nobody on the outside had deemed possible.

Only months later, when Mnookin's book was released, did many fans start to realize the depth of the problems between the president of the Red Sox and the team's general manager, whose relationship looked as dysfunctional as that of an overbearing father and his son. "Later that afternoon, Epstein paced among the cubicles outside of his basement office," Mnookin wrote, referring to Epstein's state of mind after the team's organizational meeting in mid-October. " 'What a joke,' . . . [Epstein] said to no one in particular. 'Two more weeks. Two more weeks and I might be a free man.' "

Two weeks later, he was.

And the Red Sox were a mess.

IN THE aftermath, the Red Sox made an attempt to clean up the mess. With Lucchino nowhere to be found, Henry and Epstein addressed the media on November 2 at Fenway Park, in the same room where Henry, Lucchino, and Tom Werner held their introductory press conference after being identified as the new Red Sox owners in December 2001. The session attracted reporters from all over New England—television news reporters and the local sportswriters—though many of them went home dissatisfied. Expecting some blunt explanation for Epstein's departure, some media members seemed frustrated when Henry and Epstein spoke in veiled terms.

Nonetheless, Henry questioned whether he was fit to own the franchise, while Epstein sternly looked on during the kind of circus reminiscent of previous Red Sox history. "Never in my wildest dreams did I think [Epstein's departure] would happen," said Henry, who sometimes seemed on the verge of tears. "I thought Theo was going to be the general manager here for the rest of my life."

Said Epstein: "In the end, we had some very honest talks during that last week. The way I look at it, you have to be all-in. You have to believe in every aspect of the organization to do the job with your whole heart. In the end, it wasn't a fit."

Had many media members read between the lines, they would have received the answer they were seeking. Theo Epstein didn't believe in Larry Lucchino anymore, and Lucchino probably didn't believe in Epstein either.

Following a three-year period during which the new owners and operators of the Red Sox had done everything from improving the team on the field to restoring Fenway Park, imperfections were now more easily identified. As tenacious and accomplished as Lucchino was, the entire series of events suggested that he lacked finesse, that he allowed his ego to get the best of him, that he seemed intent on keeping Epstein under his thumb after giving him the keys to the kingdom. In Epstein's case, he was probably far too sensitive and, given his age, a little immature. As for Henry, he had wilted in the face of conflict, missing countless opportunities to intervene and serve as an important liaison between his president and his general manager, both of whom he regarded highly. Later, in fact, Henry admitted that Epstein had gone to him as far back as August, when the general manager was becoming especially frustrated in attempted talks with Lucchino. Rebuffed by Lucchino, Epstein felt the need to tell Henry that negotiations were not going well, a concern the owner all but brushed off. *They'll work it out*, Henry had assumed.

In the end, they did not.

Showing typical resiliency, Lucchino quickly moved on and began the search for a new general manager, refusing to close the door on a possible Epstein return. ("We'll keep the light on in the window," Lucchino said quite gracefully.) A cancer survivor, Lucchino was nothing if not tough. As much as Lucchino's relationship with Epstein had self-destructed, Lucchino had some incredibly loyal allies, many of them young people whom Lucchino had provided with a most invaluable gift: opportunity. Lucchino wasn't afraid to hire young people, often took pride in teaching them, in the way that Edward Bennett Williams had taught him. There were as many people in the Boston organization who disliked Epstein as there were who disliked Lucchino, which made perfect sense. One had molded the other. Given the nature of their relationship and their respective responsibilities, a conflict between Lucchino and Epstein was inevitable if Epstein was the person Lucchino had long since identified him to be, a driven, smart, and hungry young man capable of great things.

It wasn't that long ago, after all, that people had said the same thing about a young Larry Lucchino.

Proceeding deliberately—just as he had throughout the pursuit of Beane—Lucchino explored a number of possibilities to replace Epstein, ranging from San Diego Padres general manager Kevin Towers (who pulled himself out of the running) to Atlanta Braves assistant

Dayton Moore to former Montreal Expos general manager Jim Beattie, the man who had traded Pedro Martinez to Boston for Carl Pavano and Tony Armas Jr. in November 1997. There was some suggestion that Lucchino wanted to hire Beattie, who had attended Dartmouth, but that Henry was less than thrilled at the prospect. When Moore later followed Towers's lead and withdrew from the race, Lucchino settled on an unusual arrangement in which former Epstein assistants Jed Hoyer and Ben Cherington were named co–general managers as part of a structure in which longtime baseball man Bill Lajoie and highly regarded evaluator Craig Shipley would have significant say.

Hired to be Epstein's right-hand man and sounding board back in the fall of 2002, Lajoie had actually resigned from the Boston organization prior to Epstein's departure, largely because he felt there was no longer a need for his services. But after Epstein resigned, Lucchino asked Lajoie to return on a three-month contract, something Lajoie agreed to on the provision that he would reevaluate his commitment to the organization at the end of that period.

Throughout the winter of 2005–6 and less than three years after the Red Sox went into the season with the closer-by-committee experiment, the Red Sox effectively operated as an oligarchy, a *management-by-committee* that ultimately reported to Lucchino, regardless of when Hoyer and Cherington were officially named. (For the record, it was the middle of December.) Further complicating matters was the fact that Epstein was maintaining some level of communication with the club, specifically with the younger Hoyer and Cherington, whom he was consulting on personnel matters despite having resigned. Henry allowed the unusual arrangement because he felt that Epstein was burned out— Epstein denied this—and he believed that it was a good way for Epstein to stay involved in matters (which the former GM clearly cared about) without having to deal with the day-to-day pressures of being general manager.

With all of those cooks in the kitchen, the Red Sox set out to retool their roster, setting their sights on a frontline pitcher. The best available free agent at the time was a hard-throwing right-hander named A. J. Burnett, who had begun his career with the Florida Marlins when Henry owned that club. Under the watch of amateur scouting director David Chadd—the talented Chadd later came to the Red Sox before moving on to the Detroit Tigers—the Marlins had become known for drafting and developing a host of good young pitchers, from Burnett to Brad Penny to Josh Beckett, the last of whom was also thought to be available by trade.

Empowered by Lucchino to act as representatives on behalf of the club, Lajoie Shipley, Cherington, and Hoyer met with Marlins officials during the annual general managers' meetings in November, the same meetings where then-GM Duquette had acquired Martinez eight years earlier. There the Red Sox, like many teams, learned that the highly regarded Beckett was indeed available by trade, though the price was considerable. In addition to a package of frontline prospects that almost certainly would have to include gifted shortstop Hanley Ramirez—the man whom Epstein and most everyone else regarded as the heir apparent—the Marlins were insisting that any team interested in Beckett would also have to take third baseman Mike Lowell, who was coming off a positively dreadful season with two years and $18 million remaining on what was originally a four-year, $32 million contract.

Even eight years after the Martinez deal between Boston and Montreal, such deals were still common in baseball, largely because financially struggling teams like the Marlins could not afford to keep high-salaried players. The difference this time was that Florida was trying to rid itself of Lowell's contract by including Beckett, then a 25-year-old right-hander coming off a 15-win season. While Beckett had not quite lived up to the expectations many had for him, he had been regarded as a future ace since the Marlins chose him with the number two overall selection in the 1999 amateur draft. Beckett zipped through Florida's minor-league system and made his major-league debut as a 21-year-old in 2001. Two years later, at the age of 23, he was named Most Valuable Player of the World Series after a complete-game shutout of the New York Yankees in the decisive Game 6, less than two weeks after Aaron Boone and the Yankees had ended the Red Sox' season.

Though Beckett was not eligible for free agency until after the 2007 season, signing him to a long-term contract was essential in order to make such a trade worthwhile. No team in its right mind would trade a player like Hanley Ramirez (who had *six years* to go before free agency) for two years of Beckett, no matter how great the pitcher's talent. On top of it all, Beckett came with some health questions—specifically, many wondered about the durability of his shoulder—which made the deal an indisputable risk.

Naturally, the upside of such a trade was also considerable. If Josh Beckett turned into the kind of pitcher that many foresaw, the Red Sox could have themselves a young Roger Clemens.

Given the complications of the deal, Sox officials engaged in extensive debate and discussion as to their best course of action. On the one hand, the Sox could try to sign a pitcher like Burnett, who was inferior to Beckett but who would require only the commitment of a long-term contract in the range of five years and $55 million (the precise deal that Burnett eventually agreed to with another team, the Toronto Blue Jays). On the other, the Sox could acquire the more talented and desirable pitcher (Beckett), albeit at a considerably higher price—a package of players built around the highly skilled Ramirez, the $18 million that came along with Lowell's contract, and the money necessary to sign Beckett to a long-term deal, however much that would prove to be.

The final choice boiled down to this: Burnett was a lot cheaper. But Beckett was a lot better.

Though fond of both Burnett and Beckett from his time in Florida, Sox owner Henry would later admit on WEEI sports radio that he argued for the signing of Burnett, primarily because it would allow the Sox to keep Ramirez in the organization. Epstein's allies in the organization emphatically stated that he, too, was against trading for Beckett, because the price was too high, but the seasoned Lajoie had long since learned that there was no substitute for a truly dominating staff ace, and that there was no way around paying a high price for a frontline starting pitcher. The Red Sox had learned that the previous winter when they ended up with Matt Clement.

Further, Lajoie believed, Lowell had suffered through a wildly uncharacteristic year in Florida and could prove a valuable asset to the Red Sox as a third baseman and middle-of-the-batting-order presence. Prior to the 2005 season, Lowell had batted .280 while averaging 25 home runs and 85 RBIs, and he had not yet turned 32. (Oddly, this made Lowell roughly the same age as Epstein.) Though Lowell had finished 2005 as perhaps the worst offensive hitter among all regular positional players in baseball—he ranked 147th among the 148 qualifying players in OPS, the sum of on-base percentage and slugging percentage used by many to assess offensive value—Lajoie believed that 2005, and not the previous five years, had been the aberration. "There were two people in evaluation within that organization that I trusted [at the time], and that was me and Shipley," Lajoie said in the spring of 2007. "We had a lot of faith in [Lowell] because we'd seen him play well [for] too many years. When I was over there [in Florida, scouting] and watching him play, he tried everything to get out of it [during a miserable '05 season]. He tried to hit the ball to right field and it would get caught, or he'd line out to the second baseman. There was nothing wrong with the player. It was just that kind of a season."

Added Lajoie: "It was myself and Craig Shipley who were the proponents of that trade, who wanted to go for it. There were some last-second attempts to stop the trade, but we decided to go through with it."

On November 24, 2005, the Red Sox formally announced a trade with the Florida Marlins in which Boston acquired Beckett, Lowell, and reliever Guillermo Mota, the last of whom was added into the deal because the Red Sox wanted the insurance of another pitcher given their concerns about the health of Beckett's shoulder. Boston gave up the supremely talented Hanley Ramirez, pitching prospect Anibal Sanchez, and two lower-level minor leaguers—Jesus Delgado and Harvey

Garcia—with all but Garcia having been brought into the Boston organization by Dan Duquette. The deal was a welcome blast of sunshine for a Red Sox organization that had been tainted by the Epstein saga, and the trade actually was completed while the former GM was on his way to the airport to travel to South America, where he was planning to watch his favorite band, Pearl Jam.

As much as Epstein was opposed to the Beckett deal, he was relieved that the Sox made the trade without including the young left-handed pitching prospect Jon Lester, who was starting to blossom in the minors. Lester was the first draft pick of the new Sox administration—he was their Nomar Garciaparra—and Epstein believed that Lester would develop into a fine major-league starter, even if the young lefty did not possess the raw talent of someone like Beckett. There had been speculation in the media that Lester was to be part of the deal instead of Sanchez, but Epstein quashed those rumors as he rode in a cab to Boston's Logan Airport. "If Lester were in the deal," mused the former Boston GM, maintaining his sense of humor in the wake of his highly publicized departure, "I would have resigned."

The comment even drew a laugh from Epstein himself.

In fact, with Beckett now in the organization, the Red Sox had positioned themselves well for the future, assuming they could sign the pitcher. Like Beckett, pitcher Jonathan Papelbon had just turned 25, and the Sox saw Papelbon, too, as a longtime anchor in their starting rotation. Lester had not yet turned 22. The three gave the Red Sox a nucleus of talented young pitchers that many teams lusted for, and it was still the club's objective—just as it had been Epstein's—to inject the pitching staff with youth. The injury to Schilling had left the Red Sox and most everyone else wondering whether Schilling's sacrifices in October 2004 had stripped them of Pedro Martinez's heir, which made the acquisition of Beckett all the more important. Even if Curt Schilling regained much of his effectiveness, there was the chance that he would no longer be the dominating ace he had been in 2004.

With Beckett now a member of the organization, the Red Sox went about the business of addressing other issues, specifically at center field and on the right side of their infield. In the case of the former, Damon had filed for free agency after an extremely productive Red Sox career that turned out better than even Dan Duquette could have hoped for. During his four years in Boston—from 2002 to 2005—Damon batted .295 with 461 runs scored, the latter more than any player in baseball but Albert Pujols (517) and Alex Rodriguez (485), each of whom made considerably more money. Further, Damon had dispelled any notion that he lacked mental toughness, something that had been a big concern when he arrived in Boston during the winter of 2001–2. There were those who had wondered whether someone like Damon could handle the pressure of Boston, whether he could thrive in it, and Damon had passed all tests with flying colors. By the time he departed, he was regarded as a fearless competitor and team leader, the latter of which completed an astonishing metamorphosis.

Back when Damon began his career in the minor leagues as a member of the Kansas City Royals organization, he had been painfully shy, something that was partially the result of a stutter. He conquered the problem during the course of his career and became, of all things a de facto *team spokesman* in a demanding media town like Boston, where he had become a national celebrity during a 2004 season in which he played with a beard.

During his time with the Red Sox, Damon also played an average of 149 games a season and never once went on the disabled list.

He had been worth every penny.

Still, with regard to their veteran free agents—again, Jason Varitek was the exception rather than the rule—the Red Sox had long since adopted the policy that they were not in the business of paying for past performance. Damon's agent, Scott Boras, was believed to be seeking a four- or five-year contract worth an average of somewhere near $12 million a year, a number the Red Sox deemed absurdly high. The Red Sox began negotiations with their center fielder offering Damon four years and $40 million, an average of $10 million per season. The terms

were identical to those that Varitek and shortstop Edgar Renteria had
signed for during the previous winter. Said one Sox official when asked
whether the proposal to Damon was merely an opening bid: "Probably
not. Four times 10 (million) is the right number for him."

Aside from Damon, Lajoie, Shipley, Hoyer, and Cherington had other
issues to deal, beginning with an annual trade request from the perpetu-
ally dissatisfied Manny Ramirez, and disgruntled left-handed pitcher
David Wells, who also asked to be traded after signing a two-year deal
with the Sox the previous off-season. Red Sox officials told both players
they would do their best to find a deal that made sense for both each player
and the club, though neither ended up being dealt away. In the case of
Ramirez, the Red Sox orchestrated an extensive dog-and-pony show during which they acknowledged discussions with a number of teams, but
never really came close to making a deal with any of them. Since Ramirez
was such a rare talent, finding equal value for him was virtually impossible, and the Sox entered most trade discussions on Ramirez asking for the
world in return. Club officials knew this would significantly hinder their
chances at making a deal, but they also knew they had all the leverage. If
they didn't make a deal for Ramirez—and they really had no intention of
doing so unless they were completely overwhelmed—they could go back
to the player and at least say they tried. And if Ramirez then tried to do
something rash like fail to report to spring training—the player and his
new agent, Greg Genske, actually did threaten this during the 2005–6 off-
season—then he would forfeit a prorated portion of his $20 million
annual salary for as long as he was out. Manny Ramirez might be an over-
sized teenager, as many Sox officials saw him, but even he wouldn't walk
away from $20 million a year.

While all of this was taking place, the Red Sox caught most everyone
by surprise when they announced that they had traded not Ramirez, but
shortstop Edgar Renteria, who had just completed the first year of his
four-year, $40 million contract. Renteria had been a major disappoint-
ment during his first year in Boston and had led all major leaguers with
an astounding 30 errors—some on WEEI talk radio began calling him

Error Renteria—but his offensive performance was better than many suggested. Renteria finished his only season in Boston with a .276 average, eight home runs, 70 RBIs, and 100 runs scored—numbers comparable to his totals of .287, 10, 72, and 84 during his final year in St. Louis—though Sox officials were both stunned and appalled by the precipitate drop in his defensive performance. Red Sox officials had almost no explanation for Renteria's fielding woes other than to suggest that he looked far less fit from the moment he arrived at spring training than the player they had expected. Said one Sox official: "From the moment we saw him we thought, 'This isn't the player we thought we were getting.' "

To make matters worse, because they had given Renteria such an exorbitant contract only a year earlier, Boston had to pay the freight in the trade that sent Renteria to the Atlanta Braves for third-base prospect Andy Marte. As a condition of the trade, the Red Sox agreed to pay $11 million of the remaining $29 million on Renteria's contract through 2008. In the end, the Braves got Renteria for the bargain-basement price of $6 million per season, while the Red Sox effectively ended paying Renteria a whopping $22 million for one year of service during which he was arguably the worst defensive player in baseball, which was a startling admission of ineptitude.

But then, the man who had signed Renteria in the first place—Epstein—was no longer with the organization.

At least not officially.

"I can't really say and I don't want to get into that because it's just something we decided to do," Lajoie said publicly when asked why the Sox so quickly cut bait with Renteria. "Probably there was an adjustment period that may have lasted longer than we hoped. There was just some overall feeling that if we could upgrade, we would try to upgrade that position."

Roughly two weeks later, when Johnny Damon surprisingly and suddenly accepted a four-year, $52 million offer to become the center fielder for the New York Yankees, the Red Sox once again appeared to be a in a spin. Though Yankees general manager Brian Cashman had publicly stated that his club was not interested in Damon—New York needed a center fielder—what Cashman had done, in fact, was wait. Knowing that Damon was wildly popular in Boston, Cashman had no intention of letting either the player or the agent use the Yankees in an attempt to get more money out of the Red Sox, so he swooped in at the last moment and made Damon an overwhelming offer that came with a deadline. The Yankees subsequently put forth an average of $13 million a year that blew everyone else out of the water, and they told Damon he had 24 hours to accept it. If he did not, they were moving on.

Damon took the deal. "They just had to come up a little bit—in between the offers [of $40 million and $52 million]," Damon said a couple of months later, after he had arrived at the Yankees' spring-training complex. "But what can you do? You're talking about $3 million a year [difference] and still playing for a winning team."

That Damon was represented by Boras only further complicated negotiations, particularly with Epstein gone. Lucchino, who distrusted Boras, with whom he had a feud, believed the agent was bluffing when he told the Sox that he had a $52 million offer in hand from the Yankees, so the Red Sox did nothing. Lucchino later denied that Boras had given the Red Sox any chance to match the deal, though the point was probably moot. Red Sox officials had already decided that they weren't going to give Damon a penny more than $40 million over four years, and to suddenly throw more money at him because he was threatening to join the Yankees would have made them look as foolish as they had during the Alex Rodriguez saga in 2003–4.

Still, in the aftermath of Epstein's departure, the Red Sox seemed to be operating without any real plan. On the one hand, they traded their shortstop of the future, Hanley Ramirez, in the blockbuster deal for Beckett; on the other, they traded away their shortstop of the present, Renteria, because they were dissatisfied with him. The Sox took on Lowell's remaining $18 million in salary to get Beckett and paid $11 million more to rid themselves of Renteria, yet they wouldn't bump their offer by, say, $6 million to $8 million (over four years) to keep Damon. Along the way, too, the Sox had traded backup catcher Doug Mirabelli to the San Diego Padres for second baseman Mark Loretta, a onetime All-Star whose skills had seemed to regress considerably during the 2005 season. (Even so, to get a starting second baseman for a backup catcher seemed an enormous coup.)

As a result of these moves, as the calendar turned from December 2005 to January 2006, the Red Sox were left with two big holes at a time of year when there seemed relatively little talent to be had. The Red Sox were roughly six weeks away from spring training and had neither a center fielder nor a shortstop, though there had been persistent rumors that the Sox had a number of candidates lined up. Roughly another month would pass before the Red Sox finally got their roster in order for the 2006 season, by which time far more dramatic developments were taking place inside the walls at Fenway Park.

Theo Epstein was coming back.

WHETHER THEO Epstein cared to admit it or not, the front page of the *Boston Herald* relayed a sentiment shared by many: "Tantrum's Over." Theo Epstein's public image had gone from noble man to spoiled brat in just two and a half months.

But the Red Sox looked just as foolish. Reached via telephone by a *Globe* reporter who wanted to know why the Red Sox had yet to issue Epstein an ultimatum—*in or out, Theo?*—Sox owner John Henry had club officials put together a press release on Friday, January 20, 2006, indicating that Epstein would be returning to the club. The peculiar release stated further that the precise nature of Epstein's responsibilities would be detailed the following week, largely because the Red Sox hadn't sorted things out yet.

When the announcement finally did come, Henry, Lucchino, and Epstein addressed the GM's return with a flurry of formal statements, each of them eager to put the operatic episode behind them. Terms of Epstein's agreement were not disclosed, though it quickly became clear that the young general manager would now report directly to Henry instead of to Lucchino, no matter how much Sox officials insisted that the structure of their operation had not changed. "This is not the same organization that Theo left," principal owner John Henry said. "There was enough discord then to give Theo legitimate reasons to move on."

Even Epstein felt as if the Red Sox had settled their differences, and he sincerely believed that the Sox had grown through the process, and that his dispute with Lucchino had inspired the Red Sox to truly look within, to map out a long-term plan and philosophy that were essential if the Red Sox were to have harmony going forward. Said Epstein later: "I'm not sure we could be where we are if we didn't go through what we did."

By the time Epstein returned, the Red Sox' roster had almost come together. While Henry was mending fences with both Lucchino and Epstein, the baseball-operations staff had signed free-agent shortstop Alex Gonzalez to a one-year, $3 million contract and had lined up a trade with the Cleveland Indians for outfielder Coco Crisp. In the acquisition of the latter, the Red Sox had given up both Guillermo Mota (from the Beckett deal) and Andy Marte (from the Renteria deal) to bring to Boston the successor to Johnny Damon, after a winter fraught with change and instability. While Crisp most recently had been playing left field and batting second for the Indians, he had been a center fielder and leadoff man for most of his minor-league career, and it was those roles that the Red Sox expected him to fill when they made the deal.

Unlike Damon, who was 32 when he left the Red Sox, Crisp was just 26 at the time of the trade and coming off a season in which he batted .300 with 16 home runs, 69 RBIs, 15 stolen bases, and 86 runs scored, all numbers that the Red Sox believed would go up. "Johnny Damon's a better player now and he might even be a better player next year [in 2007]," Epstein privately told reporters. "But by the end of the [four-year] deal [that Damon signed with the Yankees] we think Coco will be better."

By the time spring training arrived—finally and mercifully—the

Red Sox had undergone such dramatic changes since their 2004 championship season that only three positional players remained: catcher Varitek, right fielder Trot Nixon, and left fielder Manny Ramirez, the last of whom had been the subject of never-ending trade speculation. (Designated hitter David Ortiz, too, had been retained.) The Red Sox' pitching staff also had undergone massive changes, adding Beckett, Clement, and Wells while bidding farewell to, among others, Pedro Martinez and Derek Lowe, continuing the inevitable transition that had begun when owner Henry and his partners had bought the franchise.

Finally, the new operators of the Red Sox were putting their mark on the team that took the field. "I never felt like the teams in '03, '04, and '05 were my teams. They were the organization's teams, and everything we do is teamwork and part of a process," Epstein said when asked about the turnover on the club. "When you take a look at the big picture—the additions we've made—they're really the product of long-term planning over the course of many years. I don't look at [2006] as any different. The bottom line is I'd give anything to win and that's the most important thing." Added the GM of his team entering the '06 season: "We probably have more areas of risk [than in years past], but we have a lot of depth to mitigate that risk."

Spring training 2006 was relatively quiet and uneventful, though there were a few distractions. Ramirez did not report for the opening of camp with the rest of Boston's positional players, though there was little the Red Sox could do about it. While major leaguers were expected to be in camp every year by mid- to late February, they were not required to be there until March 1 based on the terms of baseball's collective-bargaining agreement between the major-league owners and the players union. Representatives for Ramirez assured the Red Sox that Ramirez would be in camp at that time; nevertheless, the club had to bargain with the player to ensure that they would have Ramirez's undivided attention when he finally showed up.

During the spring of 2006, baseball was set to unveil the first-ever World Baseball Classic (WBC), an international tournament and festival that commissioner Bud Selig hoped would someday become baseball's answer to the World Cup soccer tournament. One of Selig's chief goals as commissioner was to extend the game into global markets where it had never before existed, and indeed, baseball was making greats strides in this regard. In the inaugural WBC, there were teams from the Netherlands, Italy, Australia, and South Africa, though Major League Baseball had to manipulate the rules in order to stock the rosters of some nations. The Italian team, for example, included longtime Los Angeles Dodgers catcher Mike Piazza, then a member of the San Diego Padres. In exchange for being allowed to show up on March 1, Ramirez agreed that he would withdraw from representing the Dominican Republic in the WBC, a fact that left all parties (with the exception of Selig and the Dominicans) reasonably satisfied.

Beyond that, Boston's spring camp went off without much difficulty, though there were the usual baseball matters that needed tending to. After stringing out the Epstein negotiations, the Red Sox extended the contract of manager Francona. Though Schilling did not appear to have regained his presurgery form, he was nonetheless better, and the arrival of Beckett had lessened his workload. Meanwhile, center fielder Crisp was positively sensational throughout camp, playing with a seemingly boundless energy and enthusiasm that produced a stellar .434 batting average to go with a team-leading 11 runs and 23 hits in 19 games. "It's nice to see that extra gear in person," Francona said after watching Crisp zip around the bases during one spring game. "I'm sure he's thrilled. I know it's [only] spring training, but a lot was made of him coming over here."

There were the typical spring issues to address, with most of the Sox' concerns centering on their lineup. Over the winter, the Sox had overhauled their entire infield and the center-field position, meaning there were new players at almost every position. The Red Sox had handed over the responsibilities at first base to former backup Kevin Youkilis, allowing Kevin Millar to leave the club via free agency. With Lowell having arrived in the Beckett deal, third baseman Bill Mueller similarly was allowed to walk. Renteria's replacement, the defensively gifted Gonzalez, was equally known for being a poor hitter, though the Red Sox hoped he could at least provide some power. And while second baseman Mark Loretta was deft at handling the bat, his 2005 slugging percentage of .347 had ranked 215th among 223 major-league players with at least 400 plate appearances during the season.

Epstein was most concerned about Lowell, who was still perceived as the cost of doing business in the Beckett deal. Though Lowell ended up finishing the spring with a .327 average, early in camp he looked terribly out of sorts. The Red Sox were so concerned about his bat speed—or, more precisely, the lack thereof—that Epstein went so far as to claim a first baseman, Korean native Hee Seop Choi, just before the start of the regular season. If Lowell proved to be the bust that Red Sox officials feared, reasoned the young GM, the Sox could move Youkilis back to third base (his natural position) and play Choi at first.

The Red Sox had further hedged their bets by making another trade, this one with the Cincinnati Reds for power-hitting outfielder Wily Mo Peña. An impressive physical presence at 6-foot-3 and 245 pounds, Peña looked like a college linebacker, as if chiseled from a block of marble. In the long term, the Red Sox deemed Peña a potential replacement for Trot Nixon, who was in the final year of his contract entering 2006. In the short term, the Sox believed that Peña could add much-needed power from the right side of the plate, providing some measure of protection for the club if Lowell failed to become the run producer the team needed him to be.

The cost for Peña was steep. In a one-for-one trade that was the opposite of the Shea Hillenbrand-for-Byung Hyun Kim deal—in this one, the Red Sox traded a pitcher and received a hitter—the Sox parted ways with right-hander Bronson Arroyo, whom they had just signed to a three-year contract. While Arroyo initially believed that the deal secured his place in Boston for the immediate future, the contract actually made the pitcher *more* tradeable because it fixed his costs for a three-year period, something that was of great value to a small-market team like the

Reds. "We think he brings something to the table for us now and something, we hope, for the future," Epstein said of Peña, who had a disturbing propensity to strike out. "We think there's plenty of upside left, that he has a chance to further adapt into a full-time player." Added the GM: "I wouldn't, at some point, rule out experimenting with [Peña] at first base. But in the short term, we like him as an outfielder."

Though the Red Sox didn't say so publicly, there was some feeling in the organization that Peña could be the next David Ortiz, a late bloomer who had turned into one of the most valuable players in baseball during his time in Boston. Sox officials believed that Peña's high strikeout numbers were attributable partly to his youth and inexperience, and they hoped he could continue to develop under their watch, just as Ortiz had done. And as Ortiz had had Manny Ramirez to learn from, Peña now had both Ramirez and Ortiz, the latter of whom was all too willing to take the beefy young slugger under his wing.

By the time the smoke cleared, Epstein had tinkered enough with his roster that the Red Sox were comfortable with the team they sent on the field to start the season. The 2005 Red Sox had won 95 games, after all, and Epstein believed the team's pitching and defense had been improved considerably during the winter, primarily because those were the best buys available on the off-season market. The Boston offense was weaker, to be sure, but Epstein also believed the Sox were much improved in the area of run prevention, which should lead to victories of a different kind, but victories nonetheless.

That was assuming, of course, that everything went right.

And for a time, everything did.

LIKE MOST managers, Terry Francona was worried about the pitching. The Red Sox had as many as seven starters when they reported to camp for spring training—Curt Schilling, Josh Beckett, Tim Wakefield, David Wells, Matt Clement, Bronson Arroyo, and Jonathan Papelbon—and most people were asking Francona how he planned to use all of them. Left-hander Jon Lester was coming along too, and in a game where most teams are always looking for pitching, the Red Sox seemed to have a surplus. But deep down, as 2005 had reminded him and everyone else, Francona knew. *You can never have enough.*

By the time spring training ended, the Red Sox staff had shaken out as many had predicted, with one pitcher (Arroyo) going in a trade and another (Lester) going back to the minor leagues for additional seasoning. That left six men for five jobs, with Papelbon on the outside looking in. The other five men were all veteran pitchers earning millions of dollars every season, including Beckett, though he was only months older than Papelbon. Entering camp, Francona and Epstein had told everyone that they intended for Papelbon to be a starter, and there was a chance that things would play out that way. The Red Sox had a number of old pitchers, after all, and an injury or ailment to any one of them would open the door for Papelbon to begin making his case as the next great Red Sox pitcher.

In the absence of such of such a development, Francona knew that he had another option. Though Papelbon had initially started for the Red Sox upon joining the club from the team's Double-A affiliate in Portland, Maine, during the season, he had finished the season out of the bullpen, pitching brilliantly. In fact, Papelbon had been a closer during his college career at Mississippi State University when Epstein had scouted him during the annual Southeastern Conference tournament in 2003, and the young GM's eyes all but lit up. Almost immediately, Epstein was captivated by Papelbon's raw ability, his tenacity, his skill. Not much later, the Red Sox selected the big right-hander in the fourth round of the amateur draft and made Papelbon a starter, which was the better thing to do from a developmental standpoint. No matter how the Red Sox planned to use Papelbon in the major leagues—and starters always had more value—using him as a starter in the minor leagues would allow Papelbon to pitch more innings, to develop more rapidly and thoroughly. If the situation called for it, he could always go back to being a reliever.

At the end of the 2005 season, partly because the Red Sox needed bullpen help and partly because they were worried about Papelbon's workload, the Red Sox put Papelbon in their bullpen. The results were eye-popping. Beginning on September 1 and continuing through the postseason, Papelbon pitched 17⅓ innings over 12 appearances and allowed just two earned runs, going 3-0 with a microscopic ERA of 1.04. He struck out 15 and walked four. Red Sox officials and players were duly impressed, though they were not surprised. Earlier that year, during a spring-training game against the Baltimore Orioles, Papelbon had first caught their attention by knocking down Orioles slugger and superstar Sammy Sosa with a fastball under Sosa's chin after then–Red Sox outfielder Jay Payton had been hit by a pitch early in the game. If Jonathan Papelbon meant business then, the Red Sox were fairly certain he could handle the pressure of the big leagues. "He reminds me a little of Clemens out there," slugger David Ortiz said after Papelbon threw three scoreless innings of relief against the Toronto Blue Jays in September 2005.

Now Francona had little difficulty returning Papelbon to the bullpen. In fact, Francona *wanted* him there. One of the Red Sox' glaring deficiencies in 2005 had been the absence of power arms, especially in the bullpen—Boston pitchers finished the year ranked 21st among the 30 major-league teams in strikeouts—and Francona at the very least needed a strikeout pitcher to set up closer Keith Foulke. Additionally, Foulke had been having major problems with his knees, from which so much cartilage had already been removed that Foulke needed periodic injections of a synthetic lubricant, SYNVISC, to alleviate the pain and friction that resulted from bone rubbing against bone. By that stage, just as they had wondered about Schilling, Red Sox officials privately wondered whether Foulke ever would be the same again.

On Opening Day, a game in which Schilling pitched a masterful and encouraging seven innings in a 7–3 win over the Rangers, Foulke did little to convince Sox officials that he was ready to return to form. After Papelbon pitched an impressive, perfect eighth inning, Foulke labored through a ninth in which Rangers batters teed off on him as if they were at the driving range. Foulke was fortunate to escape the inning having allowed just two hits and one run, but the outing only reaffirmed the belief that he was a shell of his former self.

Two days later, when the Red Sox were presented with their first save situation of the season in Josh Beckett's debut with the team, Francona called on Mike Timlin to pitch the eighth before entrusting a 2–1 lead to Papelbon, who threw just 11 overpowering pitches while recording two strikeouts and a pop-up to preserve the victory. "He was electric," typically understated Red Sox catcher and captain Jason Varitek said of Papelbon. "That ball had some serious giddyup on it. He gave us a one-two-three inning and we were able to shut the door."

Said Francona amid suggestions that the club now had a closer controversy: "I don't care what it looks like. I just told you the truth and how I feel. We won and that's what we set out to do. It's a long year. I don't think Foulke is the guy we need yet and I think he's going to get there. That's part of our responsibility. I can live with myself. Sometimes, you have to do what you think is right."

In fact, there was no controversy. Francona had warned Foulke of his intentions, and the pitcher, to his credit, took the decision with remarkable grace and dignity. The simple truth was that Jonathan Papelbon was the far better man for the job—at that time and, as it turned out, any other—and everybody in the Red Sox clubhouse knew it. Including Foulke.

As the season went on, it became more and more apparent to everyone that Foulke had likely seen his last days as Red Sox closer and that the April 5 game in Texas had served as a changing of the guard. Though the Red Sox were not scoring runs with their usual potency, the club was winning games with pitching and defense—as Epstein and his interim replacements had hoped—to play themselves into first place in the American League East. Though the Sox hit some bumps—Crisp broke a finger after opening the season 8-for-24 and missed several weeks—the team kept on winning, peaking with a 12-game winning streak in June. Despite much hype concerning the potential acquisition of Roger Clemens, who eventually returned to the Houston Astros, they breezed along without a significant worry. The team entered the All-Star break with a 53-33 record that had the club on pace for precisely 100 victories, though the club was relying heavily on David Ortiz (who had 31 home runs and 87 RBIs *in the first half*) and Papelbon, who was selected to play in the All-Star Game after finishing the first half of the season with a 2-1 record, 26 saves (in 29 opportunities), and an incredible 0.59 ERA.

After so frequently losing *because* of their bullpen in recent years—the 2004 season was the exception, of course—the Red Sox now were winning thanks mainly to their brilliant new closer. "He's not afraid," Ortiz said of Papelbon, in whom he sensed an intangible from the very beginning. "That first outing with us [last year], he went out there like he's been here forever."

After a winter characterized by upheaval in the clubhouse and front office, the Red Sox were rolling along as if nothing had happened.

AS SWIFTLY as things came together for the 2006 Red Sox, they just as quickly fell apart.

Though the club won six of its first nine games after the All-Star break to improve to 59-36, general manager Theo Epstein was unwilling to sacrifice too much at the trading deadline to help a team that he believed was overachieving. Epstein had made only a handful of moves during the early part of the season, attempting to shore up any weaknesses with waiver-wire acquisitions like pitcher Jason Johnson, a journeyman right-hander who had never quite lived up to his ability. In fact, during his career, Johnson had posted one of the worst winning percentages in all of baseball among those with a minimum of 100 decisions, explaining why he was available to begin with. But Epstein was not willing to pay for anything better by giving up talent, especially with Boston's minor-league system on the verge of delivering more pitchers like Papelbon. But then, as author Seth Mnookin had revealed, Epstein wasn't expecting much from the 2006 Red Sox to begin with:

"It's probably not going to be a seamless transition. This year we had a great year. We will probably be worse next year [in 2006]."

Though Red Sox players said all of the right things as the deadline came and went, they privately expressed frustration that management had done little to support them, particularly when the New York Yankees had added multitalented outfielder Bobby Abreu. New York had overcome a mediocre start, and the addition of Abreu added much-needed depth to a Yankees lineup that, like Boston's, had thinned some. Both Francona and Schilling knew Abreu from their time with the Philadelphia Phillies. Schilling believed that Abreu, who had a reputation for being unmotivated at times, would thrive on the New York stage now that he had been thrust into a playoff race. "You watch," Schilling told a reporter privately. "He'll be the best player in baseball in the last two months."

Schilling wasn't far off. During August and September, in his first two months for the Yankees, Abreu batted .330 with seven home runs, 42 RBIs, 36 runs scored, 33 walks, and 10 stolen bases, numbers that would roughly translate into a .330 average, 21 homers, 126 RBIs, 108 runs, scored, 99 walks, and 30 stolen bases over the course of a full season.

By the time the Yankees arrived at Fenway Park in mid-August, New York had overtaken Boston in the American League East standings. Still, the Red Sox trailed the Yankees by a mere two games as the series was about to begin, though recent weeks had dealt the Red Sox a series of blows. After making it through the first four months of the season with great health, the Red Sox were hit by a succession of injuries just after the trading deadline, the most notable to catcher Jason Varitek, who underwent arthroscopic knee surgery. The Sox were wounded. Even so, they still had more than enough talent to defeat teams like the Tampa Bay Devil Rays and Kansas City Royals, then the worst clubs in the American League. Instead, just before New York arrived in town, the Red Sox went an abysmal 1-5 on a trip to Tampa and Kansas City, forcing them to play the Yankees from behind in the standings instead of from ahead.

For Epstein, the entire period of time was, to say the least, taxing. For all the criticism that former Red Sox general manager Lou Gorman had taken for trading away prospect Jeff Bagwell for reliever Larry Andersen in 1990—Bagwell would go on to have a Hall of Fame–caliber career with the Houston Astros—Gorman's intentions were good. *He was giving his team a chance.* Epstein's case could be perceived as far worse because it looked like he was quitting on his club, despite a first half in which the Red Sox had exceeded all expectations. While Epstein apologists defended the club's failure to acquire a player like Abreu—the Yankees got Abreu for a song by absorbing the balance of the player's contract, worth around $20 million—the same defenders failed to recognize that the Red Sox were willing to spend more than that to acquire Clemens, whom they had offered a prorated salary of more than $21 million.

It wasn't the money that deterred Theo Epstein, no matter what his apologists said for him at the time. Long before the season, in fact, it seemed as if Theo Epstein had resigned himself to write off 2006 for the greater good.

With the Red Sox reeling, many predicted a Yankees bloodbath in the five-game August series—and a bloodbath is precisely what they got. In the five games, New York scored 49 runs, an average of roughly 10 per game. While the Red Sox entered the series without a proven left-handed reliever—"How the fuck can you let that happen?" one Sox player wondered about management's apparent apathy—Abreu went 10-for-20 (a .500 average) with *seven* walks. Johnny Damon had 10 hits, two home runs, and eight RBIs. Jason Giambi walked six times, and young outfielder Melky Cabrera reached base nine times. All of them were left-handed hitters.

Their chances at a division title now all but destroyed, the Red Sox imploded. In the Yankees series, the Sox lost the frustrating series finale 2–1 despite a stellar outing by David Wells, who turned over a 1–1 game to reliever Foulke in the bottom of the eighth. Though he had been pitching better of late, Foulke threw a wild pitch that delivered the decisive run, leading Wells to throw up his hands in disbelief while watching from the dugout. That gesture came just days after reliever Mike Timlin had pointed a finger at the Red Sox offense by saying that Red Sox pitchers were not to blame for the team's woes, something that did not sit well with the other residents of the Boston clubhouse. On top of it all, as well as Papelbon had performed, overhyped prospect Craig Hansen (he of the 2005 draft) had fallen on his face, serving as a striking contrast to Papelbon.

On the one hand, young players could surprise you. On the other, they could disappoint. That kind of inconsistency generally made it impossible to rely on them.

"Anytime you don't win, the criticism is fair," said Epstein, who was taking more heat at the time than at any other point during his Red Sox tenure. "Our job as an organization is to win. The criticism is always fair. We're extremely critical of ourselves and I'm critical of myself." Continued the GM: "I prefer to take a broader look [than many fans and media]. We took the same principles this year that we took to make the playoffs and win [at least] 95 games three years in a row. Our goal has always been to win 95 games and make the playoffs. . . . We've gone toe-to-toe with the Yankees taking that approach [since 2003]. We're not going to change that approach and all of a sudden build an überteam."

Things got worse before they got better. Frustrated by his team's lack of professionalism while losing—the finger-pointing by Timlin and Wells especially bothered him—Francona called a team meeting before the Sox' next game, in Anaheim, against the now-named Los Angeles Angels. (Given the recent developments, it was good for the Sox to fly to the other side of the country.) In that meeting, Francona told his players that if they were going to lose, they were going to lose with dignity. He wanted no more finger-pointing and excuse making. There were bigger things in the world than baseball, and losing was frustrating to all of them. Regardless of what happened on the field, the Red Sox needed to band together.

For the the balance of the 2006 season, the Red Sox suffered no more flare-ups. Of course, the Sox did not win, either, going a miserable 25-38 over their final 63 games to finish at 85-77, just behind the Toronto Blue Jays and in third place in the American League East. Along the way, the Red Sox had plenty to worry about and talk about. Incensed by the team's lethargic performance against the Yankees in August and peeved at management for its apparent apathy—and he had a right to be—Manny Ramirez shut it down for the balance of the year, citing what many believed to be a phantom leg injury. (Ramirez was a sensational 8-for-11 with two homers and nine walks in the New York series.) The worst of the Red Sox brought out the worst in Manny, which was an unwillingness to fight the fight when things looked bleak. Said one clubhouse voice of Ramirez's late-season antics: "When things get tough, you just can't count on him."

The Red Sox had life issues to deal with too. During the Yankees series, suffering a reaction to what team doctors later described as fatigue and stress, designated hitter David Ortiz had to be taken to the hospital with an accelerated heartbeat. Under the cover of darkness, Ortiz was admitted to Mass General Hospital overnight for testing, then returned to the lineup the next day to go 3-for-6 with a home run, his 44th of the season. It was a startling demonstration of his ability and commitment. Ortiz played on until the symptoms recurred on the team's subsequent West Coast trip, when the Red Sox pulled him from the lineup and sent him back to Boston for more extensive testing. Ortiz had hoped his health would remain a private issue, but news of his problems first leaked thanks to a rumor on an unaccredited Web site. Said Ortiz when first approached about the matter: "How does that shit get out?"

At virtually the same time, unknown to most everyone outside of the Boston organization, the Sox had serious concerns about the health of Jon Lester, the young left-hander whom Epstein regarded so highly. A native of the Seattle area, Lester had pulled from a start in Anaheim with back pain that the Sox believed was the result of a fender bender in Boston earlier that summer. The Sox subsequently went to Seattle, where Lester was examined by a family doctor, who found that the pitcher had enlarged lymph nodes, an assessment that led to the diagnosis that Lester was suffering from large-cell lymphoma, a form of cancer. Lester had yet to turn 23.

The Sox were stunned. "There are a lot of personal things going on here that weigh on us a lot more than the losses and wins," Sox starter Curt Schilling said after a 7–2 loss at Oakland on August 30, the club's sixth straight loss and 12th in 14 games. While most chalked up Schilling's comment as a reference to Ortiz and the numerous injuries that had ripped out the team's insides, Schilling's use of the plural— "personal things"—was an obvious reference to Lester. A day later, the *Herald* disclosed that the pitcher was undergoing tests to determine whether he had cancer, a story that drew the paper considerable criticism from those feeling that Lester's privacy was being violated and that the paper was making a dangerous jump based on the information that Lester had enlarged lymph nodes. In fact, the *Herald* had more information that was not revealed in the story, and the Red Sox promptly announced what everyone feared (and some knew) to be true. Jon Lester was about to begin chemotherapy. His life, let alone his career, was in jeopardy.

Over the final month of the season, the Red Sox stabilized. The team went 15-14 in its final 29 games, and there were some reasons for optimism. Though Crisp's season had been derailed by injury—he hit a mere .264 with eight homers in 105 games—Lowell finished at a respectable .284 with 20 home runs and 80 RBIs, becoming far more productive than Epstein had expected. (Lajoie had been right.) Though Beckett struggled considerably in his first American League season, he won 16 games. Schilling showed signs of improvement, winning 15 games and finishing with a 3.97 ERA despite a disappointing second half.

And then there were Papelbon and Ortiz; the former recorded 35 saves and posted a 0.92 ERA in his first season as a closer despite missing roughly the last month with a worrisome shoulder ailment; the latter set a new team record by bashing 54 home runs, breaking the mark formerly held by the great Jimmie Foxx.

Nonetheless, for the first time since the 2002 season that was the stepchild of John Henry, Tom Werner, Larry Lucchino, and Theo Epstein, the Red Sox were not going to the playoffs.

And the truth was that they were not even close.

"You have to have an open, honest discussion of where we are," Sox manager Terry Francona said over the final weekend of the regular season at Fenway Park, noting that the whole league had become far more competitive. "There are some teams in our league that probably aren't going to go away, so we have to get deeper." Perhaps more than anyone in the Boston organization, Francona knew. The Red Sox had their work cut out for them.

TWO STEPS FORWARD

HAVING CONCLUDED THE DISAPPOINTING 2006 SEASON, THE RED sox immediately set out to reclaim their place as one of baseball's elite.

Along the way, they turned Daisuke Matsuzaka into an international celebrity.

Before the final days of October 2006, few people outside of Japan knew who Matsuzaka was. Even with the influx of Japanese talent into major-league baseball, most Japanese players were entirely unknown to Americans. For the longest time, at least with regard to baseball, Japan was regarded as a destination for those players who could not succeed in the major leagues, who preferred the life of the proverbial big fish in the small pond. For a baseball player, going to Japan was akin to a football player's decision to play in Canada, where he might enjoy a longer and more profitable career. So what if Japan was baseball's version of the Canadian Football League? In most cases, it beat the alternative. And the pay was good.

Still, while baseball—and the Red Sox—had dabbled in Japan long before the 21st century, things had begun to change considerably with the arrival of Japanese outfielder Ichiro Suzuki into the major leagues in 2001. Playing for a Seattle Mariners team that had lost a succession of stars in recent years—the group included Randy Johnson, Ken Griffey, and, most recently, Alex Rodriguez—Suzuki took the American League by storm in his very first season. In 157 games for a Mariners team that went an astonishing 116-46 before losing in the American League

Championship Series to (who else?) the New York Yankees, Suzuki batted a sterling .350 with 242 hits, 127 runs scored, and 56 stolen bases. He won a Silver Slugger Award as an elite offensive player at his position and a Gold Glove Award as an elite defensive player at his position. Along the way, Suzuki became just the second player in major-league history to win both the American League Rookie of the Year Award and the Most Valuable Player Award in the season, joining former Red Sox outfielder Fred Lynn (1975).

Just like that, the name Ichiro (who preferred to be called by his first name) became to baseball what Elvis became to rock 'n' roll.

As a direct result, Americans began to look upon Japanese baseball in new light. While Japanese baseball players had succeeded in the major leagues before Suzuki—right-handed pitcher Hideo Nomo, for one, spawned the craze known as Nomo-mania when he joined the Los Angeles Dodgers in 1995—Suzuki was an entirely different breed. Long before Nomo, baseball had accepted that there was a terrible shortage of pitching, the skill on which the game is built. Teams quickly learned to search the entire globe for anyone with a talented left or right arm, and even the Red Sox had made some advances in the Asian market prior to 2007. In 1999, for instance, Red Sox right-hander Tomokazu Ohka made his debut for the Red Sox, roughly a year after Korean right-hander Jin Ho Cho debuted for the team. The Sox also made it a point to promote the signings of Korean pitcher Sun-Woo Kim (he of the Cliff Floyd trade) and, later, the colorful left-handed Korean Sang-Hoon Lee. Nomo, too, pitched a season in Boston, throwing a no-hitter in his first start for the team en route to a 13-win season in 2001.

Still, Suzuki was different because he was a *positional player*, the kind of man who could (and did) contribute to his team's success on a daily basis. And despite playing in the American attic known as the Pacific Northwest—and despite hitting just eight home runs—Suzuki completely captivated the American public with a slashing offensive style and fundamental soundness that made even the most cynical and ugly Americans take notice.

Suzuki wasn't merely a good ballplayer. He was a *great* one.

Throughout the major leagues, in the wake of a phenomenon that prompted sushi vendors at Seattle's Safeco Field to create the Ichi-roll, the question in baseball was obvious: If Suzuki could be this good, how many more were there like him? In the years immediately after Suzuki's arrival, the influx of notable Japanese players—pitchers or otherwise—increased considerably. The New York Yankees signed outfielder Hideki "Big" Matsui and the New York Mets acquired infielder Kazuo "Little" Matsui. At different times, the Los Angeles Dodgers unveiled starter Kazuhisa Ishii and closer Takashi Saito. The Mariners also signed closer Kazuhiro Sasaki, while the Chicago White Sox picked up infielder Tadahito Iguchi. Even the cash-strapped, small-market Tampa Bay Devil Rays made a splash by luring away infielder Akinori Iwamura.

Japan's identity as a baseball-playing nation had changed substantially in the eyes of Americans. No longer was Japan the place to which inferior players *went*. It was the place from which superior players *came*.

All of this served as prologue to the arrival of Matsuzaka, at least in Boston, by whom the Japanese market remained relatively untapped. By the time Nomo pitched for the Red Sox, the pitcher was near the end of a career that had already endured a series of dips and turns. Ohka became a serviceable major-league pitcher despite injuries that plagued him throughout his career, but he never bordered on becoming a star. Neither pitcher had the kind of cache possessed by Matsuzaka, who was regarded in his homeland in much the same way that Americans viewed Lebron James, whose arrival in the NBA was anticipated from the time he was a teenager.

Matsuzaka had ascended to superstar status in Japan during a national high school tournament in which he performed feats that bordered on the superhuman. During that event, known in Japan as the Koshien, Matsuzaka threw 250 pitches in a 17-inning victory only *one day* after throwing a reported 148 pitches in another complete game. He entered a subsequent game in relief, and later he threw a no-hitter, all of which led to him being chosen with the first selection by the Seibu Lions. And so, in Japan, a star was born.

By the end of the 2006 baseball season, Matsuzaka's reputation in Japan had only been enhanced by his professional career. From 1999 to 2006, Matsuzaka went 108-60 with a 2.95 ERA and 8.69 strikeouts per nine innings pitched, drawing the attention of virtually every team in the major leagues. Matsuzaka had accomplished almost everything a young man could accomplish during his Japanese career—and he was still only 26—so he made it clear to his employers, the Lions, that he intended to leave them when Japanese rules first allowed, following the 2008 season. Matsuzaka was entering the prime years of his career, and in the wake of Suzuki's success in the United States—as well as that of Hideki Matsui and others—Matsuzaka believed that it was time to take his game to the next level.

Daisuke Matsuzaka wanted to go to America.

And Theo Epstein was chief among those who wanted to bring him here.

AT THE time, had anyone known to what lengths the Red Sox would extend themselves in order to make Matsuzaka a member of their franchise, the story might have received even greater attention that it did, at least at the outset. Still, as the result of an international agreement between professional baseball officials in the United States and Japan, Matsuzaka effectively was put up for sale through a process known as the *posting system*, a mechanism by which the Lions could auction off their player. Major-league teams interested in Matsuzaka were required to submit sealed bids to Major League Baseball by a specified deadline, at which point the bids would be turned over to officials in Japan. The Lions would then be told the amount of the winning bid—but not the identity of the winning team—at which point Seibu would have a decision to make: Matsuzaka or the money.

By the time all of the information became public, Matsuzaka-mania was in full force and the Red Sox looked like baseball's answer to the Corleone family, the clan that rules the underworld in *The Godfather* trilogy. Quite simply, the Sox made the Lions an offer they could not refuse. Amid speculation that the price to merely *negotiate* with Matsuzaka would require a winning bid of roughly $25 million to $30 million, the Red Sox all but pounded the table with a fistful of dollars. Boston's winning bid to secure the rights to the pitcher was a preposterous $51.11 million, a number settled on by the team's principal owner, John Henry. At a time when the Red Sox were criticized throughout the baseball world, team officials proudly thumbed their noses at their competitors, a group that included the New York Yankees and New York Mets.

The message was clear: *Sore losers.*

"What did you think of the winning bid?" one Sox administrator said with a boastful chuckle that bordered on the obnoxious. "Theo really wanted this guy."

But outbidding the world for the rights to Matsuzaka was only half the battle; now the Sox had to negotiate a contract with the player's agent, the dastardly Scott Boras. However, the Red Sox had most of the elements in their favor, largely because the rules of the posting system left Boras with little leverage in talks. Were the sides unable to reach an agreement within the allotted 30-day period, Matsuzaka would be forced to go back to Japan for at least one more season, and the Lions would have to return the $51.11 million, something neither the player nor the team wanted. And though the Red Sox desperately wanted Matsuzaka in Boston for 2007 and beyond, the club had no risk of losing the pitcher to another major-league team—as always, the Yankees were the chief concern—at least in the short term. As the rules were set up, only two outcomes were possible: Either Matsuzaka went to Boston and the deal was completed. Or the pitcher went back to Japan and the Red Sox got their $51.11 million deposit back.

Nevertheless, Epstein was wary. "Trust me," he said privately before negotiations with Boras began. "This is going to go down to the last day."

In fact, even after the Lions had accepted Boston's bid, Epstein was making similar predictions to other members of the Boston organization. Boras was known throughout the game for being a shrewd and hard negotiator, and he was sure to squeeze the Red Sox for every last penny. Already that winter, frontline pitchers like Barry Zito (who signed with the San Francisco Giants) and Jason Schmidt (Los Angeles Dodgers) were securing between $16 million and $18 million annually, a figure Boras was likely to target. The Red Sox, on other hand, were offering something more in the range of $8 million annually, the salary awarded to previous international pitchers, like right-hander Jose Contreras. When Boras and the Red Sox projected those average annual values over the length of a five- or six-year contract, the agent and the team were tens of millions of dollars apart. Meanwhile, the clock was ticking.

Accustomed to being in control of negotiations, Boras seemed increasingly frustrated as the deadline for the Matsuzaka deal approached. Unlike so many of his other negotiations, after all, Boras had no one to play the Red Sox off against. As the representative for much of baseball's elite talent, Boras had carved himself quite a niche as one of the game's premier power brokers, something he was all too eager to remind people of whenever he felt the need. His press briefings frequently came off as terribly self-serving and left attendees with the impression that Boras was insultingly arrogant, that he was, as much as anything else, a man who greatly enjoyed hearing himself talk. Team officials throughout baseball privately told stories of how Boras bored them to death with his rhetoric and propaganda during meetings about various free agents, though the large majority of those negotiations seemed to end with Boras getting precisely what he wanted for his client.

And frequently, what he wanted was beyond outrageous.

Beyond that ability to wear down potential suitors for his clients, Boras had something else beyond the obvious talent he was peddling: an indisputable fearlessness about killing a deal. On more than occasion—Red Sox catcher Varitek and outfielder J. D. Drew were chief among them—Boras allowed deadlines to come and go to strengthen his long-term bargaining position. In those cases, destroying a potential deal was the only leverage Boras had, and the decision to do so only fortified Boras's reputation as a hard-line negotiator, someone who almost always got what he wanted, someone whom all major-league teams had reason to fear. If you didn't give in to Scott Boras, major-league teams came to learn, you frequently failed to obtain what you wanted.

With regard to Varitek and Drew, Boras discouraged each player from signing with the team that drafted him until a suitable contract was offered. Both players subsequently walked away from the table—Varitek with the Minnesota Twins, Drew with the Philadelphia Phillies—and Varitek nearly did so a second time with the Seattle Mariners before agreeing to terms at the 11th hour. In each instance, there was serious question as to whether Boras did his client a long-term disservice by focusing on the contract instead of the player's development, though both players went on to have productive and fruitful careers.

Still, Boras was acutely sensitive to any suggestion that he was even remotely inhuman at the negotiating table, and it was not beyond him to call members of the media who characterized him as ruthless. During the Matsuzaka negotiations, Boras expressed his displeasure with a *Herald* columnist who suggested that Boras's only leverage in the talks was his willingness to "kill the hostage," though the assertion was indisputably true. And while Boras rambled on for minutes about the inappropriateness of the description—Boras wondered if the reporter was "a Christian," and cautioned against such terminology during a time when the world was especially sensitive to terrorism—his actions only reaffirmed the notion that in the case of Matsuzaka, he was finally involved in a dispute where he was nearly helpless, and he knew it.

To his credit, Boras persisted, intent on making Matsuzaka a landmark case that would be baseball's equivalent of *Roe v. Wade*. In Matsuzaka, Boras saw an opportunity to completely change the posting system, a process he deemed entirely unfair to Japanese players. At times, his objective seemed not to serve Matsuzaka but rather to use him, primarily as a tool to further empower players (and agents) in the negotiating process. Matsuzaka had become such an international story—the $51.11 million posting fee paid by the Red Sox was nearly four times the $13 million the Mariners had paid for Suzuki following the 2000 season—that Boras rightly saw the pitcher as a platform to implement change.

But Boras lacked the one thing he needed to make it all work: Matsuzaka's full support.

On December 13, 2006, the 30th and final day of negotiations between the Red Sox and right-hander Daisuke Matsuzaka, the pitcher agreed to a six-year contract worth $52 million, an average of $8.67 million per season. Just prior to the announcement, the Red Sox had walked away from a negotiating session on the West Coast believing that talks with the pitcher had broken down for good, only to be called back when Matsuzaka overruled his agent and told him to accept the deal. While Sox general manager Theo Epstein praised the pitcher for being so bold—"He stepped up and showed big balls," Epstein said of Matsuzaka—others in the Boston organization believed that Epstein had merely beaten Boras at his own game. "I have to give Theo a lot of credit," said manager Terry Francona. "The day we won the bid, Theo pretty much laid out how this whole thing was going to go. And he basically nailed it."

Two months after that, with dozens of Japanese media camped in the home of the Red Sox' spring-training complex in Fort Myers, Florida, Daisuke Matsuzaka reported to his first preseason camp as a major-league player. By then, Matsuzaka was known as the man for whom the Red Sox had spent a whopping $103 million—$51.11 million in the posting fee, $52 million for the contract—despite the fact that Matsuzaka had never thrown a pitch on American soil. Red Sox officials warned the American media that Matsuzaka would go through a transition, that their investment in him was over a six-year period, and that it was imperative for the Red Sox and their fans to be patient with a man who would soon be compared with, among others, Pedro Martinez.

Matsuzaka arrived in Fort Myers with a predictable air of confidence, given his reputation and accomplishments in Japan, though he could not have anticipated some of the challenges he would encounter. The major leagues were an entirely different challenge for a pitcher, particularly the American League. The demands were great. A market like Boston typically demonstrated little patience for high-priced players who failed to live up to their contracts, and Matsuzaka had the kind of contract that many major-league players dreamed about. "I've had expectations all my life," Matsuzaka said with the aid of an interpreter. "The most important thing for me is to play ball and have fun. I have done so [in the past] and I will continue to do so. . . . The scale of the contract does not determine how I play baseball. I feel responsibility a little bit, but I am not pressured." Added the guarded right-hander bluntly when asked about adjusting to the major leagues: "I have no plans to change anything at all."

That kind of stubbornness was part of what had attracted the Red Sox to Matsuzaka in the first place. Just the same, under the circumstances, an alarm should have sounded.

ALWAYS AND without exception, the money matters. In professional sports, there is simply no way around it. The best players almost always secure the largest contracts, which means there is a direct correlation between productivity and salary. The moment a player fails to meet expectations, his salary is the first thing referenced. To those on the outside, the particulars almost never matter. Nobody wants to buy a lemon.

By the time the off-season of 2006-7 had been completed, Daisuke Matsuzaka was not the only member of the Red Sox facing expectations.

Collectively, the Red Sox had a projected payroll of roughly $160 million, a club record that did *not* include the $51.11 million posting fee the Red Sox had paid for Matsuzaka. (The sum was not considered an expense under baseball's formula for calculating payroll, at least with regards to the luxury tax levied on big-spending teams.) In addition to acquiring Matsuzaka, the Red Sox had signed free agent shortstop Julio Lugo (four years, $36 million) and perennially underachieving outfielder J. D. Drew, the latter to a five-year, $70 million contract that prompted the entire baseball world to shake its head in disbelief. The Red Sox did *what*?!

All of that placed a certain amount of pressure on Epstein, even if the young GM did not acknowledge it. In the wake of Epstein's dispute with Larry Lucchino following the 2005 season and the subsequent passivity of the Red Sox front office in 2006, Red Sox followers were starting to get antsy again. More than any Red Sox team in recent history, the 2007 Red Sox entered spring training with Epstein's fingerprints all over the club. On Matsuzaka, Drew, and Lugo alone, Epstein had spent $215 million in long-term contracts. With the exception of only a few Red Sox players—Jason Varitek, Manny Ramirez, Tim Wakefield, Kevin Youkilis, and Doug Mirabelli—virtually every member of Boston's projected Opening Day roster had been brought to the organization during the administration headed by Henry, Lucchino, and Tom Werner, a period that essentially coincided with Epstein's reign as general manager.

This was Theo's team now. His ass was on the line.

Given all of the changes and improvements made by the Sox, the team enjoyed an uncharacteristically quiet spring. The Red Sox arrived at camp with decidedly few questions, as sure a sign as any that they were talented and deep. With reliever Jonathan Papelbon now earmarked for the starting rotation, the biggest question concerned the identity of the Red Sox closer, a role the Sox hoped to fill with any number of veteran relievers in camp, from Mike Timlin to Brendan Donnelly. There was also the issue of a contract extension for veteran starter

Curt Schilling, who was entering the final year of his existing deal and wanted to remain in Boston, though that had more to do with the Red Sox of 2008 than it did with the club in 2007.

The Schilling affair did not turn into nearly the distraction it could have, particularly in a Boston market where, years earlier, the contract status of first baseman Mo Vaughn had played out like a long-running soap opera. Early in spring training, Red Sox officials seemed appalled at Schilling's pronouncement that he wanted to play another season—"If he wants a contract, he should start by losing the fucking gut," said one Sox official—but the club addressed the matter swiftly and decisively. Before the team played even a single exhibition game, Epstein indicated that the Sox had no intention of negotiating with Schilling until after the season. Schilling, meanwhile, said he had no desire to make the issue a distraction as the season unfolded and assured that he would not put his individual concerns ahead of those of the team. This turned out to be one of the few occasions in baseball history (particularly in the midst of a contract matter) when both sides lived up to their word.

The issue of Red Sox closer, too, settled itself before the end of camp. As the Sox repeatedly failed to find a suitable replacement for Papelbon during the spring schedule, the young right-hander found himself feeling more and more compelled to return to his old role. Roughly 10 days before the scheduled season opener against the Kansas City Royals at Kauffman Stadium, the Red Sox announced that Papelbon would be reclaiming his role as closer, addressing the team's only significant flaw as Opening Day approached. Veteran right-hander Julian Tavarez would assume Papelbon's place in the rotation, the Sox said, and they felt both moves were in the best interests of the club. The announcement came precisely four years after the Sox' futile closer-by-committee experiment, offering further evidence that current Red Sox officials were willing to acknowledge their prior mistakes and learn from them.

"I hadn't been sleeping well since spring training started because there was always that feeling deep down in my heart that I wanted to close, and for me, it just kept getting at me and getting at me," Papelbon said. "I finally went to our captain and said, 'Tek, I'm not sleeping good at night, I've got to do something about it. Basically, I think I want to close. That's what I want to do.' He said, 'Hold on,' and Tito happened to be walking by and I said, 'If you want to give me the ball in the ninth, I want it.'"

Said Red Sox manager Terry Francona: "You have these arguments, as baseball people do, about the value [of a pitcher] to a club: starter or reliever? I normally go along with the argument of starting, but not in this situation. He's too unique. He's at the top of the list of all relievers in baseball. He impacts a ballclub unlike very few pitchers.

"If you look back at last season, this kid got a lot of action and a lot of pitches," Francona continued, acknowledging the obvious concerns about Papelbon's health and durability. "That can't happen [again]. This kid will be checked, monitored. There's going to be days I'm going to tell him he's not going to pitch and he will do his strength and conditioning exercises. The other manager doesn't know and [the media] may not know. As we do with every pitcher, we want to keep him healthy and productive, and we'll do that with Pap. I would never put our ballclub's interests ahead of one of our players' health. You can't operate that way."

Of course, after investing $160 million in a team, having a pitching staff without a closer was no way to operate. And with a new season about to dawn, the Red Sox wanted to ensure that they had addressed as many potential problems as possible.

A week and a half later, behind an unimpressive, overweight, and out-of-shape Schilling—"He looked sloppy," one Sox evaluator said of Schilling's fatness—the Red Sox opened their 2007 season with a 7–1 loss to the inferior Kansas City Royals with an aggregate performance that was, to say the least, uninspiring. The team rebounded to win its next two behind performances from Josh Beckett and Matsuzaka, the latter of whom joined newcomers Lugo and Drew in making a notable impression during his first days in a Red Sox uniform. While Matsuzaka struck out 10 in his Red Sox debut, Lugo overcame a poor Opening Day (strikeouts in his first three at-bats) to collect four hits in his final 11 at-bats.

But nothing meant more to Epstein than the impressive play of Drew, who was quietly efficient. While playing right field with effortlessness and running the bases with both ease and efficiency, Drew reached base in six of his twelve series plate appearances, going 4-for-10 with a pair of doubles and two runs scored. The performance was consistent with Drew's personality—quiet and understated—but was not lost on Red Sox officials, who had taken a great deal of criticism for signing the player in the first place. "Why don't you call those guys at WEEI (the all-sports talk radio in Boston) and ask them about him now?" One Sox official privately mused to one reporter.

Said Francona when asked about Drew while collecting his belongings as the team prepared to travel to another road series against the Texas Rangers: "I'm glad you asked me about that. I thought he was outstanding. That fucker can play. He can play the outfield and run the bases. He was *good*."

Despite losing two of three at Texas—the Sox won the series finale behind a much-improved Schilling, 3–2—the Sox returned to Boston for the first home game with a 3-3 record and in moderately good spirits, unaware that things were about to get a great deal better.

For one thing, after falling to 2-3 with consecutive series-opening losses to the Rangers, the Sox had just waved good-bye to their last losing record of the season.

For another, they were about to embark on the kind of prolonged winning streak that made the rest of their regular season all but a formality.

Thanks primarily to a pitching staff that performed brilliantly at both the beginning and end of games, the Red Sox went 33-12 over their next 45 games, a .733 winning percentage that translated into an incredible 119 victories over the course of a 162-game schedule. The Red Sox swept a mid-April series from the New York Yankees in straight sets—7–6, 7–5, and 7–6—and won against good teams and bad ones, at home and on the road. By the time the Red Sox suffered their first three-game losing streak of the season—the absence of such a streak validated the talent and depth of the Red Sox' starting rotation—the date was June 2, and the Red Sox still had record of 37-20 (the best in the game) to go along with a nine-game lead in the American League East and an even bigger 11½-game advantage over the New York Yankees.

"We're trying to win every game," said third baseman Mike Lowell, who had established himself as a leader on the club early in his second season. "I think we're doing a great job of keeping that focus."

As much as athletes and teams talk about playing "one game at a time," few really succeed in implementing the philosophy. In baseball, especially, the games come so quickly that players allow their minds and emotions to race, a problem that Lowell knew all too well.

Just prior to coming to Boston in the trade that also made Josh Beckett a member of the Red Sox, Lowell had endured his worst professional season. With the Florida Marlins in 2005, Lowell got off to such an uncharacteristically poor start that the weight of the season smothered him. By season's end, despite a few blips of productivity, Lowell finished with a miserable .236 batting average to go along with only eight home runs and 58 RBIs, totals well below his career averages. But the games kept coming, day after day after day, and even a seasoned, level-headed veteran like Lowell found himself unable to keep up with the demands of the season, finishing with a .658 OPS (on-base percentage plus slugging percentage) that ranked him an abysmal 147th among the 148 major-league players with enough plate appearances to qualify for a batting title.

During a season in which he was arguably the worst everyday offensive player in baseball, Lowell learned that the best way to combat the endless succession of games was not to speed up, but rather to do the opposite: *slow down.*

That same message was one that manager Terry Francona was constantly delivering to his players, particularly the younger and more aggressive ones who did not have enough experience to separate themselves from the happenings on the field. Francona often spoke of a player's ability to keep his emotions and thoughts under control—"The game doesn't speed up on him," was Francona's way of putting it—and paid special attention to that quality during a game. From his perch at the end of the Red Sox' dugout, Francona could see how a player responded to adversity, how he was handling emotions, whether he had the wherewithal and poise to compete or whether the challenge overwhelmed him. Like most managers who recognized that the game was played on the field by human beings susceptible to emotional and mental breakdowns, Francona especially valued those players who could handle pressure, who could fight back, who could *compete.*

In the first two months of the 2007 season, thanks to a fabulous start by his ballclub, Francona was fairly certain that he had a cast of veteran players who possessed all of those qualities. The manager also learned that some of his newer players were similarly up for the challenge.

One of those players was from Japan.

And it wasn't Daisuke Matsuzaka.

IN BOSTON, no matter how well the Red Sox played, there was always something to worry about. So even after the Red Sox addressed their biggest question of spring training when they restored Jonathan Papelbon as their closer late in March, the move triggered a predictable response: Who would serve as the bridge between the revamped Boston starters and the ferocious closer Papelbon?

The Red Sox had concerns about left-hander Hideki Okajima. Signed to a two-year, $2.5 million contract during the off-season, Okajima arrived in Boston virtually unnoticed in the midst of the Daisuke Matsuzaka saga and the signings of Drew and Lugo. On the advice of international scout Craig Shipley—the same man who had been targeting Matsuzaka for years and who was instrumental in the

Beckett deal—general manager Theo Epstein had signed Okajima to an extremely affordable contract with the simplest goals in mind. Because Okajima had a curveball that he could consistently throw for strikes, the Red Sox believed he might be the man who could fill their need for a left-handed specialist. If he could not, Epstein was reasonably confident that Okajima could aid his bullpen, perhaps as a middle reliever on the days that Red Sox starters failed to complete the sixth inning.

The Red Sox also had questions about Okajima's ability to handle a significant role, though club officials were careful to avoid making such inferences publicly. In spring training, Sox officials spoke of Okajima's being demanding, which was to say that he was relatively inflexible regarding his pitching routine and how he liked to be used. Okajima liked to have as much advance notice as possible before entering games, Sox officials learned, and he was quite particular about his routine. It seemed that everything had to be in line in order for Okajima to be effective, and that spelled potential problems down the road once the team got into the season.

During a baseball season, after all, there are countless moments that cannot be planned for. Opposing rallies sometimes mount quickly, which requires a bullpen to mobilize with similar speed. Relievers are valuable for getting batters out in a game, to be sure, but some have value because they can warm up quickly, because they can pitch frequently without losing any effectiveness, because they can deal with any situation at any time, regardless of whether they are accustomed to the role. Even if such pitchers are not consistently effective, their flexibility makes them invaluable to a bullpen because a manager can use them to help make others better too.

It didn't take long for the Red Sox to learn that Hideki Okajima was going to be worth the effort.

After allowing a home run on the first pitch to the first major-league batter he faced—Kansas City catcher John Buck on Opening Day—Okajima finished his first month as a major-league relief pitcher with

12.2 scoreless innings. The pitcher's defining moment came during an April series against the Yankees in which Okajima saved one game and helped secure another, the former when Francona, true to his word, bypassed closer Papelbon for fear of overworking him. Okajima responded by negotiating his way through the heart of the Yankees' lineup—a group that included Derek Jeter, Bobby Abreu, and Alex Rodriguez—before striking out Kevin Thompson to record his first major-league save.

On the next day, before a rejuvenated Papelbon recorded the save, Okajima struck out Jason Giambi in the middle of a Yankees rally and sprinted off the field to a standing ovation.

"We had a pretty good idea he was going to pitch well or we wouldn't have done that, but it's nice to see him respond to the Yankees–Red Sox [rivalry] and that whole bit," Francona said of his decision to employ Okajima in a more aggressive manner over the weekend. "He was valuable again today. He bounced back day game after a night game. He got Giambi in probably the biggest at-bat in the game."

The ascension of Okajima, who would become Papelbon's primary setup man over the remainder of the season, was nothing short of meteoric. Late in spring training, Francona had eschewed the notion that Okajima could emerge from a group of candidates to become Papelbon's primary setup man, opting instead to rely on a group of veteran relievers that included veterans Timlin and Donnelly, as well as left-hander J. C. Romero, the last of whom had been signed as a free agent during the winter. While Francona, like most managers, was careful about suggesting that any one player was more important to his team than another, he chose carefully when it came to his bullpen, also like most managers. In Francona's world, there were pitchers who deserved to pitch "with responsibility" and others who did not.

Like no other element of a baseball team, a bullpen can make or break a manager. A stable, reliable relief corps gives a manager options to negotiate his way through the late innings of a close game, which makes life infinitely more bearable for any skipper wearing a major-league uniform. But once the bullpen goes bad, once anarchy and uncertainty take control, a manager frequently finds himself grasping at straws in a desperate attempt to get the critical, final outs of a game.

Francona was not the only manager who believed that his fate rested largely with his bullpen; most skippers had a similar belief. Former Red Sox manager Grady Little, for one, joked that his wife would send him off to spring training every year with the same question: How does your bullpen look? For Debi Little, the answer to that question would determine whether her husband's team had a good or a bad year, a fact that made her far more shrewd and knowledgeable than 90 percent of the baseball analysts in the world.

Tell me how good your bullpen is, and I'll tell you how good you are.

In the case of Okajima, Francona had no way of knowing what he had stumbled upon. But in the earliest stages of the season, when the veteran arms in the Boston pen began failing (as history suggested they would), Francona began rolling the dice with his new reliever. He let Okajima pitch with a little "responsibility," then increased the dosage. Before long, Okajima was not merely emerging as the most reliable bridge to Papelbon in the Boston bullpen, but as one of the very best setup men in all of major-league baseball, thanks largely to the emergence of a changeup and/or split-fingered fastball that allowed the left-hander to retire both left- and right-handed batters with astonishing efficiency.

Suddenly, Hideki Okajima was not merely a situational lefty or a run-of-the-mill middle reliever. He was a vital component to a Red Sox team that was threatening to leave the rest of baseball in its wake.

Whatever the explanation for Okajima's evolution into a force—he was a good reliever during his career in Japan, not a great one—his performance over the first half of the season was nothing short of historic. After allowing only one run—the homer to Buck—in April, Okajima allowed only two runs in May, one more in June, one more in July. As the Red Sox were preparing to enter August, the fifth month of their season, Okajima had allowed fewer runs *all season* (in 47 games) than, for instance, Cleveland Indians closer Joe Borowski allowed to the Yankees during the ninth inning of a single game in April. Okajima's microscopic 0.87 ERA made him one of the most incredible bargains in all of major-league baseball.

But then, that was how the game frequently worked. For all of the money the Red Sox had spent on Daisuke Matsuzaka, Okajima was proving to be more important.

Said Red Sox general manager Theo Epstein during the peak of Okajima's effectiveness: "Obviously I'd be lying if I told you we expected this."

But so what if the details were a little twisted? In the end, the Red Sox were doing exactly what they had expected to. Winning.

AT THEIR worst, the 2007 Red Sox were not a bad team, just a mediocre one. After going a sizzling 36-15 in their first 51 games, the Red Sox went an almost perfectly mediocre 26-25 over their next 51, a stretch that took them to the end of July. So Epstein was quite aware of his team's strengths and weaknesses leading up to that time of year when baseball executives took center stage: the trading deadline.

A year earlier—and much to the chagrin of some Red Sox players—Epstein had done virtually nothing to improve his team, while the Yankees had added outfielder Bobby Abreu, a move that had a profound impact on the American League East during the final two months of the season. In 2006, the Red Sox disintegrated down the stretch while the fortified Yankees rumbled into the postseason for an 11th consecutive season, a commendable stretch during which New York won nine straight American League East Division championships. And though the 2006 Yankees ultimately failed to win the World Series—they were eliminated in the first round of the playoffs by the Detroit Tigers—New York was regarded as far more aggressive than the Red Sox.

A year later, with the Yankees enduring the kind of organizational rebuilding process that Epstein had preached only a year earlier,

Epstein was now in position to be more aggressive, to strike a decisive blow. Though the Red Sox suffered some injuries during the middle of the 2007 season—ace Josh Beckett went to the disabled list for 15 days, and Schilling missed a month to get himself into shape—the problems were relatively minimal. (In 2007, as in 2004, the Red Sox were among those major-league clubs that lost the fewest games to injury.) Nonetheless, even when the Sox did hit bumps in the road, Boston's depth paid off in the form of young pitchers like left-handers Kason Gabbard and Jon Lester, a fact that proved terribly gratifying to the young general manager of the team.

In the long run, Theo Epstein had been right. By having paid the price in 2006, the 2007 Red Sox were far better off. "I'd do it the same way again, if that's what you're asking me," Epstein told reporters who had criticized him only a year earlier.

Indeed, as much as Gabbard helped the Red Sox win games in 2006, his contribution was exponentially greater as the team approached July 31, 2007. Despite the fact that Gabbard pitched quite well for the team in 2006 and 2007—the young lefty went 5-3 with a rock-solid 3.64 ERA in spot duty with the club—the Red Sox never regarded him as one of their top prospects. So Epstein was more than willing to trade Gabbard as the July 31 trading deadline approached, a fact that further supported the general manager's stance when it came to developing young players. With Gabbard having surprised people at the major-league level, the Red Sox were now in a most enviable position: they could trade for veteran talent *and* protect their best young talent, all because Kason Gabbard had developed into a far better pitcher than anyone had expected.

Epstein's emphasis on Boston's farm system and player-development operations was paying huge dividends—and it was a good thing for the GM. After hot starts, Drew and Lugo were both having a miserable year, the latter (like Lowell with Florida in 2005) ranking among the worst offensive regulars in all of baseball during the first half of the season. Drew, meanwhile, had long since begun frustrating Sox officials with a passive nature that simultaneously made him an extremely likable young man and a positively maddening baseball player. Odd as it seemed, the Red Sox almost hoped that J. D. Drew would be a little, well, *meaner*. "I think that's just who he is," one Sox official said with a shake of the head when discussing Drew's passive approach to baseball. "I mean, he's the kind of guy you'd want your daughter to marry."

It just didn't seem like he was the kind of guy you wanted playing right field and batting fifth.

Yet, despite the disappointing play of Lugo and Drew, the Red Sox were winning, something for which Epstein still deserved credit. After a dreadful start to the season, second baseman Dustin Pedroia had emerged as a legitimate candidate to win the American League Rookie of the Year Award, a competition that might just as well have been conducted exclusively within the historic walls at Fenway Park. Red Sox rookies Pedroia, Matsuzaka, and Okajima were all brilliant, providing the 2007 Sox with both quality performances and invaluable energy. Pedroia, in particular, was everything that Drew was not: a cocky, relentless, and impassioned player who got all (and more) out of such a small frame that he quickly became a fan favorite. What Dustin Pedroia lacked in size and raw ability, he made up for in desire and baseball acumen, much to the surprise of scouts and onlookers who had never imagined that Pedroia could be so good. *"Fuck,"* emphatic Sox manager Terry Francona said late in the season when it was suggested that most people did not realize how good Pedroia was when the youngster struggled badly at the end of the 2006 season. "Who did?"

Through it all, Epstein, like his manager, had remained committed to giving Pedroia a chance, a confidence that was now paying huge dividends. With Matsuzaka, Okajima, and Pedroia having filled considerable voids in the Red Sox, Epstein could now fortify any one of the team's relatively minor deficiencies, be they in the lineup or on the pitching staff. The general manager had options at his disposal, from Chicago White Sox outfielder Jermaine Dye to White Sox starter Mark Buehrle to Texas Rangers reliever Eric Gagne—and Epstein weighed a number of factors before pulling the trigger on a deadline deal that sent a package of players, including young left-hander Gabbard, to Texas for a man regarded as a proven, big-time relief pitcher.

While Epstein might have made other deals at the deadline, he settled on Gagne for a handful of reasons. First, for as much concern as there had been about the Red Sox' offense and their ability to produce runs in the late innings of close games, Boston still ranked among the major-league leaders in runs scored, even if the Sox were not producing at the clip they did in 2003–5. Epstein believed that the Red Sox and their fans had been spoiled by the truly prolific offensive teams of his early years as general manager.

Second, the GM had long-term money tied up in Lugo and Drew, prohibiting him from making the kind of impact offensive acquisition he would prefer. Gagne was relatively cheap, even if the Sox would not admit so publicly. When the Sox made the deal, one Boston official almost chuckled at the notion that the Sox could get so much for Gabbard, who had already endured multiple surgeries on his elbow. The Red Sox also believed that they would end up with up to two compensatory draft picks when Gagne left the team via free agency following the season, meaning that they did not look at Gagne as the only player they were acquiring in the deal. In those draft picks, *the Sox essentially were getting up to two prospects, too.*

Furthermore, though the Red Sox were choosing their words carefully, they had concerns about Okajima, whose workload had been considerable to that point in the season. In the absence of another reliable setup man behind closer Jonathan Papelbon, Okajima had worked an inordinate amount for a player in his first major-league season. Sox officials were well aware that the major-league season was significantly longer than the regular season in Japan, and they feared that Okajima might tire at the end of the year. Also, because Okajima was not a power pitcher—meaning that he relied on control, finesse, and especially deception—the Sox wondered if hitters might soon begin to solve him, if Okajima's success over the first four months was at least partly because major-league hitters were seeing him for the first time.

Boston's fears about Hideki Okajima proved legitimate.

It was the demise of Daisuke Matsuzaka and Eric Gagne that they could not have entirely predicted.

OVER THE course of Red Sox history, during those times of crisis that have demanded strong leadership, too many managers have buckled under the weight of responsibility. Terry Francona remains one of the few who has not.

Nonetheless, the manager of the Red Sox annually wears a bull's-eye on his back, no matter what he has accomplished, no matter what he must endure. Second-guessing the manager is as much a part of New England as the winter snowdrifts and summers on the Cape, though most fans fail to recognize that the majority of the skipper's work is done *before* they turn on their televisions. On most days, Francona arrives at the ballpark early to go over scouting reports and update himself on injuries, and even that does not begin to measure the true challenge of the job.

On every baseball team, there are 25 players, each of whom possesses a different personality. Some require no maintenance and others require a great deal, but all require some measure of attention. Francona believes in tending to all of them, if only because he was once a player who understood the importance of communication in a baseball clubhouse. Said Francona during his earliest days in Boston: "Part of the reason you build relationships is because there comes a time when you're going to have to tell someone something they don't want to hear."

Francona got little credit for how smoothly things went for the Red Sox in 2007. While outfielder Manny Ramirez was having an incident-free year, for example, few recognized that Francona was taking time to assure Ramirez that he was appreciated, that the Red Sox needed him. On one occasion during the regular season, Francona pulled many of his starters during a lopsided Red Sox victory, with the intention of giving his players additional, invaluable rest. Extremely sensitive to such maneuvers—more than anything else, Ramirez needed love—the left fielder of the Red Sox was one of the few regulars who played the entire game, something for which his manager was grateful.

Still, with Ramirez, such things could produce resentment, a reality of which Francona was quite aware. So on a day when Ramirez might have been apt to ask the kind of question that could lead to far greater problems—"Why did *I* have to keep playing when everyone else got to rest?"—the player returned to his locker after the game to find a short note and a bottle of liquor. "You should have seen him swinging that thing around," recalled one onlooker in the clubhouse. "He couldn't have been happier."

To their credit, other Red Sox players laughed along, aware that Francona was merely doing what was necessary to keep the team both together and pointed in the right direction.

Ramirez was not the only player who required reassuring. Matsuzaka, for example, became enraged when the *Boston Herald* published photos of his wife and child, the latter of whom Matsuzaka had deemed off-limits to the Japanese press during his career in Japan. While reporters in Japan complied with the pitcher's request, the American media entered a gray area when Matsuzaka's family made a public appearance in the stands during a game at Fenway Park. The *Herald* subsequently printed a photo of the woman and child—as did a wire service and at least one Web site—which struck a nerve with the pitcher and sent Matsuzaka soaring into orbit.

While Sox officials were careful to respect Matsuzaka's requests and honor the inevitable cultural transition undergone by a player who had come from overseas, Matsuzaka's reaction nonetheless surprised them. Matsuzaka was so upset at the perceived slight that he actually suggested he would be unable to pitch, a matter that was resolved only after Francona harnessed the pitcher's emotions. The incident was the most extreme example of a number of transitional issues that surrounded the pitcher, who also did little to endear himself to the American media, particularly after the incident regarding the *Herald* and the photo of Matsuzaka's wife and child. Though he was guarded from the start, Matsuzaka's press conferences were excruciatingly dull and uninformative, particularly for the American press. Attempts to engage the pitcher were thwarted by Matsuzaka's personal media handler, Sachiyo Sekiguchi, a woman who reportedly was friendly with the pitcher's wife. Sekiguchi proved more obstruction than liaison—privately, even members of the Japanese media complained about this—so the Red Sox got only a small bump in publicity from the man for whom they had shelled out more than $103 million.

Still, in 2007, the flare-ups were relatively few, largely because things generally went *right*. Though the Yankees had begun to play quite well after the All-Star break, the Red Sox continued to move forward as the season approached late August, albeit in small steps. The team was 76-51 entering a four-game series in Chicago against the White Sox on August 24, and even Francona could not have anticipated how well his team would play in completely dismantling a Chicago team that was completely uninspired. In four weekend games—the Soxes played a doubleheader on Friday—the Red outscored the White by the incredible count of 46–7, a wipeout that left the Red Sox with an 80-51 record and, with just 31 games to play, a spongy 7½-game lead in the American League East. Even with the Red Sox about to begin a three-game series at Yankee Stadium—as it turned out, the Sox would lose all three—the Red Sox were in complete control of their fate. "It's Over!" screamed the *Boston Herald*, all but officially declaring the end of the division race in the American League East.

Sox players were not so brash. "I don't know how important it is [to have extended the division lead], but it's a much better feeling to have a lead than to be trailing," said third baseman Lowell. "Obviously, from a standings position, there's more pressure on the team that's behind. But if we get hot and explode, it doesn't dampen [New York's] spirits because they're [still] in it. Added the cerebral third baseman: "Trust me: If you can guarantee me that winning the division gets us to the World Series, then I want to win the division. But I want to be the team that's hot [in October]."

Lowell was right: despite the emphasis being placed on the American League East by Red Sox fans, who had not seen their team win a division since 1995, the title meant little. The creation of the wild-card berth had changed the postseason landscape entirely in 1998, and the Red Sox did not have to beat the Yankees during the regular season anymore. The Sox only had to beat New York *in October,* something the Sox proved during their historic championship season of 2004. And for as much ridicule as the *Herald* absorbed when the Yankees closed to within 1½ games in September—naturally, angry fans blamed the paper for their team's alleged collapse—the paper's premise was correct as the team left Chicago in late August. With a month to go, the Red Sox had secured a playoff spot.

Francona knew this, though he wasn't about to admit it. During the series in Chicago, as the Yankees were inching closer, Francona took exception with one Boston columnist who suggested that the 2007 Red Sox had not truly been tested, an opinion based largely on the fact that the team jumped to such a large lead in April and May. Such confrontations were not out of character for Francona, who, like most players, manager, and coaches, kept close tabs on the media despite insisting—repeatedly—that he neither read the newspapers nor listened to the radio. In fact, Francona knew a great deal of what was written and said about him and his team, largely because he knew the media could not merely stoke fires, but create them. In Boston, whether a manager liked it or not, dealing with the media was a huge part of the job.

"Did you write that we haven't been tested?" Francona said with a look of disbelief to the columnist while sitting behind his desk in the visiting manager's office at Chicago's U.S. Cellular Field. "This is the big leagues. Every day's a fucking test. You guys must be writing shit again." And then the manager snickered.

Still, as feisty as Francona could be, his poise was an invaluable asset to the organization when the Red Sox truly needed it. After a three-game sweep in New York that turned into a four-game losing streak, the Red Sox won four in a row and six of seven. There was still a comfortable distance between the Red Sox and the Detroit Tigers—the team chasing New York for the final American League playoff spot—and Francona recognized that the Red Sox had far bigger things to worry about than just the American League East entering the final few weeks of the regular season. Gagne had been a disaster since the Red Sox had acquired him in the trade with Texas, and Okajima was, as predicted, running on fumes. Compounding matters was the ineffectiveness of Matsuzaka, who, like his Japanese counterpart in the bullpen, appeared tired and worn by the rigors of his first major-league season.

With two weeks to go—and with the Red Sox holding a 90-60 record—the Red Sox entered a three-game series at Toronto with an array of issues. It was then that Francona elected to shut down Okajima for the purpose of giving the pitcher an extended rest; to bypass Matsuzaka so that the pitcher could similarly recharge his batteries; to put Gagne into a critical situation (in which he failed) for the purpose of trying to rebuild his confidence; and to operate with what was essentially a skeleton crew (without, among others, the injured Ramirez and Kevin Youkilis) so that the Red Sox could fully get their house in order for the only part of the season that would matter to them after the end of May, the playoffs.

While many Red Sox fans and followers succumbed to the insecurities caused by years of torture and abuse—they were panicking—Francona remained focused on the much bigger picture: a championship. "It means a lot, but it means nothing as far as winning a World Series," Francona said when asked whether a division title had any importance to him relative to a World Series. "It means a lot for what you set out to accomplish, I think. I don't think there's any getting around that, and I don't think we want to. But when it's all said and done, it won't have any bearing on how far we get into the postseason."

The manager was right again.

After departing Toronto, the Red Sox won six of their final nine games to finish with a 96-66 record and their first American League East Division title in 12 years. But also, the Red Sox were a healthy, rested, and fully prepared team entering the most important month of every baseball season. October.

MORE THAN anything else, Josh Beckett prided himself on being someone people could rely on, particularly at the most desperate times. In every sense, including literally, he was willing to put his money where his mouth was.

During a 2007 regular season in which Beckett went 20-7 with a 3.27 ERA to become baseball's only 20-game winner in two seasons, one of his more noble efforts went entirely unrecognized beyond the walls of the Red Sox clubhouse. Upon learning that a liked and respected employee in the Boston organization was enduring financial difficulty, the uniformed members of the Red Sox—players, coaches, and the manager—took it upon themselves to help a person in need. The Sox organized a clubhouse collection to buy the person a car, and players were asked to contribute only if they truly wanted to. Showing absolutely no reluctance or hesitation, Josh Beckett wrote a check for $5,000.

In the fantasy world of professional sports, of course, $5,000 represented a microfraction of a player's annual salary, but that was hardly the point. From the time Beckett was drafted out of high school by the Florida Marlins with the second overall selection in the 1999 amateur draft, he had the makings of that most desirable baseball commodity: an ace. Beckett had the right stuff, in his arm and in his soul, and his ascension to greatness as a major leaguer was seen not as a question of *if*, but *when*. In the biggest games, especially, Beckett seemed to treat every at-bat against him as a personal affront. During the 2007 playoffs, Beckett's press conferences were spotted with profanity—at times he seemed to curse purely to *prove* that he didn't give a shit—and his entire demeanor and disposition conveyed a most direct message: *Fuck you. Fuck all of you.*

"He was often referred to as cocky," said Red Sox owner John Henry, who owned the Florida team when the Marlins drafted Beckett.

"Dave Dombrowski [then the Marlins general manager] saw that as a vital ingredient because he thought that translated into confidence."

Throughout a rocky 2006 season during which he endured a rough transition to the American League, Beckett rarely seemed fazed. He chastised himself for losses far more than he praised himself for wins, a sure sign that he believed in his ability. Beckett *expected* to win. He expected to be an ace. Beckett grew up idolizing Roger Clemens, and he eventually would join an accomplished list of Sox aces that included both Pedro Martinez and Schilling, and he privately told team officials that one of his goals was to win 300 games in his career, an achievement that would almost surely land him in the Hall of Fame. Even as a budding prospect with the Marlins, Beckett was known to be so demanding of himself that the Marlins once had to lecture him about the dangers of working *too* hard after Beckett suffered a setback during his rehabilitation from an injury.

No matter what his record was, Josh Beckett regarded himself as one of the very best pitchers in baseball. And he acted like it.

Entering the playoffs, Beckett was coming off such a strong season that he was the obvious choice to start Game 1, just as Schilling had been (ahead of Pedro Martinez) three years earlier; in that sense, Game 1 marked another historic changing of the guard. Beckett went out and overpowered the Los Angeles Angels in Game 1 of the American League Division Series, pitching the Red Sox to a 4–0 victory while throwing a mere 108 pitches and recording eight strikeouts in a complete-game effort. The game established a tone and a pattern for the remainder of the postseason, namely that the Red Sox would be unbeatable any time Beckett took the mound.

In four postseason starts, Beckett would finish 4-0 with a 1.20 ERA and 35 strikeouts (against two walks) in 30 innings. In those games, the Red Sox won by a combined score of 34–5. At the most critical stage of the baseball season, it was as if Josh Beckett were issuing one rather sizable *fuck you* to the entire major leagues.

"He's maturing right in front of eyes," Sox manager Francona said during the postseason, echoing sentiments he had expressed throughout the regular season. "[It] seems like every game, he wants to make more of a name for himself."

The numbers alone did not do justice to what Beckett meant for the Red Sox.

Having dispatched the Angels in the minimum three games—the final count of the Division Series was Boston 19, Los Angeles 4—the Red Sox advanced to the American League Championship Series against the Cleveland Indians, who had defeated the Yankees in four games in the American League's other semifinal series. Having assumed that the Yankees had overcome their early-season difficulties, many baseball prognosticators had identified the Yankees as the the Team to Beat entering the 2007 postseason. But New York's flaws were once again exposed. The Yankees lacked the necessary pitching to match up with Cleveland's two-headed monster of left-hander C. C. Sabathia (the eventual AL Cy Young Award winner) and right-hander Fausto Carmona, so when the mighty Yankees offense managed just four runs in the first two games of the series, New York lost both games. After the Yankees rebounded to win Game 3, veteran right-hander Paul Byrd sufficiently stymied their attack in Game 4 during Cleveland's series-clinching win.

In a relative instant, after marching through the final 80 games of the regular season with a record of 54-26 and causing more than a few eternal Sox skeptics to constantly peek in the rearview mirror, the Yankees disappeared entirely from view. There would be no repeat of the historic AL Championship Series that took place between Boston and New York in October 2004.

If the absence of the Yankees resulted in a letdown among some Boston fans, the players in the Red Sox clubhouse experienced no such symptom. Beckett would not let them. Picking up where he had left off against the Angels, Beckett allowed just two runs in six innings of a resounding 10–3 Boston win in Game 1 against Cleveland, a victory that prompted more than a few to wonder if the Red Sox were going to flatten the Indians the way they had the Angels. Indeed, the Red Sox were clicking on all cylinders, scoring runs and getting production from the veteran players around whom the team was built. After terrorizing the Angels in the AL Division Series, the offensive tandem of numbers three and four hitters David Ortiz and Manny Ramirez went a combined 4-for-4 with five walks while reaching base in all 10 of their plate appearances in Game 1, finishing with three RBIs and four runs scored. It certainly seemed as if nobody had an answer for the Red Sox.

For all of the concerns about the Boston offense during the regular season, Red Sox hitters were firing on all cylinders through the first four games of the postseason. At the center of it, unsurprisingly, were Ortiz and Ramirez, the accomplished veteran sluggers who had played such a big role in leading the Red Sox to the 2004 world title but who, for an assortment of reasons that included injury (a knee ailment for Ortiz, a rib-cage-muscle strain for Ramirez) had experienced relatively lackluster years during the regular season. During the series against the Angels, in just three games, Ortiz and Ramirez seemed to do a month's worth of damage, combining to go 8-for-15 with four home runs, seven RBIs, eight runs scored, and 11 walks, reaching base safely in an ungodly 19-of-26 plate appearances.

"I think there were a couple of storylines in this series. One is that when we have our three-four hitters clicking at the same time, it makes us a different team," Sox general manager Theo Epstein said after the Sox demolished the Angels. "When [Ramirez] gets locked in, it's really hard to get through the middle of our order."

Said Sox owner John Henry: "People have talked about, 'Are you going to trade Manny? Are you going to trade Manny?' Manny's bat—you saw the difference in the lineup when he's out there. They can't pitch around David. They have to pitch to David and Manny."

But any thought of a Red Sox sweep was promptly quashed the next night, when a resilient Cleveland club overcame deficits of 3–1 and 6–5 before exploding for seven runs in the 11th inning of an eventual

13–6 victory. The series then shifted to Cleveland, where the Indians won Game 3 (a 4–2 final) behind a masterful performance from right-hander Jake Westbrook (the first starter to truly shut down Boston during the playoffs) and Game 4, by a 7–3 score after jumping to a 7–0 lead in the bottom of the fifth inning with their second seven-run outburst in 14 innings. The victories gave the Indians a commanding series lead of three games to one, and even the most experienced members of the Red Sox admitted that Boston might be facing its first true crisis of the season. "We haven't had our backs against the wall all year, until now, because during all that panic stuff about the division at the end of the [regular season], we were never in danger of missing the playoffs," Red Sox starter Curt Schilling said even before the Sox lost Game 4. "I think this is our first true character test given our lead all year."

That said, having endured the trial that was the 2004 ALCS against the Yankees, the Red Sox remained unshaken. According to respected *Sports Illustrated* reporter Tom Verducci, Ortiz addressed the team following the Game 3 loss at Cleveland's Jacobs Field, reminding his teammates that "we're a great team . . . and don't you fucking forget that" and stressing to the younger Sox players that, as a club, the team was a "bad motherfucker." A day later, after the Game 4 loss, Ramirez took his turn stepping to the forefront, telling a gaggle of reporters that a Red Sox loss to the Indians in Game 5 would be "no big deal." Win or lose, the Red Sox would show up for spring training again in 2008, Ramirez assured, and they would try to win the championship, just as the Red Sox had done following their backbreaking loss to New York in October 2003.

While having their fun with what they perceived as Ramirez's apathy, many media members missed the more important points: First, Ramirez was right. Second, the Red Sox were as loose as ever, a quality that had served them well in 2004 and sufficiently liberated them to play their best baseball of the year.

And there was an even greater reason to believe the Red Sox had more than a little fight left in them.

Beckett was pitching Game 5.

FROM THE start of March through the end of October, the Red Sox played more than 200 games, including undocumented split-squad games during spring training. Without question, the single most important one took place on October 18.

For all that Beckett had accomplished in both October 2007 and his postseason career to that point, his effort in Game 5 against the Indians was a *fuck-you* performance of the greatest magnitude. Staked to 1–0 lead in the top of the first inning, Beckett allowed a run to the Indians in the bottom half before shutting down Cleveland the rest of the way. On a night when the Red Sox made a succession of potentially fatal mistakes— they ran the bases poorly and failed to execute a sacrifice bunt, among other transgressions—the Sox nonetheless took a 2–1 lead into the seventh inning. The Red Sox then rallied for a pair of runs in the seventh and three more in the top of the eighth before Beckett took the mound for the bottom half, when he promptly set the Indians down in order.

By that point, with the Red Sox holding a 7–1 lead and Papelbon about to enter the game, Beckett had piled up 11 strikeouts against just one walk while throwing 109 pitches, a preposterous 74 of which were strikes. The Indians tried virtually everything against him, including the gamesmanship of having Beckett's former girlfriend, Danielle Peck, sing the national anthem and "God Bless America" during the seventh-inning stretch, the latter while Beckett stood just a few feet away on the pitcher's mound.

None of it worked. "I don't get paid to make those fucking decisions," an all-but-snarling Beckett said after the game when asked about the appearance of Peck, a Cleveland-area native. "She's a friend of mine. That doesn't bother me at all. Thanks for flying one of my friends to the game so she could watch it for free."

The room exploded with laughter.

Using Beckett's performance as a springboard—in much the same way that the 2004 Sox catapulted off the heroics of David Ortiz and, to a lesser extent, Dave Roberts—the Red Sox never looked back. With the series shifting back to Boston thanks to Beckett's magnificence, the Red Sox throttled the Indians in Games 6 and 7, winning by the respective scores of 12–2 and 11–2. After Cleveland's seven-run outburst in Game 4, in fact, the Red Sox outscored the Indians 33–5 over the final 31 innings of the series, a roll that only got more impressive when the Sox steamrolled the National League champion Colorado Rockies by a 13–1 score in Game 1 of the World Series.

During that four-game stretch, the greatest common factor was Beckett, whose bookend performances (in Game 5 against Cleveland, Game 1 against Colorado) highlighted a dominating stretch during which the Red Sox manhandled the two best remaining teams in baseball by the aggregate count of 46–6. The Red Sox then steamed forward to make the World Series anticlimactic, just as they had in 2004, defeating the Rockies in Games 2, 3, and 4 by scores of 2–1, 10–5, and 4–3, finishing the 2007 baseball season with a seven-game winning streak. Coupled with Boston's four-game sweep of the St. Louis Cardinals in 2004, the victory gave Boston an eight-game World Series winning streak—only nine years earlier, remember, the Red Sox were the franchise that had managed to lose an astonishing 13 postseason games in a row over 10 years—and left manager Terry Francona with a career playoff record of 22-9, which gave him the highest postseason winning percentage in history (.710) among managers with at least 20 games at the helm.

Many Red Sox contributed to the team's second world title in four seasons—third baseman Mike Lowell was named Most Valuable Player of the World Series, making the Beckett-Lowell trade with Florida look even better—but Beckett's efforts were singular in many regards. With the four victories, Beckett improved his career postseason record to 6-2 with a 1.73 ERA, the latter of which placed him behind only Mariano Rivera and Sandy Koufax among major-league pitchers with at least 70 career postseason innings over a 75-year span. Entering 2008, Beckett's teams had won all six postseason series in which they had played, including two World Series, during which Beckett had a career record of 2-1 with a 1.16 ERA. On top of it all, he had been the indisputable Most Valuable Player of the 2003 World Series (with the Florida Marlins) and the 2007 American League Championship Series (with the Red Sox), only further establishing his place as the best big-game hunter in baseball.

He left even Red Sox heroes of the past awestruck. "I have not seen Beckett pitch all year, but let me tell you: he's some kind of good," the Los Angeles Dodgers' Derek Lowe said of Beckett while watching the 2007 playoffs from his Florida home three years after helping to propel Boston's 2004 World Series run. "Out there in [Los Angeles], we don't get to see all that much during the season. He's got to be the best pitcher in our game. I really believe that, as far as what he does, and he consistently does it in October."

From Cape Cod to Tokyo, nobody was about to argue.

FOR ALL that took place in Boston during the spring, summer, and fall of 2007, the most extraordinary may have been this: the Red Sox were never visited by ghosts. Even as the New York Yankees gained steadily on the Red Sox in August and September, even when the Indians came within one win of ending Boston's season during the American League Championship Series, there were no comparisons drawn between the Red Sox of 2007 and those of 1946 or 1948, 1967 or 1975, 1978, 1986, or 2003. Three years after the exorcism that was their historic championship of 2004, the Red Sox were now enjoying a new era in their history, free of the baggage that had weighed them down for so long.

Only the most experienced Red Sox players recognized the change—

which was precisely the point. Once defined by a telling phrase traced back to longtime *Boston Globe* baseball reporter Peter Gammons—"25 players, 25 cabs"—the Red Sox were now both unified and successful. The younger players, in particular, did not know any better than to focus on the future.

"*Fractured* is probably the best way to describe it," Curt Schilling said when asked about the perception of the Red Sox before he joined the organization in 2004. "From the clubhouse to the front office, there was that whole 25 players, 25 cabs thing. But when I came here, I knew right away that it was different."

Said manager Francona: "I do think that in games of huge magnitude, our guys don't get overwhelmed. It doesn't assure that you're going to win, but it is a good feeling. You look out there and you see Jason Varitek behind the plate, guys like Beckett and Schilling, they do what they're supposed to do."

Consequently, and only validating the theory that children are a largely a product of the environment in which they are raised, the youngest and most inexperienced Red Sox played freely and relatively flawlessly during the most critical time of year. During Boston's seven-game winning streak that began with Game 5 of the AL Championship Series, more than a few observers noted that many of the critical Boston performers were members of Red Sox Youth, newly sprouted players like Dustin Pedroia and Jacoby Ellsbury, even Okajima and Matsuzaka. When closer Jonathan Papelbon made his Red Sox debut in 2005, for example, the Red Sox were the reigning world champions, winners instead of chokers. The same was true of everyone from Lester to Beckett, who were never asked to suffer for the sins of Red Sox past.

From 2003 to 2007, the Boston uniform had become considerably lighter and brighter.

"That's a great thing to have associated with your organization," general manager Epstein said proudly in an uncharacteristically placid October moment at Fenway. "It establishes a real culture of winning and overcoming obstacles throughout the organization. You can't teach that."

Nonetheless, it has to be learned.

And over time, it has to be built.

EPILOGUE

MONTHS AFTER BOSTON WON ITS SECOND WORLD TITLE in four years—and one month before the start of spring training 2008—Theo Epstein had the Red Sox right where he wanted them.

"We were talking about this in the office the other day," Epstein said. "If you look at it, I think our last five years have been better than anybody else's in baseball. At the same time, I'm not sure we'd trade our next five for anyone else's, either."

There was little sense in arguing the point. Epstein was right.

In a glaring contrast to the tumultuous off-season that followed the Red Sox' championship season of 2004, the winter of 2007–08 was uncharacteristically silent. At times, the calm seemed downright eerie. The Red Sox entered the off-season with two major contractual issues—Curt Schilling and Mike Lowell—and both had re-signed with the club before Thanksgiving. Schilling took an incentive-laden contract that would pay him a base salary of $8 million in 2008, a decrease in guaranteed earnings of $5 million from the previous year. Lowell—the man whose $18 million in salary was deemed an additional cost for obtaining Josh Beckett—was signed to a three-year, $37.5 million contract that would pay him an average of $12.5 million per season through 2010.

"There's a premium for frontline pitching, so let's be realistic: I mean, Josh was the key to that deal," Lowell said back in May when asked about his career in Boston and the prospect of remaining with the

Red Sox. "But I like to think there was some belief that I'd be able to produce. [The Marlins] didn't trade me because I was old. They traded me because of the contract. I'm aware of how things work.

"It's an appealing situation [in Boston]. I like the way the organization does things," Lowell added. "We go for a World Series every year. We're not rebuilding, ever, here. I want to be in that flow I had in '03 [when he and Beckett were on a championship Marlins team]. I don't want that to be the only time in my career."

Of course, it wasn't. And for the 2007 World Series MVP, there is the chance that more World Series titles could be on the way.

As for Schilling, his return to the club hit an unexpected snag just before the start of spring training, when it was learned the pitcher had a shoulder injury expected to sideline him for at least half—and perhaps all—of the 2008 season. Though Schilling finished 2007 with a 9-8 record and 3.87 ERA, he had gone 3-0 with a 2.92 ERA in the postseason, when his grit and experience annually proved most valuable. Still, while the Red Sox held out hope that Schilling could return to the club before the end of the 2008 campaign—in time, perhaps, to once again help them in the playoffs—the Red Sox also found themselves in good position to withstand a blow of such magnitude.

Where the Red Sox of the past might have been crippled by an injury to one of their projected front-line starters, the Red Sox of 2008 had both depth and youth to fall back on.

Strongly positioned throughout the winter, the Red Sox engaged in various off-season trade talks, most notably with the Minnesota Twins for ace left-handed pitcher Johan Santana, a two-time Cy Young Award winner whom the Twins were being forced to peddle for economic reasons. (It was Pedro Martinez and Beckett all over again.) The Red Sox offered a variety of packages built around any one of three budding major leaguers—outfielder Jacoby Ellsbury or pitchers Clay Buchholz and Jon Lester—stressing to the Twins that they could have only one from that group. Minnesota officials subsequently used the offer in an attempt to drive up the price with the far more desperate New York Yankees, which seemed to please Red Sox officials to no end. Thanks to the shrewd management of their minor-league and player-development system, after all, the Red Sox didn't *need* Santana as much as the Yankees did, leaving Boston with a win-win outcome in which the Red Sox either acquired the pitcher or drove up the price for New York.

With the roles of the clubs now switched from their traditional places in history, the Red Sox sat by and watched with amusement as Hank Steinbrenner (the son of Yankees owner George Steinbrenner) demon-strated astonishing dexterity by publicly changing direction almost every day. "No," one Sox official said when asked if he knew Steinbren-ner's son at all, "but I'm starting to like him more and more every day."

As it turned out, Santana ended up with the New York Mets, who ac-quired the pitcher from Minnesota for a package of four young players at the end of January. That outcome suggested that the Yankees, like the Red Sox, were now committed to nurturing their young, following the lead of a Boston organization that now seemed to be setting the pace throughout the major leagues.

For Epstein, in particular, the relative tranquillity of the off-season was a welcome change from the first five winters of his career as Red Sox general manager. But tranquil didn't mean without rewards. Shortly after the season concluded, the trade publication *Baseball America* rated the Red Sox' farm system as the second best in baseball, which was to say that only one other organization was blessed with more talent. Of course, that pronouncement came after a major-league season in which the Red Sox led virtually wire to wire in the American League East and won the World Series, putting Boston smack dab in the middle of a time line perfectly balanced with past achievement and future promise.

On top of it all, roughly a year after being married to his longtime girlfriend, Marie Whitney, Epstein became a father when the couple welcomed a baby boy, Jack, on December 12, 2007. The Red Sox an-nounced the child with only a very short press release—that was what

Epstein preferred—before the general manager of the Red Sox took a brief leave from his job to get acquainted with his newest acquisition.

Five years after being named general manager of the Red Sox and inheriting a work started by Dan Duquette, Theo Epstein was once again learning that the world can indeed change.